# MARK

# BELIEF

*A Theological Commentary*
*on the Bible*

GENERAL EDITORS

*Amy Plantinga Pauw*
*William C. Placher*[†]

# MARK

WILLIAM C. PLACHER

WESTMINSTER
JOHN KNOX PRESS
LOUISVILLE · KENTUCKY

*First edition*
Published by Westminster John Knox Press
Louisville, Kentucky

10 11 12 13 14 15 16 17 18 19—10 9 8 7 6 5 4 3 2 1

*Book design by Drew Stevens*
*Cover design by Lisa Buckley*
*Cover art: © David Chapman/Design Pics/Corbis*

**Library of Congress Cataloging-in-Publication Data**

Placher, William C. (William Carl), 1948-2008.
Mark / William C. Placher. — 1st ed.
    p. cm. — (Belief : a theological commentary on the Bible)
Includes index.
ISBN 978-0-664-23209-2 (alk. paper)
1. Bible. N.T. Mark—Commentaries. I. Title.
BS2585.53.P54 2010
226.3'07—dc22
                                                            2010003671

# Contents

# Publisher's Note

William C. Placher worked with Amy Plantinga Pauw as a general editor for this series until his untimely death in November 2008. Bill brought great energy and vision to the series, and was instrumental in defining and articulating its distinctive approach and in securing theologians to write for it. Bill's own commentary for the series was the last thing he wrote, and Westminster John Knox Press is grateful to Wabash College, especially Dean Gary Phillips and Professor Raymond Williams, for their generous cooperation in bringing this manuscript to publication. The only part missing from the table of contents Bill had laid out was a concluding "personal epilogue." The Press has decided to publish "the shorter ending" of Bill's commentary on the Gospel of Mark, rather than attempt to provide a closing epilogue in another hand. Thus his commentary, like the Gospel of Mark itself, ends without a sense of final closure. It is most fitting that Bill's splendid commentary inaugurates this series, and Westminster John Knox Press wishes to dedicate the entire series to his memory with affection and gratitude.

# Series Introduction

*Belief: A Theological Commentary on the Bible* is a series from Westminster John Knox Press featuring biblical commentaries written by theologians. The writers of this series share Karl Barth's concern that, insofar as their usefulness to pastors goes, most modern commentaries are "no commentary at all, but merely the first step toward a commentary." Historical-critical approaches to Scripture rule out some readings and commend others, but such methods only begin to help theological reflection and the preaching of the Word. By themselves, they do not convey the powerful sense of God's merciful presence that calls Christians to repentance and praise; they do not bring the church fully forward in the life of discipleship. It is to such tasks that theologians are called.

For several generations, however, professional theologians in North America and Europe have not been writing commentaries on the Christian Scriptures. The specialization of professional disciplines and the expectations of theological academies about the kind of writing that theologians should do, as well as many of the directions in which contemporary theology itself has gone, have contributed to this dearth of theological commentaries. This is a relatively new phenomenon; until the last century or two, the church's great theologians also routinely saw themselves as biblical interpreters. The gap between the fields is a loss for both the church and the discipline of theology itself. By inviting forty contemporary theologians to wrestle deeply with particular texts of Scripture, the editors of this series hope not only to provide new theological resources for the church, but also to encourage all theologians to pay more attention to Scripture and the life of the church in their writings.

We are grateful to the Louisville Institute, which provided funding for a consultation in June 2007. We invited theologians, pastors, and biblical scholars to join us in a conversation about what this series could contribute to the life of the church. The time was provocative and the results were rich. Much of the series' shape owes to the insights of these skilled and faithful interpreters, who sought to describe a way to write a commentary that served the theological needs of the church and its pastors with relevance, historical accuracy, and theological depth. The passion of these participants guided us in creating this series and lives on in the volumes.

As theologians, the authors will be interested much less in the matters of form, authorship, historical setting, social context, and philology—the very issues that are often of primary concern to critical biblical scholars. Instead, this series' authors will seek to explain the theological importance of the texts for the church today, using biblical scholarship as needed for such explication but without any attempt to cover all of the topics of the usual modern biblical commentary. This thirty-six-volume series will provide passage-by-passage commentary on all the books of the Protestant biblical canon, with more extensive attention given to passages of particular theological significance.

The authors' chief dialogue will be with the church's creeds, practices, and hymns; with the history of faithful interpretation and use of the Scriptures; with the categories and concepts of theology; and with contemporary culture in both "high" and popular forms. Each volume will begin with a discussion of *why* the church needs this book and why we need it *now*, in order to ground all of the commentary in contemporary relevance. Throughout each volume, text boxes will highlight the voices of ancient and modern interpreters from the global communities of faith, and occasional essays will allow deeper reflection on the key theological concepts of these biblical books.

The authors of this commentary series are theologians of the church who embrace a variety of confessional and theological perspectives. The group of authors assembled for this series represents more diversity of race, ethnicity, and gender than any other commentary series. They approach the larger Christian tradition with a critical respect, seeking to reclaim its riches and at the same time to acknowledge its shortcomings. The authors also aim to make available to readers a wide range of contemporary theological voices from many parts of the world. While it does recover an older genre of writing, this series is not an attempt to retrieve some idealized past. These commentaries have learned from tradition, but they are most importantly commentaries for today. The authors share the conviction that their work will be more contemporary, more faithful, and more radical, to the extent that it is more biblical, honestly wrestling with the texts of the Scriptures.

William C. Placher
Amy Plantinga Pauw

# Abbreviations

| | |
|---|---|
| AB | Anchor Bible |
| *ANF* | *Ante-Nicene Fathers* |
| AV | Authorized (King James) Version |
| BNTC | Black's New Testament Commentaries |
| *CBQ* | *Catholic Biblical Quarterly* |
| *CD* | Karl Barth, *Church Dogmatics* |
| FC | Fathers of the Church |
| IBT | Interpreting Biblical Texts |
| *JBL* | *Journal of Biblical Literature* |
| LCC | Library of Christian Classics |
| LCL | Loeb Classical Library |
| LW | *Luther's Works* |
| *NPNF* | *Nicene and Post-Nicene Fathers* |
| NRSV | New Revised Standard Version |
| NTL | New Testament Library |
| SP | Sacra pagina |

# Introduction:
## Why Mark? Why Now?

The Gospel according to Mark tells the story of Jesus of Nazareth, a first-century Jew—who he is, what it means that he is the Son of God, and what it means to follow him. It lays claim to be the most important of all stories. What military victory or intellectual breakthrough could be as important as the news that the Creator of the whole universe came to live among us? What guide to health or wealth or happiness could matter as much as the way to eternal salvation?

Still, we can read the story of Jesus in other Gospels, and for that matter in all sorts of Christian and non-Christian writings. Why read Mark in particular? Mark's story, moreover, has been told for nearly twenty centuries. Is it somehow particularly relevant to our time?

At least four types of factors make *Mark in particular* worth reading *just now in particular:* historical, political, literary, and theological. To summarize: (1) Historical: Of all the sources available to us, Mark gets us closest to Jesus' own lifetime. (2) Political: The great theologian Karl Barth used to say that theology should be done with the Bible in one hand and the newspaper in the other. The newspapers these days are full of stories of war and torture in the Middle East and church debates about whom to ordain and whom to exclude. Indirectly, Mark turns out to have a lot to say about such topics. (3) Literary: Mark is an odd text—abrupt, sometimes clumsy, written in Greek totally without literary polish, yet astonishing in its complexity, its allusiveness, its anticipation of the techniques of "postmodern" literature. Written by an ill-educated author long ago, it has amazing similarities to the work of some of the most

1

sophisticated storytellers of our time. (4) Theological: One of the most important themes in recent theology has been a rebellion against pictures of God as unchanging, unaffected by the vicissitudes of the world in favor of an idea of God as, in Alfred North White-head's beautiful phrase, "the great companion—the fellow-sufferer who understands."[1] We encounter such a God not only in twentieth- and twenty-first-century theologians, but also—more than any-where else in the New Testament—in the Gospel according to Mark.

## *History*

For most of Christian history, Mark was the neglected Gospel. Augustine, with his enormous authority, noticed how much of Mark can also be found in Matthew. Since he believed that Matthew was an eyewitness to Jesus' life, he concluded that Mark "looks like his attendant and epitomizer. . . . By himself, separately, he has little to record."[2] Why consult a truncated copy, therefore, when the fuller original was available? Matthew and Luke seem to provide more complete accounts of Jesus' teaching; John apparently has a far more sophisticated theology. All three are written in better Greek. Why bother much with Mark? As one measure of the results, there is evi-dence of fewer than twenty commentaries on Mark in the whole time before the nineteenth century, compared with hundreds for Matthew or John.

In the early eighteenth century, an English Deist named Thomas Chubb, like Mark a man without much formal education, proposed that Mark was really the first Gospel to be written, a conclusion that gradually drew support among nineteenth-century German schol-ars and now seems the dominant (though not universal) scholarly opinion. Most scholars now agree that this Gospel was written in northern Palestine, Syria, or Rome between 65 and 75, and that at least Matthew and Luke, possibly even John, had Mark's text avail-able to them. Though early Christian authors make various claims,

---

1. Alfred North Whitehead, *Process and Reality* (New York: Macmillan, 1929), 413.
2. Augustine, *The Harmony of the Gospels* 1.2.4 (*NPNF*, 1st ser., 6:78).

we do not really know who wrote it. (It will be easiest to follow tradition and call its author "Mark," which was, after all, the most common name in the Roman Empire, and to assume that "he" was, like nearly all authors of the time, male.)

Whoever the author was, he probably knew people who knew Jesus. In the face of contemporary skepticism, this may be worth emphasizing. Jesus died thirty-five to forty-five years before Mark wrote. Many of the earliest Christians lived in Palestine and Syria. Good historical evidence puts Peter in Rome and sets his death in 64, under Nero's persecution, when Mark was there if the Gospel was written in Rome. Mark tells how Jesus' cross was carried part of the way by "Simon of Cyrene, the father of Alexander and Rufus" (15:21). Since Alexander and Rufus get no introduction or further reference, it seems likely they were members of Mark's community, known to his first listeners. ("Listeners" seems a better word than "readers" since the Gospel, in accordance with the practices of the time, was probably at first read aloud to a group far more often than it was read in private by one individual.) Mark was thus writing, first of all, for people who knew the sons of the man who had carried Jesus' cross.

To be sure, he was not trying to write history the way a modern historian would. No one in the ancient world did. Thucydides, in many ways the most cautious and skeptical of ancient historians, frankly admitted that in reporting the speeches in his history of the Peloponnesian War, "my method has been, while keeping as closely as possible to the general sense of the words that were actually used, to make the speakers say what, in my opinion, was called for by each situation."[3] In other words, he made up what he thought speakers should have said. Ancient writers generally, including historians— and in this perhaps they were just more honest than we are today— understood their purpose as affecting their readers in some way, accomplishing something, rather than representing some independent reality.[4]

---

3. Thucydides, *History of the Peloponnesian War* 1.22, trans. Rex Warner (London: Penguin, 1972), 47.

4. "A literary work is not so much an object, therefore, as a unit of force whose power is exerted upon the world in a certain direction" (Jane P. Tompkins, *Reader-Response Criticism: From Formalism to Post-Structuralism* [Baltimore: Johns Hopkins University Press, 1980], 204).

Mark wanted to convey the identity of this man Jesus. To do that best, he was willing to juggle chronology, combine features of several stories, and no doubt make up some episodes that would vividly convey a point he thought worth making. As John Calvin once put it, "No fixed and distinct order of dates was observed by the Evangelists in composing their narratives. The consequence is, that they disregard the order of time, and satisfy themselves with presenting, in a summary manner, the leading transactions in the life of Christ."[5]

People still tell stories the same way. A personal example: my father died when I was in high school. I can recall some things he said word for word, and I have one letter he wrote me. But some of the things I remember most precisely stuck in my mind because they were uncharacteristic of him. And that one surviving letter (written when I had won an award) is weirdly formal and would give a badly distorted impression of our relationship. If you wanted to know about the sort of man my dad was, you would do better to trust my general descriptions and the stories I tell about how he was most himself, even if I am fudging some of the details to make them even more "characteristic" of him.

I therefore distrust projects like the Jesus Seminar. They want to work through the Gospels, find the particular sayings and actions that seem most historically trustworthy, and build a picture of Jesus out of them alone. But the most historically reliable details may not be at all the most characteristic.[6] Indeed, the rules of the Jesus Seminar specify that the passages most likely to be from Jesus himself are those at odds with the teaching of first-century Judaism or the early church. As a historical device, this has merit up to a point—such sayings are less likely to have come from any source other than Jesus himself. Pushed to the limit, however, its bias is quite unfairly against ways in which Jesus was a Jew of his time or in which the church followed his teachings. One other complicating factor: Mark's view is that the most important thing about Jesus was the special relation-

5. John Calvin, *Commentary on a Harmony of the Evangelists, Matthew, Mark, and Luke*, trans. William Pringle, Calvin's Commentaries (repr. 3 vols. in 2; Grand Rapids: Baker, 1989), 1:239. See also 2:89.
6. Hans W. Frei, *The Identity of Jesus Christ* (Philadelphia: Fortress, 1975), 141.

ship he had with the one he called his Father—and the reality of that relationship lies beyond what a historian can determine.

Mark thought he knew what was really important about Jesus, and I want to listen to what he has to say—all of it, set down the way he chose to tell it—even if I doubt some of what he tells happened at all as he describes. I am less interested in such details than in trying to learn from Mark who Jesus was.

Like the Jesus Seminar, those who focus their attention on texts that did not make it into the Bible have been getting a great deal of attention lately. Articles in popular magazines describe with great excitement the picture of Jesus to be found in the *Gospel of Thomas* or the *Gospel of Judas*. It is therefore worth emphasizing that all these texts were written, at least in their present form, much later than Mark. Moreover, they were generally written by "gnostic" Christians inclined to think that the real truths lie at a spiritual level and therefore even less interested than Mark in historical details. The fascination some folks have with a possible nonbiblical fragment, when we have the whole of the New Testament before us, often puzzles me. In one famous case, the distinguished scholar Morton Smith now seems to have forged a fragment of the "Secret Gospel of Mark" he claimed to have discovered, though it influenced a surprising number of scholars eager to show the dangers of trusting too much to the Bible.[7]

## *Politics*

Nearly everyone remembers the picture: a Middle Eastern man standing on a box, arms stretched out like a cross, a bag over his head, electric wires attached to his hands. Many people, including even the young woman who took the picture, had the same reaction: "He looks like Jesus!"

---

7. See the still controversial Stephen C. Carlson, *The Gospel Hoax: Morton Smith's Invention of Secret Mark* (Waco, TX: Baylor University Press, 2006). "But maybe Smith forged it. Few others in the late twentieth century had the skill to pull it off. Few others had enough disdain of other scholars to want to bamboozle them" (Bart Ehrman, *Lost Christianities: The Battles for Scripture and the Faiths We Never Knew* [New York: Oxford University Press, 2003], 89).

The story behind the photograph turns out to be complicated. It comes from an American prison camp in Iraq, Abu Ghraib. The young Army Reserve troops who took it and others like it were acting out of complex motives—partly joking around, partly trying to document horrors that disturbed them, partly just following their generation's instinct to photograph everything.[8] In the case of this prisoner, the electric wires were not connected to anything. (He seems, incidentally, to have been a taxi driver caught in the wrong place at the wrong time.) But these young prison guards had been told to soften up prisoners for questioning, with no clear limits on what they could do. Experienced interrogators find that offering prisoners tea and talking with them in a friendly way nearly always generates more useful information than beating them.[9] But the word had come down from Washington that guards needed to be tougher. Mysterious nonmilitary personnel turned up at Abu Ghraib from time to time with anonymous prisoners whose presence was not to be recorded; these prisoners' screams could be heard from secret rooms, and at least one of them died. The young people who took the pictures have been sent to jail. Neither the actual torturers nor the people in Washington who gave the key orders have even been officially investigated.

Americans today, therefore, read the Gospel of Mark—this story of a Middle Eastern man tortured to death by the most powerful empire of his time—when we are the most powerful nation of our time, and *our* forces are torturing people, sometimes to death. What does that imply about our values and the sort of people we have become?

Wherever Mark wrote, between 65 and 75 (my own amateur guess would be 68 or 69), he wrote in the midst of imperial violence affecting Christians and Jews. When much of Rome burned in 64, Emperor Nero dealt with a rumor that he had started the fire himself

---

8. "He looked like Jesus Christ. At first I had to laugh so I went on and grabbed the camera and took a picture. One of the guys took my asp and started 'poking' his dick. Again I thought, okay that's funny then it hit me, that's a form of molestation. You can't do that. I took more pictures now to 'record' what is going on" (Sabrina Harman, letter to her lover, Kelly, October 20, 2003, quoted in Philip Gourevitch and Errol Morris, *Standard Operating Procedure* [New York: Penguin, 2008], 110).

9. See Jane Mayer, *The Dark Side* (New York: Doubleday, 2008), 119 and elsewhere.

in the midst of a drunken party by shifting the blame to the small Christian community. The historian Tacitus tells how Christian prisoners "were covered with wild beasts' skins and torn to death by dogs; or they were fastened on crosses, and, when daylight failed, were burned to serve as lamps by night."[10] Eusebius refers to a very early tradition from Clement of Rome that both Peter and Paul were killed at the time.[11]

Palestine saw even more violence. In 66 Eleazar, a captain in the Jewish forces at the temple in Jerusalem, refused to perform sacrifices there to the Roman emperor. A rebellion began against both the Romans and the higher Jewish authorities, and the rebels burned the public archives where records of all debts were kept, got the Roman garrison in Jerusalem to surrender, and then killed them. After four years of brutal warfare, the Romans defeated what must have seemed to them a terrorist operation on their vulnerable border with the Parthian Empire, burned the Jerusalem temple, and razed it to the ground. Such news would have reached Rome quickly as well. If we read Mark with our newspaper headlines, and therefore a great power's violence in the Middle East, in mind, we are thus not imposing an agenda on the text but connecting to its own time's concerns.

Those of us who belong to many mainline churches read in another context too. Though matters of war and torture seem surely more important than the sexual orientation of our ministers, it is the latter question that threatens to divide several of our denominations at the national or worldwide level. Issues about homosexual orientation or practice never come up in Mark or the other Gospels, a fact that in itself makes it stranger that this should be our potentially church-dividing question. Purity, however, is one of Mark's central topics. The Pharisees, sometimes cast among the villains of his story, were in many ways among the most admirable Jews of Jesus' time. Unlike those who wrote off ordinary people as incapable of real piety, the Pharisees encouraged *all* Jews to follow the laws God had given them—and a good Jew thinks of these laws as a gift rather than

10. Tacitus, *Annals* 15.44.4, trans. John Jackson, LCL (Cambridge: Harvard University Press, 1962), 4:285.
11. Eusebius, *Ecclesiastical History* 2.25.2.

a burden. They therefore had a popular following all over the country, which is why they are the opponents Jesus so often encounters early in Mark.

Only when we recognize the Pharisees for the pious, virtuous folk they were can we see how radical was Jesus' opposition to them. As the great NT scholar Joachim Jeremias put it, "the numerous words of judgment in the gospels are, almost without exception, not directed against those who commit adultery, cheat, etc., but against those who vigorously condemn adultery and exclude cheats from the community."[12] In a society where concerns about propriety focused on the rituals surrounding meals, Jesus casually invited *everyone* to dinner, from prostitutes to the tax collectors who collaborated with the hated Romans in cheating the people. Where rules about eating or the Sabbath were concerned, he had a certain insouciance. Such things mattered little. Far more often, Jesus condemned those preoccupied with respectability rather than those society judged unrespectable. As we read Mark, therefore, we have to think about the implications of this attitude for the debates of our own time—debates about sexuality, but also all the debates about how we sort out insiders and outsiders and how we treat them.

## *Literature*

Anyone who studies Mark in Greek soon learns that he did not write very well. One writer cites over two hundred "harsh constructions."[13] Mark "gave no place to the artistic devices and tendencies of literary and polished writing," Martin Dibelius wrote.[14] Mary Ann Tolbert classifies this Gospel among the popular ancient novels, a "fairly crude, repetitious, and conventionalized narrative."[15] It is

12. Joachim Jeremias, *New Testament Theology*, trans. John Bowden (New York: Charles Scribner's Sons, 1971), 151.
13. Howard Clark Kee, *Community of the New Age: Studies in Mark's Gospel* (Philadelphia: Westminster, 1977), 50, citing J. C. Hawkins, *Horae Synopticae*, 2nd ed. (1909; repr. Grand Rapids: Baker, 1968), 131–38.
14. Martin Dibelius, *From Tradition to Gospel* (New York: Charles Scribner's Sons, 1935), 1.
15. Mary Ann Tolbert, *Sowing the Gospel: Mark's World in Literary-Historical Perspective* (Minneapolis: Fortress, 1989), 65.

with some hesitation, therefore, that I propose that Mark was a literary genius, admittedly of an odd sort, emerging as he did from the ranks of the little educated. Even his "mistakes"—the long rows of sentences, each beginning, "And immediately . . .", the shifts to the historical present uncharacteristic of good Greek style—make the story dramatic. Mark often switches from one story to another and then back to the first in a way that leads his readers to compare the two narratives and illuminates both of them. He comes back to a rare word he used much earlier and thereby connects two distant passages in a remarkably sophisticated way. Such devices are in any event there in the text (and some modern literary theorists would insist that that is all that matters), but I also think the author knew what he was doing. Those who prefer polished writing are impatient with Mark's tendency to leave ambiguities ambiguous and annoyed with his enigmatic ending. If we have come to admire Kafka and Joyce, however, we can hardly criticize Mark on such grounds.

Jean-François Lyotard, in a famous essay, defined "postmodernism," that word intellectuals have been tossing around so much lately, as a suspicion of "metanarratives."[16] That is, before the late nineteenth or early twentieth century, Western writers tended to think that history was ultimately about one big thing: the triumph of Christianity, or the gradual victory of science over superstition, or class struggle that would lead to the eventual triumph of the working class, or whatever. That story was not just one narrative among others but the all-inclusive metanarrative. More recently, Lyotard claims, people are more inclined to think that history is just one damned thing after another. There may be islands of local meaning—this love affair does culminate in a happy marriage, this investigation does catch the criminal. But things in general do not add up to one meaningful whole.

By that definition, it may be impossible to believe fully both in God and in postmodernism, since belief in God would seem to involve having things ultimately add up. But Mark comes about as

16. Jean-François Lyotard, *The Postmodern Condition*, trans. Geoff Bennington and Brian Massumi (Minneapolis: University of Minnesota Press, 1984), xxiv.

close as possible. He repeatedly introduces ambiguities. He presents Jesus as a teacher who uses parables as his key pedagogical technique, and then has Jesus tell us that the parables are designed to keep people from understanding. Just when we expect a dramatic climax...he stops. Perhaps he really was the first postmodern writer.

He seems to have invented a new genre of writing when he wrote the first Gospel. We take the "four Gospels" so much for granted as part of the New Testament that we forget that no one before Mark had ever written a "gospel." Given Paul's relative indifference to the narrative of Jesus' life, it was by no means obvious that Christians would write works anything like Mark's. Scholars sometimes try to classify it among the forms of Hellenistic literature, but the results often have a quality of desperation. Mark is like ancient biographies—except that it does not discuss most of Jesus' life; Mark is like popular romances—except that its topic is serious and it does not involve romance. And so on. The literary critic Erich Auerbach (a secular Jew who cannot be accused of Christian bias) seems to reach the best conclusion: Mark "fits into no antique genre.... too serious for comedy, too everyday for tragedy, politically too insignificant for history—and the form which was given it is one of such immediacy that its like does not exist in the literature of antiquity."[17] In a culture where anyone but kings and queens and lords could appear in drama only in bit parts or low comedy, this text tells a story of infinite importance focused on fishermen and a small-town carpenter's son. When Willy Loman's wife cries out, in *Death of a Salesman*, that "Attention must be paid"[18] to the trials of her rather ordinary traveling-salesman husband, or when Marcel Proust plumbs the philosophical implications of the most ordinary events, they are asserting a principle that, in all of Western literature, first appears in Mark.

---

17. Erich Auerbach, *Mimesis*, trans. Willard R. Trask (Princeton: Princeton University Press, 1953), 45.
18. Arthur Miller, *Death of a Salesman* (repr. New York: Penguin, 1999), 39.

# *Theology*

"Only the suffering God can help," Dietrich Bonhoeffer wrote from his prison cell shortly before the Nazis killed him.[19] His understanding of God as suffering with us has become a commonplace of contemporary theology, but it challenges one of the most basic assumptions of most past centuries. Christian theologians before the twentieth century generally insisted that God is unchanging, immutable, and certainly incapable of suffering. God, they believed, is all-powerful and all-knowing—how could such a God be subject to injury? God is eternally perfect—how could such a God suffer change?

The Bible sees God differently. God tells the prophet Hosea that Israel's unfaithfulness makes him feel pain like that Hosea feels when his wife is unfaithful. Isaiah describes a God who "will cry out like a woman in labor" and "gasp and pant" (Isa. 42:14). In Philippians Paul talks about Christ "who, though he was in the form of God . . . humbled himself and became obedient to the point of death—even death on a cross" (Phil. 2:6, 8). Mark, most starkly of all the Gospels, presents Jesus as at once the Son of God and a human being who ends up abandoned by his friends, subject to a painful and humiliating death, and crying out at the end to ask why God has forsaken him. The other Gospels all try to soften the story somewhere along the line. In Mark it is precisely the appalling way Jesus dies that leads a first human being to proclaim that he is God's Son (Mark 15:39).

When so many twentieth-century theologians—Bonhoeffer, Barth, Balthasar, the process thinkers, feminists, liberationists, Moltmann . . . the list goes on and on—speak of a God who suffers, therefore, they are not inventing a new way of thinking about God but recovering an important biblical theme.[20] Still, one can speculate on why something so long apparently hidden to wise forebears has become in our time so clear to so many. Did the tragedies of the

19. Dietrich Bonhoeffer, "Letter to Eberhard Bethge, July 16, 1944," *Letters and Papers from Prison*, enlarged ed., trans. Reginald Fuller and John Bowden (New York: Macmillan, 1972), 361.
20. See Ronald Goetz, "The Suffering God: The Rise of a New Orthodoxy," *Christian Century* 103, no. 13 (1986): 385–89.

century just past—the trenches of World War I, the Holocaust, the Gulag, and all the rest—make it harder to worship a God defined as somehow untouched by human suffering? When Christianity's influence shrinks in more powerful and wealthy nations even as it grows among the world's poor, is it more difficult to imagine a God characterized by power and incapable of suffering? Whatever the reason, when we come to believe in a God understood first of all in terms of suffering love, we will find Mark waiting for us, with a story he is eager to tell.

What follows is a theological commentary on the Gospel according to Mark. Like John Calvin—and Martin Luther and Desiderius Erasmus and many others—I will comment on the best scholarly guess as to the "original autograph"—the text someone back in the first century wrote. Thus, for instance, the commentary will end at Mark 16:8 rather than continuing to passages scholars agree to be later additions; it will not treat the version used through most of Christian history as the "canonical" text.

At every stage, I will be dependent on the work of modern historical-critical scholars to illumine many features of the text. I am in awe of their learning. Still, I confess that their work often strikes me, as Karl Barth said of the biblical commentaries of his time, as "no commentary at all, but merely the first steps toward a commentary."[21] To put the matter more colloquially, they often seem to stop just when they get to the good stuff. Christians do not primarily read Mark, I am assuming, to learn about Koine Greek or first-century history, but to learn about Jesus, what he reveals to us about God, and what we learn from him about how to live. A book that does not focus on such questions seems to a theologian "merely the first steps toward a commentary." I will try to take more steps than that. Still, this is a commentary on Mark. Where a work of systematic theology would appropriately draw from every biblical text, a commentary focuses on the book at hand, and in this case in particular will keep comparisons with other Gospels to a minimum.

21. Karl Barth, *The Epistle to the Romans*, trans. Edwyn C. Hoskyns, 2nd ed. (repr. London: Oxford University Press, 1968), 6.

# 1:1–1:13

# *Good News!*

## 1:1

### *Title*

George Buttrick, the great Harvard teacher of preachers, used to say that every preacher, just before entering the pulpit, should think, "I have *wonderful* news to tell these people." So Mark begins with "good news"—the most natural translation of the word we usually render "gospel."

"The beginning of the good news of Jesus the anointed one, Son of God" (my trans.)—whether this is the title or the first line of what follows (a matter debated among scholars), every word counts, and most of what follows is already here summarized.

"Beginning" contains a suggestive ambiguity and a dramatic implicit reference. The ambiguity: At an obvious level, "beginning" refers to the fact that this sentence is the first of the story that will follow. But this opening also serves, formally or informally, as the title of the *whole* book, so this first word invites us to think that the *whole story* that follows is a beginning. Indeed, when we get to the last sentence, it will turn out that Mark really has no ending: it opens to the future, challenging its audience to continue the story. A book with "beginning" in its title warns us right at the start not to expect closure at the end.

The implicit reference: Mark's first audience was familiar with a book that started with *archē* (beginning)—Genesis, the first book of the Torah, in its Greek translation. Starting another book that way suggests a comparison between this story of a recently crucified teacher and the story of God's creation of the whole universe, the beginning of God's sacred Word. History, creation itself, is beginning again. Can what follows possibly be *that* important? So Mark claims.

*Euangelion*—"good news" or "gospel"—did not refer to just any sort of good news. "Tomorrow will be sunny," or even, "The cancer does not seem to have spread," would not have counted. Most uses in classical Greek refer to the news of a military victory; one scholar even proposes that the most literal translation would be "good news of victory from the battlefield."[1]

The Septuagint translation of Isaiah uses the root *euangel* [phonetic, evangel] to offer a different image of good news as announcing peace and salvation:

> How beautiful upon the mountains
>     are the feet of the messenger who announces peace,
> who brings *euangelion*, who announces salvation.
>
> (Isa. 52:7)

It is from this prophet that Mark quotes:

> The spirit of the Lord GOD is upon me,
>     because the LORD has anointed me;
> he has sent me to bring *euangelion* to the oppressed,
>     to bind up the brokenhearted,
> to proclaim liberty to the captives,
>     and release to the prisoners.
>
> (Isa. 61:1)

Here "gospel" is good news not just of victory but of victory's hoped-for fruits: peace and an end to oppression. Mark takes that path even further. The contemporary peace activist Ched Myers writes, "The 'good news' of Mark does not herald yet another victory by Rome's armies; it is a declaration of war upon the political culture of the empire."[2] This story will describe a different kind of victory. This

1. M. Eugene Boring, "Mark 1:1–15 and the Beginning of the Gospel," *Semeia* 52 (1990): 56.
2. Ched Myers, *Binding the Strong Man: A Political Reading of Mark's Story of Jesus* (Maryknoll, NY: Orbis, 1990), 124.

warrior Jesus is a servant whose weapon is love and whose victory lies on the other side of a cross; his story will be good news very different from that proclaimed by imperial heralds—or by presidents or hedge-fund managers or fan magazines telling about the stars—and will thereby raise questions about the ultimate importance of those other forms of news.

Already in Paul's earliest known letter, 1 Thessalonians, written within twenty years of Jesus' death, Paul used *euangelion* as if it were the natural term for the basic Christian message (see for instance 1 Thess. 2:2 or 3:2—six times in all in a very short letter). Christians must have been using the word in that sense very early indeed. Mark, however, seems to have been the first to use *euangelion* as the name of a book, a usage not picked up by what we call the other "Gospels" and indeed so far as we know not used in a generic sense ("four Gospels") until the middle of the second century.[3] We take the term for granted and lose the surprise and puzzle it might have occasioned among Mark's first listeners/readers at the beginning of a book. "Gospel" was one of Mark's favorite words (1:1, 14, 15; 8:35; 10:29; 13:10; 14:9) and for him captured what he wanted to say—he had wonderful news to tell, news of a kind, he was signaling his readers, that no previous form of writing could appropriately convey.

> For I am not ashamed of the gospel; it is the power of God for salvation to everyone who has faith, to the Jew first and also to the Greek.
> —Romans 1:16

His wonderful news was about *Jesus*. Listen to John Wesley's definition: "*The gospel* (that is, good tidings, good news for guilty, helpless sinners), in the largest sense of the word, means the whole revelation made to men by Jesus Christ; and sometimes the whole account of what our Lord did and suffered while he tabernacled among men."[4] The good news is not abstract, not first of all about

---

3. Justin Martyr, *First Apology* 66.3 (*ANF* 1:185).
4. John Wesley, "Sermon 7: The Way to the Kingdom," *The Works of John Wesley*, 3rd ed. (repr. Grand Rapids: Baker, 1979), 5:84–85.

human beings in general or some particular type of human beings, but about one particular individual, identified by a name. The popular modern chorus "There's Something about That Name," written by Gloria and William Gaither, emphasizes the point by repeating "Jesus, Jesus, Jesus" along with the titles "Master" and "Savior."[5]

Indeed—the *name* matters, as a token of a particular person. Mark has nothing to say about his own authority, or some authenticating source from which he heard his good news. The authority of the story comes not from the person telling it but from the person about whom it is told. As Karl Barth wrote, the New Testament binds its message "strictly and indissolubly to this name . . . presenting it as the story of the bearer of this name. . . . Without this name it is left insecure and unprotected. It is exposed to the suspicion that it might be only a postulate, a pure speculation, a myth."[6] But no—there was this human being, who lived within the lifetime of some in Mark's original audience, and the story, with all it implies, concerns him.

> In the Christian "God with us" there is no question of any other source and object than that indicated by this name.
> —Karl Barth
>
> *CD*, IV /1:17.

This Jesus, Mark tells us, is the *Christ*, the Greek translation of the Hebrew *mashiach*, "Messiah" or "anointed one." To a purely Gentile audience, the word would have meant merely "someone smeared with oil,"[7] a puzzling word for such a significant context. By Mark's time, Christians may have treated it just as part of Jesus' name. But in ancient Israel kings (and also priests and prophets) were ritually anointed with oil, so in the first instance the anointed one was the king. As kings who should have served the Lord and the people too often failed to do so, however, the people's hope turned to the future, to a king someday who would be what a king should be—a messiah.

5. William J. and Gloria Gaither, "Jesus, Jesus, Jesus, There's Just Something about that Name," *Chalice Hymnal* (St. Louis: Chalice Press, 1995), no. 115.

6. Karl Barth, *Church Dogmatics*, IV/1, *The Doctrine of Reconciliation*, trans. G. W. Bromiley (Edinburgh: T. & T. Clark, 1956), 16–17. (Hereafter cited as *CD*.)

7. Donald H. Juel, *The Gospel of Mark*, IBT (Nashville: Abingdon, 1999), 100.

As the Jewish scholar Martin Buber explained, "The history of the kings is the history of the failure of he who has been anointed to realize the promise of his anointing. The rise of messianism—the belief in the anointed king who realizes the promise of his anointing—is to be understood only in this context."[8] Jews in Jesus' time meant many different things by "Messiah," but any who used the word hoped for a coming one who would transform the world—defeat the Romans or restore the Law or whatever, but anyway change everything.

Buber published those remarks, in an essay titled "Biblisches Führertum," in Germany in 1933, when talk of *biblical* leadership implied a dramatic contrast with and criticism of Germany's new "Leader." But "Messiah," properly understood, was always a critical term, with its implication that Israel's actual anointed ones had failed to match the ideal of monarchy. To say that Jesus is the Messiah, then, meant at least two things. First, it indicates that we need to understand who Jesus was and is in a Jewish context. "Messiah" is a term from *Jewish* history. In Barth's words, "The Word did not simply become any 'flesh,' any man humbled and suffering. It became Jewish flesh."[9] Given the tragic history of Christian anti-Semitism, this cannot be emphasized enough. Second, in the face of every kind of human leadership, reference to "Messiah" implies that something immensely better is possible, that we should not ultimately settle for what is only somewhat better.

The term thus poses problems. Jews, Buber said, cannot believe that the Messiah has come: "We know more deeply, more truly, that world history has not been turned upside down to its very foundations—that the world is not yet redeemed."[10] The identification of Jesus as Messiah already in this first line of the Gospel raises a difficult question for Christians: If the Messiah has indeed come in this man Jesus, why does the world not look different?

Jacques Derrida, Jew by tradition and postmodernist by faith, pushed the matter further. The Messiah, he said, has to be a critique

---

8. Martin Buber, "Biblical Leadership," in *The Martin Buber Reader*, ed. Asher D. Bienann (New York: Palgrave Macmillan, 2002), 40.
9. Barth, *CD* IV/1:166.
10. Martin Buber, *Der Jude und sein Judentum* (Cologne: J. Melzer, 1963), 562.

of present imperfection; that is how the term functions—and therefore anyone who actually appears cannot really be the Messiah.[11] His
paradox poses another challenge to a Christian reader of Mark. If
this Jesus challenges earthly powers, how can those who follow him
avoid becoming yet another earthly power? A radical Christian fighting for a change in government in Latin America once told one of his
revolutionary comrades, "Of course, you understand that once you
win and take control of the government, I will have to be opposed
to you!" That does seem to be the logic of following a messiah—but
can one responsibly have such a politics?

In most early manuscripts, though not some of the most ancient
ones, Mark's first line concludes, "Son of God." Since the term
unquestionably appears later in the text, it seems best to save discussion of it until then. Reflection on the first verse has already raised
many issues. Can the good news about this Jesus really be as important as Mark claims? How can that be, given that the world does not
seem to have changed much since he came? Dare Christians, inevitably creating their own sort of institution, claim to be his followers?

## 1:2–8

### The Messenger

Verses 2–3 are not in fact "written in the prophet Isaiah"; Mark com-
bines phrases from Isaiah 40:3, Exodus 23:20, and Malachi 3:1. It
is unlikely that he just made a mistake. Here as elsewhere he is not
much concerned about the details that might preoccupy a biblical
literalist. He wants to set his story in the context of Israel's history,
and particularly not just one passage but the whole set of texts modern scholars call "Second Isaiah," the most hopeful and universalistic
of the prophets.

Second Isaiah, this great anonymous prophet, speaks tenderly,
offering words of comfort to a people then in exile. Israel has already
"received from the LORD's hand double for all her sins" (Isa. 40:2),

11. See Jacques Derrida and Maurizio Ferraris, *A Taste for the Secret*, trans. Giacomo Donis
(Cambridge: Polity, 2001), 22.

and now they can indeed anticipate good news. What follows in Mark will be full of Second Isaiah's themes: the forgiveness of sins, the clearing of a path through the wilderness and the pacification of wild animals, the tearing open of the heavens so that the Spirit can descend, the nearness of God's rule, and the extension of good news to all the nations.

Malachi, in contrast, warns of judgment. Although chronologically other prophets followed Malachi, this book came at the end of the collection of Hebrew prophets. By beginning with a fragment from Malachi, Mark is thus in effect starting up where prophecy left off. Malachi wrote at a time, roughly 450 years before the birth of Jesus, when the small Jewish community around Jerusalem was impatiently wondering why God was not acting on their behalf. "Where is the God of justice?" they cried (Mal. 2:17). God will indeed act, the prophet proclaims, but you may not enjoy the results. "The messenger of the covenant in whom you delight—indeed, he is coming, says the Lord of hosts. But who can endure the day of his coming, and who can stand when he appears?" (Mal. 3:1–2). Thomas Jefferson once remarked, "I tremble for my country when I reflect that God is just."[12] Indeed, any nation, any group, any individual, but especially those of us who are privileged, ought at least to pause nervously before praying to God to establish justice.

Exodus 23:20 falls somewhere between these two prophets in tone. God will send an "angel" (the word can also be translated "messenger"), and, if the people obey him, "then I will be an enemy to your enemies and a foe to your foes" (Exod. 23:22). On the other hand, if they rebel against him, "he will not pardon your transgression" (Exod. 23:21). The three contexts of Malachi, Second Isaiah, and Exodus 23 together, then, add up to a message that could be summarized in the old phrase, "Be careful what you wish for." God is about to do a great thing. Good news! But not the good news people expect or will find comfortable.

The messenger of this ambiguous good news is John the Baptizer, the only figure Mark (here and again in chap. 6) ever lets divert him

12. Thomas Jefferson, *Notes on the State of Virginia*, query 18, in *The Complete Jefferson*, ed. Saul K. Padover (New York: Duell, Sloan, and Pearce, 1943), 677.

from his single-minded focus on Jesus. William Abraham writes, "John does not show up with grandeur and force in a limousine or an army tank; he does not dine at the best restaurants; and his wardrobe is not that of the brightest and best. He represents a reversal of all earthly values. . . . Thus he clears the way for a clean and uncluttered look at the one who is to come."[13] John also appears in the work of the Jewish historian Josephus,[14] and his baptism of Jesus was sufficiently embarrassing to early Christians (why did the sinless Jesus need to be baptized?) that they are hardly likely to have invented the story. So John and his baptism of Jesus seem as historically well established as anything in the Gospels.

The meaning of his activity is far less clear. Some Jewish groups—the Essenes, for instance—engaged in regular ritual washings. Gentiles who became Jews underwent a number of rituals, including a kind of baptism. But neither of these practices is the same as John's "baptism of repentance for the forgiveness of sins," which thus seems to be something new. The symbolism of sin as like dirt, what Paul Ricoeur calls "a quasi-material something that infects as a sort of filth,"[15] is a widespread human phenomenon. The psalmist prays, "Wash me thoroughly from my iniquity, and cleanse me from my sin" (Ps. 51:2). Shakespeare's Lady Macbeth cannot shake the image of the blood of her victims on her hands: "Out, damned spot! . . . What, will these hands ne'er be clean?"[16] Thus some sort of washing is a natural enough ritual for sinners seeking to repent, and John may well have invented his own.

The Baptizer brings to mind the prophet Elijah, that "troubler of Israel" (1 Kgs. 18:17) who denounced the corruption of King Ahab and fought for the pure worship of the Lord. Elijah too wore a leather belt around his waist, and either he or his clothing (the translation is not quite clear) was hairy (2 Kgs. 1:8). Elijah too went east of the Jordan into the wilderness and ate only what ravens brought him—a diet as unattractive as locusts. In the last verses of Malachi (4:5–6),

13. William J. Abraham, "First Sunday after the Epiphany," in *The Lectionary Commentary: The Third Readings: The Gospels*, ed. Roger E. Van Harn (Grand Rapids: Eerdmans, 2001), 163.
14. Josephus, *Jewish Antiquities* 18.116–19.
15. Paul Ricoeur, *The Symbolism of Evil*, trans. Emerson Buchanan (Boston: Beacon, 1967), 25.
16. William Shakespeare, *Macbeth* 5.1, in *The Norton Shakespeare*, ed. Stephen Greenblatt et al. (New York: Norton, 1997), 2609.

which are the final verses of Catholic and Protestant versions of the Old Testament, the Lord promises to send Elijah back to call people to repentance before "the great and terrible day of the LORD." Thus John as a kind of Elijah surrogate picks up the story of divine revelation, stands in judgment against the powerful of his time, and reinforces the idea that a deeply ambiguous divine intervention is near at hand.

The prophets who begin with Elijah, Walter Brueggemann writes, abruptly halt the royal narrative of 1 and 2 Kings to present a counterforce to monarchy. Elijah, Micaiah, and Elisha "are completely unexpected, uncredentialed, and uninvited characters in the royal history of Israel. According to the tale told, they enact the raw, unfiltered power of Yahweh that lies complete beyond the command of the royal houses. Indeed, their presence in the narrative serves to expose the inadequacy and lameness of the kings as shapers of history."[17] The same can be said of the Baptizer. Yet John's function here is almost entirely to proclaim that the one coming after him is greater. The rabbis taught that a student owed his teacher any service except untying his shoe.[18] The Baptizer declares not just that he should do even that, but that he is not worthy to do it.

> Lo, I will send you the prophet Elijah before the great and terrible day of the LORD comes. He will turn the hearts of parents to their children and the hearts of children to their parents, so that I will not come and strike the land with a curse.
> —Malachi 4:5–6

## 1:9–11
### *Baptism*

As already noted, the theologians of the early church were nervous about the fact that Jesus had been baptized. If baptism washes away sins, why did the one they judged to be sinless get baptized? Gregory of Nazianzus concluded that in this case the cleansing action went the other direction. Just as, when lepers touched Jesus, they did not

---

17. Walter Brueggemann, *1 and 2 Kings* (Macon, GA: Smith and Helwys, 2000), 207.
18. Babylonian Talmud *Ketubot* 96a, quoted in Joel Marcus, *Mark 1–8*, AB (New York: Doubleday, 2000), 152.

make him unclean, but he cured them, so in this case, "He needed no fortifying rites himself—his purpose was to hallow water."[19] John Chrysostom saw only one more instance of a general pattern in which God becomes human, and "in these humiliations his exaltation most shines forth."[20]

What happens is worth some detailed attention. Those who practice baptism by immersion will note with pleasure that Jesus comes up out of the water. The verb describing what happens to the heavens is an exceedingly forceful one, meaning "ripped apart" or "torn open." Both Matthew and Luke tone it down to something like "opened." But as Donald Juel noted, "What is opened may be closed; what is torn apart cannot easily return to its former state."[21] In Mark's version, the relation of heaven and earth has been permanently changed. Pictures of the Spirit descending in the form of a dove fill the history of Christian art, and Luke certainly imagines a bird. Mark, on the other hand, could mean only that the Spirit came down in the way that a dove would. That meaning is ambiguous; at another point most recent translations just seem to get the text wrong: the Spirit descends *in* or *into* (*eis*) Jesus, not *on* him. Mark means that something entered Jesus, not that a bird perched on his head.

The image of the dove evokes the dove that returned to the ark with a freshly plucked olive leaf (Gen. 8:11) to signal to Noah that the floodwaters had subsided and there was now solid ground bearing vegetation. But in this case, Chrysostom writes, "the dove also appears, not bearing an olive branch, but pointing out to us our Deliverer from all evils, and suggesting gracious hope. For not from out of an ark does she lead one man only, but the whole world she leads up to heaven."[22]

The tearing of the heavens, like the quotation from the prophets, is more ambiguous. When Second Isaiah prayed, "O that you would tear open the heavens and come down . . ." (Isa. 64:1), he was hoping

19. Gregory of Nazianzus, "Oration 29: On the Son" 20 (*NPNF*, 2nd ser., 7:308).
20. John Chrysostom, *Homilies on Matthew* 12.1 (*NPNF*, 1st ser., 10:75).
21. Donald H. Juel, *Mark*, Augsburg Commentary on the New Testament (Minneapolis: Augsburg, 1990), 33.
22. John Chrysostom, *Homilies on Matthew* 12.3 (*NPNF*, 1st ser., 10:77).

for the vindication of Israel against its enemies. In contrast, Donald
Juel used to tell about the seminary student whose first reaction to
this passage was, "It's scary. God is loose in the world." That reaction
does not seem entirely wrong. Can any of us be confident enough of
ourselves to welcome God's presence among us without hesitation?

In Mark God directly speaks twice and acts twice. At Jesus' baptism, God tears open the heavens and declares Jesus "my Son, the
Beloved." At the transfiguration God again declares, "This is my
Son, the Beloved" (9:7), and at
the moment of Jesus' death God
tears the veil of the temple in two
(15:38). Two proclamations and
two tearings: God breaks open barriers and identifies Jesus as God's
beloved Son. Beyond that, Jesus
carries the story.

> Whenever I attempt to
> think about Abraham I am . . .
> overwhelmed.
>
> —Søren Kierkegaard
>
> *Fear and Trembling*, 35.

Reference to a "beloved son" calls to mind the terrifying story
in which God tells Abraham to take his beloved son to the top of
Mount Moriah and offer him as a sacrifice (Gen. 22). Søren Kierkegaard worried at great length about the paradox of Abraham's faith:
he did not think it was all a game but set off taking God's command
seriously, and yet he did not despair but retained a faith in God that
ultimately he would not lose his son. "He had faith that God would
not demand Isaac of him, and yet he was willing to sacrifice him if
it was demanded. He had faith by virtue of the absurd, for human
calculation was out of the question, and it certainly was absurd that
God, who required it of him, should in the next moment rescind the
requirement."[23] Kierkegaard's insistence on the paradoxical character of Abraham's mind-set provides a useful way of thinking about
the paradox of Jesus, who is both human and divine, who will, by the
end of Mark's story, both be as one with God and cry out that God
has forsaken him.

In Mark the voice from heaven at the baptism addresses Jesus
alone. Mark's story of Jesus' baptism, indeed, gave aid and comfort

---

23. Søren Kierkegaard, *Fear and Trembling*, ed. and trans. Howard V. Hong and Edna H. Hong
(Princeton: Princeton University Press, 1983), 35–36.

to the early heresy called adoptionism, the belief that Jesus was born simply a human being, whom God adopted as in some honorary sense his Son at the time of his baptism because of his previous life of virtue. A leather merchant named Theodotus came to Rome from Byzantium teaching this doctrine about 190, and it was further developed by a third-century bishop of Antioch named Paul of Samosata. The adoptionists wanted to avoid any challenge to the oneness of God, and claiming that Jesus was divine from birth and thus by nature seemed to them to represent just such a challenge. Indeed, Mark's account of Jesus' baptism raises all sorts of questions about the relation of this Son to the voice from heaven and the Spirit that descends into him, topics with which the early church struggled as it developed the doctrine of the Trinity.

# FURTHER REFLECTIONS
## *Father, Son, and Spirit*

It is a commonplace of modern theology to note that the Bible never mentions the Trinity, and indeed neither the word "Trinity" nor the complex set of ideas Christians developed under that term in the church's first four centuries appear in the Bible. Still, it is a mistake to conclude that the church invented this idea of Trinity without any scriptural warrant. (I will have something to say later about the male language of "Father" and "Son"; in tracing the historical issues it seems impossible to avoid.)

Consider Mark's account of Jesus' baptism. Jesus comes out of the water, the Spirit descends in him, and a voice from heaven proclaims him "my Son, the Beloved." In Augustine's words, "Here then we have the Trinity in a certain way distinguished: the Father in the Voice, the Son in the Man, the Holy Spirit in the Dove."[24] Christians inherited from Judaism a clear monotheism; at the core of Jewish faith is the affirmation, "Hear, O Israel: the LORD is our God, the LORD alone."[25] Yet, as Augustine argued, it is not simply God who was crucified and bur-

---

24. Augustine, *Sermons on New Testament Lessons* 2.1 (*NPNF*, 1st ser., 6:259).
25. Deut 6:4. See Athanasius, *Discourses against the Arians* 3.24.7 (*NPNF*, 2nd ser., 4:397).

ied and rose again, or who descended at Jesus' baptism and again at Pentecost, or who spoke from heaven at Jesus' baptism and again at the transfiguration.[26] So there is one God, but the Son and the Holy Spirit are different from the Father. To simplify, that leaves two options: either the Son and the Spirit are not really God, or else we need a way to talk about a God who is both one and three.

So, to focus on the Son, does Mark present the Son as really God, or just a good man God honors with the name of Son (adoptionism) or a divine being of some sort, but one lesser than God (Arianism)? Mark's story of Jesus' baptism does not yet answer that question. Nor is the question best answered, as many have tried to do, by attending to the titles Mark ascribes to Jesus—Son of God, Messiah, Lord, and so on. They are worth discussing, but Mark derives their meaning from the way he uses them in his narrative, rather than bringing terms that already have a clear definition into his story. It is the narrative that answers the question, and it does so in that, as the story unfolds, we see God acting in Jesus so fully and directly that it becomes impossible not to think of Jesus as God. It is Jesus who heals. How people stand with respect to God's kingdom depends on how they stand with respect to Jesus. It is Jesus who saves. If this Jesus is not truly God, then God becomes an abstract figure in the background, and it is Jesus who loves us and Jesus whom we should worship. But then it is Jesus, and not the one God, who is our Lord.

If the Son is really God (and the Spirit too, but that argument has to reach beyond Mark to Acts and John and Paul's Letters), and if there is one God, but the Son is not the Father, and the Spirit is neither the Father nor the Son, how do we talk about this God who is both one and three? After literally centuries of debate, Greek-speaking Christians settled on saying that God is one *ousia* but three *hypostases*. Christians who spoke Latin said that God is one *substantia* but three *personae*. So in English we usually speak of God as one "substance" but three "persons."

The thought of unpacking the technical meaning of all these metaphysical terms is intimidating, but also apt to lead astray. The

26. Augustine, *The Trinity* 1.2.7, *The Works of Saint Augustine*, part 1, vol. 5, trans. Edmund Hill (Brooklyn: New City Press, 1991), 69.

theologians who developed the terminology keep insisting that they do not know what it means either. Take Augustine, for example:

> When the question is asked "Three what?" we apply ourselves to finding some name of a species or genus which will comprise these three, and no such name occurs to our minds, because the total transcendence of the godhead quite surpasses the capacity of ordinary speech. . . . And so, for the sake of talking about inexpressible matters, that we may somehow express what we are completely unable to express, our Greek colleagues talk about one *ousia*, three *hypostases*, while we Latins talk of one *essentia* or *substantia*, three *personae*.[27]

Similarly, Gregory of Nyssa admitted, "Whoever searches the whole of Revelation will find therein no doctrine of the divine nature,"[28] and therefore, "for how could a name be found for that which is above every name," we use "whatever name our intelligence by pious effort be enabled to discover to indicate the transcendent nature."[29] The Trinity offers something more like a set of rules than a metaphysical theory:[30] Recognize that the Father does things that the Son does not do, the Son does things that the Father does not do, and so on—and yet they are all one God. Find some convenient labels for the oneness and the threeness, but do not claim to understand their relationship. Do not begin with the definitions of terms and try to make Mark's story fit them, but begin with the story and let the concepts and the relations among them emerge from it.

# 1:12–13

## *Temptation*

No sooner has Jesus been baptized and heard the voice from heaven than "the Spirit immediately drove him out into the wilderness." That "immediately" (*euthys*) is one of Mark's favorite words; he uses

27. Ibid., 7.3.7 (224–25).
28. Gregory of Nyssa, *Answer to Eunomius' Second Book* (*NPNF*, 2nd ser., 5:261).
29. Gregory of Nyssa, *Against Eunomius* 2.3 (*NPNF*, 2nd ser., 5:103).
30. George A. Lindbeck, *The Nature of Doctrine* (Philadelphia: Westminster, 1984), 18–19.

it forty-one times compared with ten times in all the rest of the New Testament. Translators trying to "improve" Mark's prose tend to find synonyms (for instance, "just as he was" in 1:10) to avoid Mark's constant repetition of the word, but thereby they lose some of the energy with which that repetition drives the story forward. And immediately.... And immediately.... And immediately.

The Spirit *drives* Jesus into the wilderness. The verb is strong, the same one later used for driving evil spirits out of the possessed. This is no casual trip. The remarkably brief story of his temptation (one of those places where one must resist reading Matthew or Luke into Mark) continues the ambiguities of this whole introductory section. Jesus goes into the wilderness. The wilderness is a dangerous place, undomesticated, unsafe, the abode of demons (Isa. 34:14), and indeed Jesus encounters Satan there. Yet Israel remembered the wilderness as the place where they had been closest to God (Jer. 2:2), and pious folks and lovers of solitude down the centuries have sought out wilderness for contemplation. As Chrysostom put it, "For the wilderness is the mother of quiet; it is a calm and a harbor, delivering us from all turmoils."[31] Similarly, one can imagine the wild beasts as dangerous, like the howling creatures, goat demons, hyenas, and jackals with which Isaiah threatens Babylon in the time after its defeat (Isa. 13:21–22) or the wild beasts Christians in Mark's time faced in the Roman Coliseum. But Isaiah also promises an eschatological time of peace when:

> The wolf shall live with the lamb,
>     the leopard shall lie down with the kid,
>     the calf and the lion and the fatling together,
>     and a little child shall lead them.
>
> (Isa. 11:6)

This is a return to the time of innocence prior to the fall. Is Mark implying that Jesus was surrounded by threatening wild beasts or that even the wild animals ministered to him? Once again, he leaves ambiguity.

---

31. John Chrysostom, *Homilies on Matthew* 50.1 (*NPNF*, 1st ser., 10:310).

There is no ambiguity about the figure of Satan, the one who tempts him. In Job 1 and Zechariah 3, "the Satan" ("the adversary," at this point a title rather than a name) is one of the heavenly beings, a sort of prosecuting attorney in the divine court, whose job is to test and ask hard questions, but whose work is an assignment from God. In the intertestamental period, Jews increasingly came to think of Satan as truly God's opponent and enemy, though never an equal and indeed always one of God's creatures. This is the picture presented in Mark 3:23–26.

But what does it mean that Jesus was tempted? It is a tough theological question. Jesus, Christian faith teaches, is the Son of God incarnate, fully divine as well as fully human. Yet Mark affirms the fact that he was tempted, just as Hebrews assures us that "we do not have a high priest who is unable to sympathize with our weaknesses, but we have one who in every respect has been tested as we are, yet without sin. . . . He is able to deal gently with the ignorant and wayward, since he himself is subject to weakness" (Heb. 4:15; 5:2). We find it hard to imagine what it means to be tempted, "yet without sin"—perhaps in part because we ourselves so regularly succumb to temptation.

> Therefore Christ was tempted so that a Christian not be conquered by the tempter.
> —Augustine
>
> "Second Sermon on Psalm 90."

Pope Gregory the Great explained it like this. Temptation moves to fulfillment in three stages: suggestion, delight, and consent. I see someone drop a wallet and realize that I could pick it up and keep it. I think with pleasure how much I would enjoy having more money. So I say to myself, "Yes, I will pick it up and keep it." Jesus, Gregory says, experienced suggestion—he recognized how he could do wrong. But it never occasioned delight in him, and so he never consented.[32] Augustine said that sin resulted only at the stage of consent.[33] The point is that one can be tempted, really tempted, without falling into

---

32. Gregory the Great, "Homily 16 on the Gospels," in *The Sunday Sermons of the Great Fathers*, ed. and trans. M. F. Toal (repr. Swedesboro, NJ: Preservation Press, 1996), 2:33.
33. Augustine, "On Continence" 5 (*NPNF*, 1st ser., 3:381).

sin. To say that Jesus was never tempted denies his humanity; to say that he fell into sin denies his divinity.

Yet how the same person could be both human and divine is perhaps the greatest mystery of all in Mark's story. Classic Christian theology teaches that Christ is two natures in one person. To put it in different terms, he is two *whats* but one *who*.[34] There is not one person who grows tired and another who cures the sick, but *one* who who acts and suffers. Yet, when we ask *what* that one person is, there are two answers: the son of Mary, and the Son of God, human and divine. Only as both natures can the one person experience temptation and defeat Satan.

---

34. David S. Yeago, "Jesus of Nazareth and Cosmic Redemption: The Relevance of St. Maximus the Confessor," *Modern Theology* 12 (1996): 167.

# 1:14–3:6

# *Healing the Rejected Ones*

In the introduction to Mark, we encountered voices from heaven and angels, Satan and wild beasts. Now, as Jesus' ministry begins, we are in more ordinary territory, among the common folk of the villages of Galilee. Jesus proclaims the coming of God's reign, calls disciples, heals, and enters into controversies. We learn about who he is by hearing about what he does. Among other things, we learn that he has a strange compelling power, a particular concern for society's outsiders, and a willingness to challenge the religious and cultural rules of his time.

## 1:14–15
### *Proclaiming God's Reign*

Scholars focused on Mark's structure debate whether verses 14 and 15 are the end of the introduction or the beginning of the first section describing Jesus' ministry. The plausibility of arguments on both sides makes it easiest to think of this passage as a transition. These verses conclude the introduction by providing an introductory summary of what comes next, Jesus' activity of preaching, teaching, and healing. Mark tells us that Jesus' public activity began only after John the Baptizer had been "handed over." "Arrested," the usual translation, hides the first appearance of one of the key words in this Gospel—*paradothēnai*, "handed over" or "delivered up." In passages where Paul seems to be quoting even earlier formulas, he speaks of how Jesus "was handed over to death for our trespasses"

(Rom. 4:25), and on the night when he "was handed over" shared bread and the cup with his disciples. The phrase must be one Christians used very early to describe what happened to Jesus. Mark uses it here of John, several times of Jesus, and in Mark 13:9 and 11 of those who will follow Jesus. The passive verb leaves its subject unclear. John was handed over—by whom? By the end of the Gospel it is clear enough that this verb signals action directed by God, part of God's plan. Thus here, just as Jesus begins his public activity, Mark indicates that this is not a random moment. John's arrest is a signal: after the prologue the director is opening the curtain on the first scene.

In an early scene of the best movie ever made (I think) about Jesus, Pier Paulo Pasolini's *The Gospel according to St. Matthew*, Jesus is walking at a brisk pace just short of a jog down a road. Some farmers traveling the opposite direction stop to look, and, as he passes them, almost over his shoulder, he says, "Repent, the kingdom of God is at hand," and just keeps on moving. The scene captures something of Mark's style—the constant "and immediately . . ." with which he pushes his story forward—but also something of the strange power of this Jesus, who declares and compels rather than explaining and persuading. John called people to repent and be baptized; Jesus calls them to repent and believe. Believe what? The good news of God— that God's reign is at hand.

## FURTHER REFLECTIONS
### *The Reign of God*

The reign or kingdom of God lies at the core of Jesus' preaching. In Mark, the first words Jesus speaks proclaim it. I use "reign" rather than "kingdom" for two reasons. First, it avoids introducing a male image that is not in the original Greek, where *basileia* can apply equally to the rule of kings and queens. Second, "kingdom" seems primarily a spatial term—the boundaries of a kingdom run to the river or the mountains—whereas Mark uses *basileia* more as a temporal category, whose important boundary is its beginning. In English a ruler's "reign" has more of that temporal focus.

Just when Mark thinks the reign of God begins is one of the central questions in interpreting the Gospel and is inseparable from the question of what the term means. At the end of the nineteenth century and beginning of the twentieth, theologians like Albrecht Ritschl and Adolf von Harnack in Germany and Walter Rauschenbusch in the United States thought of God's reign as something that could emerge gradually in history through human efforts assisted by God's grace. Rauschenbusch, a Baptist political and social activist who worked in the slums of New York, was particularly eager to emphasize that Jesus had not preached just inner spiritual transformation. Any first-century Jew, Rauschenbusch said, would have understood the reign of God to mean a transformation of society. "Jesus, like all the prophets and like all his spiritually minded countrymen, lived in the hope of a great transformation of the national, social and religious life around him." Jesus modified the dominant view, however, in that he rejected all violence, focused on all humankind rather than just Israel, hoped to work by beginning with small centers of influence rather than a general transformation, and "postponed the divine catastrophe of judgment to the dim distance and put the emphasis on the growth of the new life that was now going on."[1] So, Rauschenbusch argued, we can pick up Jesus' task by working for social reform in our own communities.

In his radical 1892 book *Jesus' Preaching of the Reign of God*, the German NT scholar Johannes Weiss took a dramatically different view. The New Testament, he argued, pictures God's reign as beginning dramatically at some future moment by direct divine intervention. As Mark puts it:

> the sun will be darkened,
>     and the moon will not give its light,
> the stars will be falling from heaven,
>     and the powers in the heavens will be shaken.
> Then they will see the "Son of Man coming in clouds"
>     with great power and glory.
>
>                                        (Mark 13:24–26)

---

1. Walter Rauschenbusch, *Christianity and the Social Crisis* (London: Macmillan, 1913), 64.

Albert Schweitzer's famous book, *The Quest of the Historical Jesus*, originally published in German in 1906, developed this "futuristic" or "consistent eschatological" account of what the New Testament (and Jesus himself) meant by the reign of God. Schweitzer concluded that Jesus desperately wanted God's reign to begin and had despaired of the standard ways of initiating it. Jesus believed, however, that God could not let the Messiah die, and that he was the Messiah. Thus by setting up his own death, Jesus meant to force God's hand and bring in the reign of God.

The problem was, Schweitzer admitted, that if that is what Jesus meant, then he was wrong. Jesus expected this dramatic, public event as he was on the cross or at any rate within the lifetime of some of those around him: "There are some standing here who will not taste death until they see that the kingdom of God has come with power" (Mark 9:1). Yet here we are, two thousand years later. Schweitzer concluded that, nevertheless, Jesus offered a model of commitment to a personal cause, even if a misguided one, and in that sense we can still follow him. "Our relationship to Jesus is ultimately of a mystical kind. . . . we can achieve a relation to such a personality only when we become united with him in the knowledge of a shared aspiration, when we feel that our will is clarified, enriched and enlivened by his will, and when we rediscover ourselves through him."[2] And this brilliant man, great theologian and one of Europe's great organists as well, went off to spend most of his life as a medical missionary in West Africa.

Taking a very different point of view, the English scholar C. H. Dodd argued in 1935 for a "realized eschatology" in which Jesus was teaching that the reign of God had already come: "Jesus intended to proclaim the Kingdom of God not as something to come in the near future, but as a matter of present experience. . . . In the ministry of Jesus Himself the divine power is released in effective conflict with evil."[3] To say that God's reign "is at hand" could mean either that it is about to come or that it already has come; Dodd imagined the

2. Albert Schweitzer, *The Quest of the Historical Jesus*, trans. W. Montgomery et al., ed. John Bowden (Minneapolis: Fortress, 2001), 486.
3. C. H. Dodd, *The Parables of the Kingdom* (New York: Charles Scribner's Sons, 1961), 31, 35.

Aramaic original behind the Greek and concluded it would imply that the kingdom was already present. As to passages like Mark 9:1, Dodd put the emphasis on how some "will not taste death *until they see* that the reign of God has come"—the kingdom has come already; what will happen before they die is that some of the people with him will realize the fact. Thus Dodd's eschatology (theory about the end times) is "realized" in that it was already real in Jesus' ministry, not a future event for which we need to wait.

Few followed Schweitzer in his conviction that Jesus was wrong but worth following anyway, and Dodd himself, in later work, backed off "realized eschatology" in favor of "eschatology in the process of realization." The problem with either "futuristic eschatology" or "realized eschatology" is that the Gospels contain *both* passages that seem to talk about the reign of God as a future event *and* texts that seem to assume that it is already present and at work in Jesus' ministry. Voting for one side or the other involves ignoring some of the evidence.

The best solution seems to be what a number of scholars call "proleptic eschatology." "Prolepsis" is a literary term referring to an anticipation, early in a story, of an important later event. For instance, from the start of the Harry Potter books, the scar on Harry's forehead comes from a fight with Voldemort in which Harry, amazingly, was not killed. So we anticipate that in the end Harry is the one who will defeat Voldemort in some sort of combat—after all, he already did, proleptically. So the central parables in which Mark explains God's reign involve the planting of seeds. The seed is planted, really there in the ground, coming to life, but it is so far small and hidden, not yet the bush or tree that will emerge. Similarly, the transformation of the world is already happening as Jesus heals the sick and challenges the established authorities. But the activity of this one wandering preacher in an obscure province of the empire is not what the reign of God will be when it is fulfilled, for ultimately it really will transform the world.

In different ways, though, all these interpretations agree with one of Rauschenbusch's points—the reign of God is not just something that happens in people's hearts. As the NT scholar John Meier puts it, "These sayings proclaim more than a rosy-fingered dawn impinging on one's consciousness."[4] The reign or kingdom of God was rarely discussed among Jews before the time of Jesus, but the term would have evoked political and social change, not just inner, spiritual transformation. William Abraham makes the point,

> The language is clearly political in content, for it concerns a kingdom. The kingdom is not about philosophy, ethics, or abstract spirituality; it is about God's rule in history here and now. There is a hard edge to kingdom discourse; it suggests that we cannot reduce what is at stake to interior piety or the world to come. Current public and political issues are in view. To his hearers this would be obvious, for in Israel religion and politics, ethics and politics, were inextricably connected.[5]

What Jesus is beginning is the transformation of this world. That is why those in charge of this world as it was ended up killing him.

## 1:16–20
### *Calling the First Disciples*

Having proclaimed the core of his message, Jesus begins his ministry by calling disciples. *Mathētēs*, the word here for "disciples," never appears in the Septuagint (the Greek version of the OT), and in the New Testament comes up only in the Gospels and Acts. It was a rare enough word that Mark's first readers/listeners would have had to learn its meaning by what followed. Being a disciple of Jesus, it emerges, means receiving his call, physically following him (and thereby giving up job, home, and normal ties to family), and risking the suffering that may ensue.

The story's most dramatic feature is the sheer abruptness of the call. Jesus says, "'Follow me.' . . . And immediately they left their nets and followed him." Mark rarely uses his favorite phrase, "And

4. John P. Meier, *A Marginal Jew: Rethinking the Historical Jesus*, vol. 2, *Mentor, Message, and Miracles* (New York: Doubleday, 1994), 451.
5. William J. Abraham, "First Sunday after the Epiphany," in *The Lectionary Commentary: The Third Readings: The Gospels*, ed. Roger E. Van Harn (Grand Rapids: Eerdmans, 2001), 172.

immediately . . .," to such powerful effect. No discussion or explanation, no packing, no good-byes to family and friends. One pictures
Zebedee standing in his boat with his mouth open in surprise as his
sons depart. Dietrich Bonhoeffer asks, "How could the call immediately evoke obedience? The story is a stumbling block for the natural
reason, and it is no wonder that frantic attempts have been made to
separate the two events [the call and the following]. By hook or by
crook a bridge must be found between them. Something must have
happened in between, some psychological or historical event."[6] Even
Saint Jerome imagined that "there was something divine in the Savior's countenance that men, seeing, could not resist," for people to
follow him like this.[7] But no, Bonhoeffer continues, "This encounter
is a testimony to the absolute, direct, and unaccountable authority
of Jesus." Because it is Jesus who calls, they obey. Nor do they understand any particular content to that obedience other than simply following: "It gives no intelligible program for a way of life, no goal or
ideal to strive after. It is not a cause which human calculation might
deem worthy of our devotion."[8]

Bonhoeffer argues than in this episode faith does not precede
obedience.[9] So often Christians think that, if only we had a deeper
faith, like those we most admire, we would go out and feed the hungry, serve the gospel. Bonhoeffer insists that we should not try to
cultivate our faith so that some day we will be able to obey. Rather, in
obedience we will find our faith growing. What we first need to do,
this story tells us, is to follow Jesus.

Zebedee and his sons had a boat and hired men. They were not
poor, and James and John did not stop to negotiate the terms on
which they could return to their inheritance. To follow Jesus is to risk
great cost. Jesus calls them to become fishers of people. The phrase is
appropriate, Calvin writes, "For men stray and wander in the world,

---

6. Dietrich Bonhoeffer, *The Cost of Discipleship*, trans. R. H. Fuller (New York: Macmillan,
    1963), 61.
7. Jerome, "Homily 83: On Mark 11.15–17," *The Homilies of Saint Jerome*, trans. Marie Liguori
    Ewald, 2 vols., FC 48, 57 (Washington, DC: Catholic University of America Press, 1964–
    1966), 2:180.
8. Bonhoeffer, *Cost of Discipleship*, 62.
9. Ibid., 69.

as in a great and troubled sea, till they are gathered by the Gospel."[10] Yet in earlier scriptural passages (Jer. 16:16; Ezek. 29:4; Amos 4:2), the image is a negative one, like the trappers of animals. After all, once caught the fish usually dies. Is such a connotation intentional? It is hard

> I am now sending for many fishermen, says the LORD, and they shall catch them; and afterward I will send for many hunters.
>
> —Jeremiah 16:16

to tell. Those who are "caught" in discipleship of Jesus will come to great joy, but only, we will learn, on the other side of suffering.

## 1:21–28
### *Healing a Man with an Unclean Spirit*

Jesus has proclaimed his central message and called his first disciples. Now he begins his ministry, and he begins it at the heart of his society: at a synagogue, and on the Sabbath. He teaches and cures— two of his ministry's central activities—and he does so in a way that reinforces what we learned in his call of his first disciples. Twice in a few verses observers remark that he has authority. *Exousia*, the word for "authority," was often applied to kings and especially associated with what God would have when his reign came. This section mentions no opposition, but there are hints of things to come. He has authority, not like the scribes. His fame begins to spread. Is it only because we know the rest of the story so well that these things seem ominous?

A man with an unclean spirit did not belong in a synagogue. He was ritually unclean, and this was sacred space. Indeed, like the children or mentally ill people we often try to keep out of church, he promptly disrupts things by yelling his head off. The spirit or spirits within him recognize Jesus as "the Holy One of God." (It is unclear whether the references to "us" imply several spirits in this man or fear of Jesus on behalf of evil spirits in general.) Evil spirits never have any problem knowing who Jesus is; "the demons believe—and

---

10. Calvin, *Harmony of the Evangelists*, 1:244.

shudder" (Jas. 2:19). As Augustine explains, "The devils confessed Christ. . . . They had faith but not charity; hence they were devils."[11] The Catholic tradition follows Augustine here, holding that faith is incomplete apart from charity. Protestants tend rather to emphasize that "faith" means more than just knowing the facts about God. As Calvin says, "faith consists in assurance rather than comprehension";[12] it involves personal trust and confidence. So, when the Heidelberg Catechism asks, "What is true faith?" the response is, "It is not only a certain knowledge by which I accept as true all that God has revealed to us in his Word, but also a wholehearted trust which the Holy Spirit creates in me through the gospel, that, not only to others, but to me also God has given the forgiveness of sins, everlasting righteousness and salvation, out of sheer grace solely for the sake of Christ's saving work."[13] Whether, with Catholics, one adds charity to faith, or, with Protestants, one expands faith's definition, either way it involves a trusting heart as well as a knowing brain. And the devils do not have it.

English translations usually water down the blunt forcefulness of Jesus' response: "Shut up" or "Muzzle it" and "Get out." The evil spirit(s) spoke truly enough, and Jesus' insistence on secrecy about his identity is a theme in Mark to which we will have to return. For the moment, perhaps it is enough to quote Athanasius: "For although what they said was true . . . yet He did not wish that the truth should proceed from an unclean mouth, and especially from such as them, lest under pretence thereof they should mingle with it their own malicious devices."[14] Evil spirits are not to be trusted, even when they are telling the truth.

11. Augustine, *Lectures on the Gospel of John* 6.21 (*NPNF*, 1st ser., 7:46).
12. John Calvin, *Institutes of the Christian Religion* 3.2.14, ed. John T. McNeill, trans. Ford Lewis Battles, 2 vols., LCC 20–21 (Philadelphia: Westminster, 1960), 1:560.
13. Heidelberg Catechism, q. 21, in *Creeds and Confessions of Faith in the Christian Tradition*, ed. Jaroslav Pelikan and Valerie Hotchkiss (New Haven: Yale University Press, 2003), 432.
14. Athanasius, *To the Bishops of Egypt* 1.3 (*NPNF*, 2nd ser., 4:224, translation altered).

# 1:29–34
## *Healing in Simon's House*

"Peter had a mother-in-law, and therefore had a wife too," Martin Luther once remarked in the midst of debates about priestly celibacy.[15] There may be good reasons for some Christians to live a celibate life (so that they are free of worries about inheritances for their children, so that they can dedicate themselves better to their vocations, and so on), but those in the Christian tradition, like Tertullian and Jerome, who argued that celibacy is *intrinsically* a better state have always been embarrassed by the fact that the first and most honored of the disciples was married.

Simon's mother-in-law is in bed with a fever—a much more serious issue in the preantibiotic ancient world. Jesus heals her by touching her and lifting her up—none of the chanted secret formulas characteristic of a magician, and not even a prayer. As with the calling of disciples, his authority suffices. Deborah Krause remarks that, when she teaches this story, "many women snort under their breath at the detail in Mk. 1:31 about her 'serving them.'" They see that Jesus "healed her just in time for supper!"[16] True enough. Yet, as Krause and others point out, some qualifications may be in order. A first-century Jewish matriarch would have been ashamed not to be in charge when guests came to her home; whether or not this was psychologically healthy (and perhaps she *should* have enjoyed what authority was available to her in a patriarchal society), it was a fact. That word "serve" (*diēkonei*), moreover, is an interesting one. It is the origin of our word "deacon," the church office created in Acts 6 to supervise the distribution of food among Christians, though most English translations render it "deacon" when applied to men and "servant" when applied to women. Mark uses the verb only of women and angels and Jesus, never of the male disciples. So it is far from clear that the word denigrates Simon's mother-in-law.

15. Martin Luther, "The Tyranny and Burden of Celibacy," *Table Talk* (no. 3777, February 24, 1538), ed. and trans. Theodore G. Tappert, LW 54 (Philadelphia: Fortress, 1967), 271.

16. Deborah Krause, "Simon Peter's Mother-in-Law," in *A Feminist Companion to Mark*, ed. Amy-Jill Levine (Cleveland: Pilgrim Press, 2001), 39.

# 1:35–39
## *Praying and Preaching*

Is it all nearly too much? In Pasolini's *Gospel according to St. Matthew* all sorts of cripples and lepers and madmen virtually pile on top of Jesus in a horrific scene. Such an image is horribly unfair to the handicapped (I have used demeaning words as the only way to describe the impression the scene creates), but the narrative does contrast the evening when "the whole city was gathered around the door" with the next morning, when Jesus arises while it is still dark and goes out to a deserted place to pray. Simon and his companions have to "hunt" for him—the verb does not mean just "looking" but is used for the tracking and pursuit of animals. Jesus is pressed in from all sides. Social workers, emergency room nurses, and others like them know how the demands of their clients can become overwhelming. Eugene Boring notes, "In the preceding scenes, he does not pray to God but acts *as* God. . . . But divine beings do not pray. Mark here juxtaposes the picture of the weak human being and the preceding picture of the powerful Son of God, so that already in these opening scenes there is a mini-summary of the Gospel as a whole."[17] Mark's story presents the Christology that would become orthodox in a narrative form. This one Jesus is both human and divine—as the Council of Chalcedon would teach more than four centuries later, one person in two natures. One agent acts and suffers, and that one agent is both human and divine. Moreover, he is not less divine for being also human. As Karl Barth puts it,

> He (the Redeemer) descended to earth out of sympathy for the human race.
> . . . What is this passion which He suffered for us? It is the passion of love (*caritas est passio*).
>
> —Origen
>
> Quoted in Jürgen Moltmann, *The Way of Jesus Christ* (San Francisco: HarperSanFrancisco, 1990), 179.

---

17. M. Eugene Boring, *Mark*, NTL (Louisville: Westminster John Knox, 2006), 68.

> In being neighbor to man . . . He does not need to fear for His
> Godhead. On the contrary . . . God shows Himself to be the
> great and true God in the fact that He can and will let His grace
> bear this cost, that He is capable and willing and ready for this
> condescension, this act of extravagance, this far journey. What
> marks out God above all false gods is that they are not capable
> and ready for this. In their otherworldliness and supernatural-
> ness and otherness, etc., the gods are a reflection of the human
> pride which will not unbend. . . . God is not proud. In His high
> majesty He is humble.[18]

God is not first of all power, or transcendence. God is love.

So Jesus comes away from the deserted place and travels around
Galilee, proclaiming the message and casting out demons. This
one person who is both human and divine acts in obedience to his
calling.

# 1:40–45

### *Healing a Leper*

Medical historians debate just what disease this story is about. Hansen's disease, the modern term for leprosy, comes on slowly and is
incurable. The discussion of "lepers" in Leviticus 13 refers to a condition that appeared suddenly and sometimes went away. Leviticus,
however, may not settle questions about Jesus' time; Hansen's disease
seems to have arrived in the Middle East between the time Leviticus
was written and the time of Jesus. So the medical evidence is confusing. But the victims of whatever disease this was had a rough time of
it under Jewish law: "The person who has the leprous disease shall
wear torn clothes and let the hair of his head be disheveled; and he
shall cover his upper lip and cry out, 'Unclean, unclean.' . . . He shall
live alone; his dwelling shall be outside the camp" (Lev. 13:45–46).

Since we do not know the nature of the disease, we cannot know
how infectious it was, but something more than medical concern
about infection is at work here. Think of how reluctant people have

---

18. Barth, *CD* IV/1:159.

been to touch AIDS patients, even though it is clear the disease cannot be transmitted by touch. Even some cancer patients talk about
their longing for human touch and how, strangely, many people do
not want to hold their hands. Our instinct to keep our distance from
what we fear runs deep. But Jesus either lacked that instinct or over-
came it. He stretches out his hand, touches the leper, and cures him.
He might have healed simply by speaking a word, Calvin writes, but
he touches "to express the feeling of compassion." After all, we are
all sinners, but "he did not only deign to touch us with his hand, but
was united to one and the same body with us, that we might be flesh
of his flesh."[19]

In some early manuscripts, Jesus acts here out of pity; in others,
he reaches out in anger. The general scholarly rule is to think that
the more difficult reading is the original one. A copyist might think,
"'Anger' cannot be right; I will change it to 'pity,'" but it is hard to
imagine someone doing the opposite. Surely, though, Jesus would
not be angry at the leper. Might he, however, have been angry at the
rules that compelled lepers, already physically afflicted, to live alone
outside the town, to dress in rags, and to approach others shouting,
"Unclean, unclean"? The further burdens we place on those already
suffering are just the sort of thing that did make Jesus angry.

## 2:1–12

### Healing a Paralytic

Many of us remember this story from childhood Sunday school with
particular vividness. Perhaps the idea of tearing open a roof appeals
to children. Given the thatched roofs of the time, the task would have
involved neither great difficulty nor permanent damage. Still, the
paralytic's four friends remind one of fraternity boys in both their
virtues and their vices. They are loyal to their friend and determined
to get him cured, crowd or no crowd. And they are a little indifferent
to property and propriety. Mark suggests Jesus is rather like that too.
In any event, Jesus does not criticize their destructiveness but com-

---

19. Calvin, *Harmony of the Evangelists*, 1:374.

mends their faith, and thus we get further insight into the meaning of faith, what Theodore Jennings calls "this holy impatience, this all out, go for broke determination that the lame be made to walk."[20] It is their faith and not that of the paralytic (which is never mentioned, incidentally) that is at issue. Those who favor infant baptism and believe that the parents' faith can serve for the child's thus often cite this text.[21] But its implications concerning faith stretch wider. Faith has so much power, Cyril of Jerusalem declared in the fourth century, that "some have been saved by others believing." Therefore do not despair if your faith is weak or halfhearted but trust in God and it will be enough.[22]

For the first time Jesus encounters opponents. A "scribe," like a "secretary" in our society, could mean anyone from a low-level taker of notes to a high official (secretary of state). The scribes here represent the educated guardians of the Law. When Jesus forgives the paralytic's sins, they insist that no one "can forgive sins but God alone." They are right, in more than one sense. Technically, even the prophets who had healed never claimed the ability to forgive sins, and, according to one Jewish text, even the Messiah would have to pray to God to secure the forgiveness of sins.[23] Thus, when Jesus asks whether it is easier to forgive sins or enable a paralytic to walk, the surprising answer is that all sorts of magicians and prophets can heal the lame, but only God can forgive sins. After all, as the early Christian writer Irenaeus noted, sin is against God, and, "In what way can sins be truly remitted unless He against whom we have sinned has Himself granted remission."[24] But also, of course, we readers, who already know about the voice at Jesus' baptism, recognize that the scribes got it exactly right—only God can forgive sins, and in Jesus God is there among them.

20. Theodore W. Jennings Jr., *The Insurrection of the Crucified* (Chicago: Exploration Press, 2003), 29.
21. See Calvin, *Harmony of the Evangelists*, 1:393.
22. Cyril of Jerusalem, *Catechetical Lectures* 5.8 (*NPNF*, 2nd ser., 7:31).
23. "Thargum of Yonathan" 53.4, *The Fifty-Third Chapter of Isaiah according to the Jewish Interpreters*, vol. 2, *Translations*, ed. and trans. S. R. Driver and Adolf Neubauer (1877; repr. New York: Ktav, 1969), 5.
24. Irenaeus, *Against Heresies* 5.17.1 (*ANF* 1:545, translation altered).

Jesus does not here identify himself, however, as the Son of God. Instead, he uses the much-debated phrase "Son of Man." In all four Gospels, this term appears only in Jesus' own words, and in the rest of the New Testament it appears only three times. It seems as if the early church did not find much use for the phrase but remembered that Jesus himself had used it. In Jewish texts, "Son of Man" can just mean "a human being," as when a psalm says, in the old masculine-language translation (AV):

> What is man, that thou art mindful of him?
> and the son of man, that thou visitest him?
> (Ps. 8:4)

Similarly, in Ezekiel God calls to the prophet as "son of man," or, in the NRSV, "mortal" (e.g., 2:1, 3, 6), and might just as well say, "Hey, you."

Chapter 7 of Daniel, however, presents a very different picture. The prophet has a vision of four beasts, each more terrifying than the one before (and each, scholars assume, representing one of the empires—Babylonian, Persian, Hellenistic, and either Seleucid or Roman—that had ruled Israel). But then the Ancient of Days (AV), or the Ancient One (NRSV), takes his throne and puts an end to the rule of the beasts. After that,

> I saw one like a [son of man] human being
> coming with the clouds of heaven. . . .
> To him was given dominion and glory and kingship,
> that all peoples, nations, and languages should serve him.
> (Dan. 7:13–14)

Here the son of man is an eschatological figure, the future ruler who will establish justice and peace. Unlike the Messiah, who is usually pictured as a human ruler and warrior, the son of man comes down from heaven.

Other Jewish texts, written just before the time of Jesus, picked up the theme of the Son of Man. *First Enoch*, for instance, as it survives in an Ethiopic version, declares of the Son of Man,

> He is the light of the gentiles and he will become the hope of
> those who are sick in their hearts . . . for he has preserved the
> portion of the righteous because they have hated and despised
> this world of oppression and hated all its ways of life and its
> habits. . . . In those days, the kings of the earth and the mighty
> landowners shall be humiliated on account of the deeds of
> their hands.[25]

This author too hopes for a figure coming down from heaven, but
he emphasizes that the new age he inaugurates will involve a radical change in the present social and
economic order.

Two questions emerge about
Jesus' use of this term (both Jesus as
we encounter him in Mark, and the
actual Jesus who lay behind Mark's
story). Did he use "Son of Man"
to mean just "a human being" or
"this eschatological figure"? Did he
mean it to apply to himself, or was
he talking about a future figure? I
agree with what seems a majority (but by no means a consensus) of
scholars in thinking that Jesus (both actual and narrated) meant by
"Son of Man" an eschatological figure but also himself. Thus his use
of this phrase means something like, "God is going to send someone
who will transform the world and put an end to oppression, and I am
that someone." The scribes who worried about his blasphemy did
not know the half of it.

> As I watched in the night visions,
> I saw one like a human being
> coming with the clouds of
> heaven.
> And he came to the Ancient One
> and was presented before
> him.
> —Daniel 7:13

# 2:13–17

## *The Calling of Levi*

Just as Jesus was walking along the sea in 1:16 when he called his first
disciples, so here again he is walking along the shore as he calls Levi,
a tax collector, to follow him. First-century tax collectors did not just

---

25. *First Enoch* (Ethiopic) 48:4, 7–8, trans. E. Isaac, in *The Old Testament Pseudepigrapha*, ed.
James. H. Charlesworth, 2 vols. (Garden City, NY: Doubleday, 1983–1985), 1:35–36.

generate the slight discomfort we feel around representatives of the Internal Revenue Service. The Roman Empire hired out the work. You bought the right to collect these taxes or tolls and owed the government a specified sum. Your own income came from whatever you could get out of the people over and above what you owed your imperial masters. Thus tax collectors were inevitably both collaborators with the hated Romans and crooks squeezing out of ordinary folks more than the government had demanded. Right there in front of the "whole crowd," Jesus calls such a man to follow him. Moreover, he then sits down with his disciples to eat at Levi's house with a bunch of other "sinners and tax collectors" (the paired phrase gets repeated three times in two verses; Morna Hooker remarks that it is as if sinning were another job one might have[26]). Eating with people, as will become ever clearer in Mark's future stories, was a serious business for first-century Jews. Eating with the polluted was polluting. Yet Jesus seems unconcerned. He does not even make appeals for repentance or reform. No prior qualifications are necessary for eating with Jesus.

His critics here come from "the scribes of the Pharisees"—the phrase is an odd one, and some manuscripts "improve" it to read "the scribes *and* the Pharisees," but it could mean simply some scribes from the Pharisee party. This is Mark's first reference to the Pharisees, who will play an important role in his story, so some account of them is in order. But it is not easy. John Meier concludes in what sounds like despair, "The dirty little secret of NT studies is that no one really knows who the Pharisees were."[27] Two of the greatest recent scholars in such matters sharply disagree. Jacob Neusner argues that the Pharisees were those who sought to eat ordinary meals according to the ritual holiness laws of the temple. E. P. Sanders insists that no one could really have done that.[28]

At least it is worth correcting a traditional misunderstanding. Many Christians have cast the Pharisees unambiguously among the

---

26. Morna D. Hooker, *The Gospel according to Saint Mark*, BNTC (London: A. & C. Black, 1991), 95.

27. John P. Meier, *A Marginal Jew: Rethinking the Historical Jesus*, vol. 3, *Companions and Competitors* (New York: Doubleday, 2001), 311.

28. Ibid., 311–12.

villains of the story. (Even worse, they have then identified the Pharisees with Jews in general and used criticism of the Pharisees as a starting point for anti-Semitism.) They are supposedly the persnickety legalists, always fussing about every detail of the Law. Well— yes and no. Pious Jews think the Law is really a gift, not a burden. It should be a joy to live one's life in service of God, in just the way God wants. Some pious Jews in Jesus' time believed that expecting ordinary people, above all peasants up in notoriously lax Galilee, to obey the details of the Law was a lost cause. In contrast, the Pharisees seem to have been a more popular party, eager to persuade all sorts of Jews that they could find the satisfaction that comes from a life of obedience. Because they are out among the people, they are the ones with whom Jesus is initially arguing. This point is worth emphasis because we grasp how radical Jesus was only when we recognize the apparent good sense of his opponents. He was not sitting down to eat with people who had once, twenty years ago, violated subparagraph b of paragraph 137 of the ritual law. He was eating with *tax collectors* and *sinners*. Most pastors today would get in the same trouble if they tried something similar.

## 2:18–22

### *A Question about Fasting*

Of all the spiritual dangers against which most contemporary Christians need to be warned, excessive fasting surely lies far down the list. *Any* form of fasting has come to be rare for most Christians, and so this passage seems to have little to do with us. But fasting of some sort (not eating for a time, or not eating some foods) was a common practice among the Jews of Jesus' time and has been valued not only in the Catholic tradition but by Luther, Calvin, Wesley, and many other Protestants. My sense is that since the late twentieth century many Christians have been rediscovering fasting.[29]

---

29. For this and much of what follows, see Marjorie J. Thompson, *Soul Feast* (Louisville: Westminster John Knox Press, 1995), 69–81.

Most of us so rarely, if ever, experience real hunger that we lose any sense of the basic satisfaction of eating. The Russian theologian Alexander Schmemann noted that moderate fasting "makes us light, concentrated, sober, joyful, pure. One received food as a real gift of God. One is constantly directed at that inner world which inexplicably becomes a kind of food in its own right."[30] Macrina Wiederkehr makes much the same point:

> Fasting is cleansing. It cleans out our bodies. It lays bare our souls. It leads us into the arms of that One for whom we hunger. In the Divine Arms we become less demanding and more like the One who holds us. Then we experience new hungers. We hunger and thirst for justice, for goodness and holiness. We hunger for what is right. We hunger to be saints.[31]

> Fast not to stir up strife and contention. You eat indeed no flesh; but you devour your brother. You drink no wine; but you cannot refrain from doing injury to others. . . . Anger is a kind of inebriation which does no less trouble the mind than real drunkenness.
>
> —Basil
>
> "Homily on Fasting."

Discipline in eating is but one example of the self-control that those who live in a society so full of so much might well develop. Fasting is not just about food, St. Basil wrote in the fourth century. "True fasting is to refrain from vice. Shred to pieces all your unjust controls. Pardon your neighbors. Forgive them their trespasses."[32]

Jesus was not against fasting. But at least at this point in his ministry, his disciples apparently did not fast, and in this they differed from the Pharisees or John's disciples. Fasting is not a good in itself. If it serves some of the purposes just mentioned, well and good. If it becomes a source of pride or distracts us, through hunger, from the ways we could be helping our neighbor

30. Alexander Schmemann, *Great Lent* (Crestwood, NY: St. Vladimir's Seminary Press, 1974), 98.
31. Macrina Wiederkehr, *A Tree Full of Angels* (San Francisco: HarperSanFrancisco, 1991), 37.
32. Basil, "Homily on Fasting," quoted in *Mark*, Ancient Christian Commentary on Scripture: New Testament 2, ed. Thomas C. Oden and Christopher A. Hall (Downers Grove, IL: InterVarsity Press, 1998), 33.

or doing God's will, then it is not a good practice. So the normally mild-mannered nineteenth-century English theologian Frederick Denison Maurice impatiently denounced high-church Anglicans like John Henry Newman for urging fasting on workers who were overworked and underfed in the normal course of things. "How can we insult God and torment men with such mockery?"[33]

Jesus' disciples, drawn from the ordinary people of an oppressed country and called to follow without any planning or preparation, may not have needed any special discipline of fasting. In the daily course of their lives they had experienced enough hunger to learn to value food. Moreover, Jesus wants to emphasize the sheer joy of God's good news. A properly trained Pharisee may understand that scrupulously following the Law brings its own kind of joy, but for ordinary folks it feels as if it is all about limits and barriers. "Reluctant obedience to God's command is not obedience," Barth notes, and therefore Jesus wants to emphasize that "the command of God is a festive invitation."[34] It is as if there is a wedding at hand, and it is time for a party.

Mark makes clear how radical Jesus' project was in another way. The business of politics and social reform, whether liberal or conservative or anything else, is to figure out what kind of patch to put on an old cloak, what kind of old wineskin will hold new wine. One always starts with a given set of circumstances. Human beings are inevitably not in the business of starting completely afresh. Only God can do that.

## 2:23–28

### *A Question about the Sabbath*

The same sorts of issues arise about the Sabbath. Just as some Christians today are finding a value in fasting in the midst of over-abundance, so some are newly attracted to the idea of Sabbath in the midst of over-busyness. There was a time when the fact that one

33. Quoted in Alec R. Vidler, *F. D. Maurice and Company* (London: SCM, 1966), 97.
34. Barth, CD II/2:588.

could shop or go to a movie on Sunday felt like liberation, but now that every commercial enterprise runs full-tilt and nonstop that can seem more like a burden. A day of rest, a time for pausing and reflecting, seems like a good idea.[35]

For Jews, Abraham Heschel has written, the Sabbath provides "a day of detachment from the vulgar, of independence of external obligations, a day on which we stop worshipping the idols of technical civilization, a day on which we can use no money, a day of armistice in the economic struggle with our fellow men and the forces of nature."[36] Similarly Luther, in his Large Catechism, declares that, in addition to providing a time set apart for worshiping God, we should keep Sabbath since "Nature teaches and demands that the common people—man-servants and maid-servants who have attended to their work and trades the whole week long—should retire for a day to rest and be refreshed."[37] At the same time, Jews and Christians alike can set up detailed rules that change a freedom into a burden.

Such reflections provide a context for reading what turns out to be a very odd story. To start with, just what were Jesus' disciples doing? A literal translation would be something like "began to make a way, plucking the ears of grain," or even, "began to build a road, plucking the ears of grain." We think of them, hungry, eating the grain, but the story at this point does not mention either hunger or eating. A king had a right (what we would call "eminent domain") to make a road through private property. Taken literally, that hardly makes sense here, but perhaps the idea of Jesus as king and his way being prepared, just as John the Baptizer did, is somewhere in the background.

The Pharisees object that the disciples are working on the Sabbath. It is not clear if their objection is justified. Deuteronomy (23:25) says that one can pluck grain by hand but not use a sickle.

35. See Dorothy C. Bass, "Keeping Sabbath," in Practicing Our Faith, ed. Dorothy C. Bass (San Francisco: Jossey-Bass, 1997), 75–89.
36. Abraham Heschel, The Sabbath: Its Meaning for Modern Man (1952; repr. New York: HarperCollins, 1999), 19.
37. Martin Luther, The Large Catechism of Martin Luther, trans. Robert H. Fischer (Philadelphia: Fortress, 1959), 20.

The Pharisees honored oral interpretation as well as written law, and later evidence indicates that at some point any sort of reaping or threshing on the Sabbath was prohibited.[38] Thus we cannot quite tell either what the disciples were doing or whether the Pharisees' condemnation of it rested on an appeal to oral interpretation or was just a mistake.

Jesus' response, however, adds confusion to confusion. He appeals to a precedent: in 1 Samuel 21:1–6, he says, David and his companions were hungry and so they "entered the house of God, when Abiathar was high priest," and ate the bread set apart there for only priests to eat. This gets the original story wrong on almost every count. David was by himself, with no companions. The story does not mention hunger. David did not enter the house of God; the priest was Ahimelech rather than Abiathar; and, though David took the bread with him, the story does not mention that he ate it.

Is this all a joke? A mistake? By Jesus? By Mark? Mark so rarely misremembers texts that I doubt he is doing so here. I infer, then, that the point of his reply is to show that these Pharisees, eager to burden the common people with the details of the Law, are actually so ignorant of Scripture that they do not notice one misquotation after another. Such matters have not altogether changed, and those who quote a particular biblical passage as a means of condemnation often turn out not to know its context or relation to other biblical texts.

Heschel pointed out that ancient Jewish rabbis (we should say "besides Jesus," since Jesus too was a Jewish rabbi) knew "that excessive piety may endanger the fulfillment of the essence of the law."[39] In declaring, "The sabbath was made for humankind, and not humankind for the sabbath," Jesus was not breaking with Judaism but could have been quoting a number of rabbinic texts. The line of division here runs not between Christians and Jews but between those in both traditions for whom laws about the Sabbath provide a blessing to which we should attend and those in both traditions who lose sight of the point of the laws in legalism.

---

38. *Shabbat* 7:2, *The Mishnah*, trans. Jacob Neusner (New Haven: Yale University Press, 1988), 187.
39. Heschel, *Sabbath*, 17.

# 3:1–6

## *Healing a Man with a Withered Hand*

Tension builds in the story. Four times Jesus or his disciples do something that could be counted as working on the Sabbath: healing the man with the unclean spirit, healing Simon's mother-in-law, the disciples plucking grain, and now healing a man with a withered hand. The first two produce no opposition, the third raises an objection, and now his opponents are watching him in advance to see if he breaks the Sabbath rules. Jesus never says, "Oh, forget this business about the Sabbath." He accepts the Sabbath's basic value but finds a reason why the legislation in question does not apply in this case.

Technically, Jesus violates no law here because he does no work. He tells the man to stretch out his hand, and the hand is cured. No spitting, touching, or commanding a cure. Jewish law, moreover, specified that better reasons could "override" the Sabbath law.[40] The Maccabees fought on the Sabbath to save their country. Male babies should be circumcised eight days after birth even if it was the Sabbath.[41] When life was in danger, that took precedence over the Sabbath regulations, and, after all, even a sore throat, left untreated, might lead to death—so most medical treatments could be permitted.[42]

A man with a withered hand, however, will not take a turn for the worse overnight. Jesus is going beyond particular exceptions to a more general principle that it is good to help people when you can. As Luther wrote, "There is always an exception to divine laws in case of need. . . . God created the body, the soul, and all their material belongings, and . . . he wants you to take care of them, so that if any of them is endangered, you may know at once that his precepts are precepts no longer."[43] "How much more ought one boldly to break all kinds of laws when bodily necessity demands it, provided that nothing is done against faith and love."[44]

40. *Pesahim* 6:1–2; Neusner, *Mishnah*, 239.
41. *Shabbat* 19:1–3; Neusner, *Mishnah*, 202.
42. *Yoma* 8:6; Neusner, *Mishnah*, 278.
43. Martin Luther, "The Judgment of Martin Luther on Monastic Vows, 1521," trans. James Atkinson, in *The Christian in Society I*, ed. James Atkinson, LW 44 (Philadelphia: Fortress, 1966), 389–90.
44. Martin Luther, "Preface to the Old Testament" (1545), trans. Charles M. Jacobs, *Word and Sacrament I*, LW 35 (Philadelphia: Muhlenberg, 1960), 241.

When Jesus asks if it is wrong to break the Sabbath laws for a good reason, however, his opponents remain silent, and he is angry and grieved at their hardness of heart. As John Wesley put it, "He was angry at the sin, and in the same moment grieved for the sinners. . . . With anger, yea, hatred, he looked upon the thing; with grief and love upon the persons."[45] Early theologians worried about whether Jesus ought to have felt such emotions. Much of Greek philosophy pointed in a different direction. The Stoics cultivated the ideal of *apatheia*, in which the good person rose above worldly joys and sorrows. Aristotle taught that God dwells in unchanging perfection, unaffected by anything whatever. Some theologians thus argued that emotions could only be part of Christ's humanity, not of his divinity. But the anger and grief here seem to be the action of the one person, Jesus Christ. And they are not incompatible with the character of the God of the Hebrew Scriptures, who can sorrow or grow impatient at the infidelity of his people. As Augustine wrote, "If these emotions and feelings, that sprung from love of the good and from holy charity, are to be called faults, then let us allow that real faults should be called virtues."[46]

Mark has thus shown the pattern of Jesus' ministry. He heals, he forgives sins, he challenges legalism, he eats with sinners. These activities are more related than at first they might seem, for handicaps and diseases generally rendered people in ancient Israel "unclean"—at worst forced in every way to the margins of society, at best excluded from full participation in religious activities. In every way, Jesus is breaking down barriers. He does not ask the afflicted outsiders he encounters to repent or to perform cleansing rituals. He

> We should feel "a displacency at every offence against God, but only love and tender compassion to the offender."
> —John Wesley
>
> "Sermon 40," *Works of John Wesley*, 6:18.

---

45. John Wesley, "Sermon 40: Christian Perfection," *The Works of John Wesley*, 3rd ed. (repr. Grand Rapids: Baker, 1979), 6:18.
46. Augustine, *City of God* 14.9, trans. Henry Bettenson (Harmondsworth, Middlesex: Penguin, 1972), 563.

simply welcomes them and cures them. Who could object? Well, it turns out many could—then and now. There are those who like barriers, want to be clear on their superiority to "others," want to enforce all the rules. The "Herodians" (a word Mark seems to have made up for the occasion) followed a notoriously scandalous half-Jewish king who clung to political power. The Pharisees believed in following the Law. They had almost nothing in common. No matter. As this section ends, they are conspiring to destroy this Jesus. A section that began with John handed over to prison ends with the word "destroy," but this time the target is Jesus.

# 3:7–6:13

# *Parables and Deeds of Power*

## 3:7–12
### *The Messianic Secret*

The last section ended with Pharisees and Herodians conspiring to destroy Jesus. This one begins with a passage full of violent language—"crush," "press upon him," "fell down," "shout"—if anything, the English translations underplay the force. Jesus here is at once powerful and vulnerable, driving out unclean spirits left and right yet oddly fragile in the face of the crowds. In a world beyond what human beings can see, he is master; it is in the human world that he seems at risk.

The unclean spirits proclaim him as the Son of God, "But he sternly ordered them not to make him known." It is a pattern we have already seen—Jesus apparently wants to keep his miracle-working powers and his true identity secret. Ever since the German scholar William Wrede published *Das Messiasgeheimnis in den Evangelien* in 1901,[1] scholars have debated why, in the Gospels and especially in Mark, Jesus so regularly tries to silence those who want to tell who he is or what he can do. This is again one of those places where Mark is either incompetent or very sophisticated (I, as usual, will vote for sophistication), since Jesus tries, surely in vain, to hush up public events witnessed by crowds—and sometimes, with no discernible pattern, lets the word be spread. Approaching the matter as historians, Wrede and others have argued that Mark was working around an awkward problem. By Mark's time, Christians identified Jesus as the Messiah and the Son of God, but their community

---

1. See William Wrede, *The Messianic Secret*, trans. James C. G. Greig (London: James Clarke, 1971).

still remembered that during his lifetime Jesus had not made such claims. Hence Mark tells a story in which voices keep proclaiming Jesus' identity, but he keeps silencing them. The Gospel becomes, in Martin Dibelius's famous phrase, "a book of secret epiphanies."[2]

My concern is with how these "secrets" function within Mark's story, and there the point seems to be to protect Jesus' good news from being misunderstood. Yes, he is the Messiah—but proclaim that in Galilee around the year 30 and most people will expect a warrior king to defeat the Romans. Jesus is a different kind of Messiah, one who suffers and dies, and it is only when circumstances make his inevitable suffering clear that he can reveal who he truly is.

# 3:13–19a

## *Appointing the Twelve*

Mark's first section about Jesus' ministry begins with the calling of his first followers. This section too begins with a story about calling. All four Gospels give a list of "the twelve" (Mark's use of the term "disciples" seems to refer to a larger group than just the Twelve), but the names are slightly different every time. The individuals involved seem to matter less than the fact that there were twelve of them, a number, Barth says, "not to be understood arithmetically but symbolically."[3] In Jesus' day only two and a half of the traditional twelve tribes of Israel claimed to survive, but eschatological dreams of Israel's restoration always involved all twelve (see for instance Isa. 49:6 and Ezek. 45:8; the same is true in Maccabean and Qumranic texts; it is a consistent theme in all Jewish writing of the time). Thus Mark here presents Jesus as enacting a symbolic reestablishment of the whole people of Israel—done, just as Moses established Israel's law, from a mountaintop. Even before they do anything, just by being twelve, this group anticipates the reign of God.

In a fascinating book the English theologian Austin Farrer explored Mark's numerical symbolism, finding complex patterns

---

2. Martin Dibelius, *From Tradition to Gospel* (New York: Charles Scribner's Sons, 1935), 230.
3. Barth, CD II/2:445.

that even Farrer later concluded had read too much into the text.[4] One of Farrer's points is that everyone always referred to "twelve tribes," but there were really thirteen. Jacob had twelve sons, but each of Joseph's two sons was, in Genesis, assigned a tribe of his own. The "tribe" of Levites, down to Jesus' time, had no territory of their own but were assigned to assist the priests in religious rituals (see Num. 18:21–24; Deut. 10:8–9). Thus Jews sometimes dodged the problem of how many tribes there were by referring to "the Levites and the twelve tribes." Farrer notes, then, that Mark here has Jesus calling twelve, but a chapter earlier, he called Levi, who is not included in the list of the Twelve. (We identify Matthew with Levi, but that equation comes from Matthew's Gospel, not Mark.) Is Mark either affirming the full correspondence between those Jesus calls and Israel's tribes, or injecting a subtle reminder that there was always something not quite right about the numbering of the tribes, or both? Hard to say, though it is interesting that "Levi," the name associated with the tribe most identified with ritual purity, should here belong to a despised tax collector. All that can be certain is the eschatological gesture involved in naming twelve followers.

Simon here gets his nickname Peter, based on *petros*, the Greek word for "rock." We might have called him "Rocky." Matthew's Gospel offers an explanation that would become standard in the church: Peter has the solidity of a rock, "and on this rock I will build my church, and the gates of Hades will not prevail against it" (Matt. 16:18). Mary Ann Tolbert, however, points out that Mark says none of this, and indeed the closest reference to "rock" in this Gospel is to the "rocky ground" on which some seed is scattered, springs up quickly, but then withers away because it has no depth of soil (Mark 4:5). Indeed, the impulsive Peter we encounter in Mark in many ways has more in common with such seed than with rock as secure foundation.[5] Neither Peter nor the Twelve nor male disciples in general are altogether admirable figures in Mark.

Mark refers to James and John as *Boanerges* or "Sons of Thunder," though no one can quite figure out either how *Boanerges* would be

4. Austin Farrer, *A Study in St. Mark* (London: Dacre, 1951), 317–47.
5. Tolbert, *Sowing the Gospel*, 145.

translated to mean that or why they should be called it. Since so much has been made of the name Simon the Zealot, a word about him may also be in order. The Zealots as a radical political party out to defeat the Romans by any means necessary did not come into existence until 67 or 68. Depending on when and where Mark was writing, he might have known about them, but he would have known that this was a new group that had not existed in Jesus' time, when "Zealot" generally meant just someone passionately committed to following Jewish law. The text cannot be stretched to make one of Jesus' disciples a revolutionary. What we know is that they are a mixed bag of rather ordinary men, and that Mark sees them as generally rather dull and uninspired.

The most dramatic item in this list of twelve comes right at the end: "and Judas Iscariot, who betrayed him." We cannot recover the sheer shock some of Mark's first readers/listeners would have experienced when they learned that one of the Twelve was also Jesus' betrayer. No one knows the meaning of Judas's second name, Iscariot. It might allude to a terrorist group, the *sicarii*, named after the knives they used; but they did not come into existence until the 40s or 50s. It sounds vaguely like a Semitic word meaning "to lie" or another meaning "to hand over" (as Judas handed Jesus over to the authorities), but both these connections are a bit of a stretch. It could just mean "red" and refer to someone who worked with red dye or had red hair, or it could identify Judas as from the town of Kerioth—if there was such a town.[6] In the end, we do not know.

Why would Jesus (deliberately?) choose someone who would betray him? Why would Mark tell this story? Calvin thought of at least three reasons. When we remember that Jesus himself chose Judas, we will not grow uneasy when powerful people in the church become corrupt. The memory of Judas should warn church leaders against complacency—just because they have a high position does not mean they cannot fall victim to serious sin. And the story of Judas shows that the church does not depend on human excellence—it rests on God's grace.[7]

6. Meier, *Marginal Jew*, 3:210.
7. Calvin, *Harmony of the Evangelists*, 1:255–56.

The Twelve as a group play an odd role in Mark's story. They keep missing the point. They fail to understand. In the end, they run away. Scholars debate whether Mark's picture of them is ambiguous or altogether negative. A generation ago, Theodore Weeden argued that Mark's picture of the disciples grew out of a conflict in his own community, where some of the leaders thought that following Jesus had led them to have special spiritual gifts and other forms of power—what Luther called a "theology of glory" rather than a "theology of the cross." Mark, according to Weeden, represented those in the community who believed that following Jesus leads on an ordinary path, and to suffering. Thus the Twelve in his story represent the community leaders he judged to be misguided, and their mistakes expose the flaws in their position.[8]

A little later, Werner Kelber proposed that the Twelve represent the Jerusalem church, which showed reluctance to include Gentiles longer than most other Christian communities, and Mark is using the Twelve to show the errors of the Jerusalem leaders.[9] More recently, John Donahue has suggested that the Twelve should not be identified with some particular party in the early church but with the experience of Christians generally, in particular those reading the Gospel. One initially experiences enthusiasm at the good news of this Jesus, but then realizes that following him will lead to suffering. We trace our own experience in the ups and downs of the Twelve. Donahue thinks Mark was writing in a time of persecution, when some Christians had caved in, in the face of danger. That even the Twelve made mistakes and wrong turns was therefore a way of promising hope even to Mark's cowardly contemporaries.[10] Perhaps the core of

> Contextually the Gospel of Mark is clearly written with memories of persecution vivid in the minds of its readers. . . . The failure of the disciples thus paradoxically becomes good news for a community struggling with failure and apostasy.
>
> —Donahue and Harrington
>
> *The Gospel of Mark*, 34.

---

8. Theodore J. Weeden Sr., *Mark: Traditions in Conflict* (Philadelphia: Fortress, 1971).
9. Werner H. Kelber, *The Kingdom in Mark* (Philadelphia: Fortress, 1974), 64.
10. John R. Donahue and Daniel J. Harrington, *The Gospel of Mark*, SP (Collegeville, MN: Liturgical Press, 2002), 32–34.

Donahue's interpretation offers the most helpful analysis for Christians today. So often our tendency is to contrast the mess we find
in some aspect of the current church with the good old days when
all was well. Mark keeps reminding us that even the first Christian
community, the Twelve Jesus chose himself, consistently misunderstood and in the end ran away, denied, and betrayed. The church has
always rested on the triumph of God's grace over human failings.

# 3:19b–35
## *Jesus' Family/Conflict with Demons*

What follows is a rich and complex passage that introduces several
of Mark's rhetorical techniques. Mark here first uses the word "parable," which will play a key role in several later chapters. He also uses
intercalation, the "sandwich" technique, for the first time. He begins
by talking about Jesus' family, shifts to a discussion of Beelzebul, and
then returns to Jesus' family. This device of sandwiching a second
story in between the beginning and end of a first story forces readers
to think about the relation between the two stories, and Mark will
use it regularly.

Mark is harsher than any other Gospel when it comes to Jesus'
family. We do not know why. They were almost certainly not followers of Jesus during his lifetime; the picture of hostility would be
unlikely to have been invented without some basis in fact. By Mark's
time, though, Jesus' brother James had become a leader in the church
at Jerusalem, notoriously reluctant to welcome Gentiles easily into
Christianity. Mark, who was friendly to the Gentile mission, may be
reminding readers of James's problematic background. Early Christians often faced difficulties with their families when they joined
the church; Mark may be offering the comforting thought that even
Jesus had to struggle with his family.[11] In any event, even if Jewish
law (Deut. 21:21) specified that rebellious sons should be stoned to
death, Mark here clearly implies that there are causes for which it is

11. Joel Marcus, *Mark 1–8*, AB (New York: Doubleday, 2000), 279–80.

worth turning against your family. It was a decision early Christians often had to make.

I suspect, incidentally, that the NRSV misses Mark's subtlety here. It translates the obscure phrase meaning "the ones with him" in 3:21 as "family," since it turns out, starting at verse 31, that these people are his family. But could this be the kind of trick Mark would enjoy? We hear that some people connected with Jesus think he has gone crazy and are trying to restrain him—then the subject changes, and only later do we find out that these people are in fact his own family, making the story build to a surprising climax.

Scribes down from Jerusalem join the chorus of critics. Jesus can cast out demons only because he is in league with them, they say, and with particularly powerful demons like Beelzebul and Satan. "Beelzebub," by the way, which means "lord of the flies," appears only in the Vulgate Latin translation, not in any Greek manuscripts, where the name is always "Beelzebul," which probably means "lord of the house" and refers to an old Canaanite deity. (The reference to "a house divided against itself" may be a pun on this name.)

If the demons were fighting against one another, Jesus replies, then these internal conflicts would surely weaken them. Jesus' decisive power against them shows that he represents another sort of force altogether. The good news here is that, if Jesus can rescue property from Satan, then Satan must be already tied up and defeated. Oddly, it is Satan who is the householder in this parable, and Jesus who is the thief who ties him up so that he can make off with his belongings. Sinners do in a sense belong to Satan. The Jesus who rescues sinners is not a defender of the status quo but one who challenges it, who breaks the laws of property. Moreover, he tells sinners that he has already redeemed them. As Barth puts it, to the sinner, "The Word of grace simply tells him that the table is spread for him and for all, but that a few places—his own included—are still vacant, and would he be so good as to sit down and fall to, instead of standing about and cleverly or foolishly prattling."[12] The strong man is defeated, dinner is prepared, we need only sit down and eat.

---

12. Barth, *CD* IV/3.1:247.

Love bade me welcome: yet my soul drew back,
  Guiltie of dust and sinne.
But quick-ey'd Love, observing me grow slack
  From my first entrance in,
Drew nearer to me, sweetly questioning
  If I lack'd anything.

A guest, I answer'd, worthy to be here;
  Love said, You shall be he.
I, the unkinde, ungratefull? Ah, my deare,
  I cannot look on thee.
Love took my hand, and smiling did reply,
  Who made the eyes but I?

Truth, Lord, but I have marr'd them: let my shame
  Go where it doth deserve.
And know you not, sayes Love, who bore the blame?
  My deare, then I will serve.
You must sit down, sayes Love, and taste my meat:
  So I did sit and eat.[13]

Mark here then provides at least one hint of how he understands what Jesus does to accomplish our salvation. Sinners are the property Satan holds; in Augustine's phrase, "those who had been held by the devil in diverse sins and iniquities."[14] Since they chose their course into Satan's power voluntarily, Augustine even says that Satan "deservedly" held them.[15] But Christ has defeated Satan (in what sort of battle is an issue to which we must return), and sinners can therefore be made free.

Many things, then, can be forgiven—but not "the sin against the Holy Spirit." John Wesley wrote, "How immense is the number in every nation throughout the Christian world of those who have been more or less distressed on account of this scripture!"[16] Pious

13. George Herbert, "Love (III)," *The Works of George Herbert* (Oxford: Clarendon, 1961), 188–89.
14. Augustine, *The City of God* 20.7 (*NPNF*, 1st ser., 2:426).
15. Augustine, *On the Trinity* 13.15.19 (*NPNF*, 1st ser., 3:177).
16. John Wesley, "Sermon 86: A Call to Backsliders," *The Works of John Wesley*, 3rd ed. (repr. Grand Rapids: Baker, 1979), 6:524.

Christians like John Bunyan have tortured themselves with the thought that they somehow committed the one unforgivable sin.[17] Wesley thought they need not worry—in Mark's context, this sin was clearly the belief that Jesus worked his miracles by the power of an unclean spirit, and Wesley thought it unlikely that even dissolute Christians had believed *that*. The recent Catechism of the Catholic Church, on the other hand, following Augustine,[18] defines this sin as the deliberate refusal to accept God's mercy.[19] This nearly makes the matter circular: if you consciously and deliberately refuse to accept God's forgiveness, then almost by definition you do not receive it. In any event, this unforgivable sin proves not the sort of thing one could commit casually or by accident.

> Whosoever therefore shall be guilty of impenitence against the Spirit, in whom the unity and fellowship of the communion of the Church is gathered together, shall never have forgiveness.
>
> —Augustine
>
> "Sermon 71."

Verse 28 begins with the word "Amen," a transliteration of a word meaning "true," translated in the NRSV as "Truly." In the first century the word was usually used as we use it, at the end of statements, to emphasize or agree. "Amen, brother," means, "I agree with you." But Mark has Jesus use it thirteen times at the *beginning* of a statement. Joachim Jeremias thought that this went back to the historical Jesus and represented a special claim to authority.[20] It certainly conveys the authority of Jesus' teaching.

Having digressed into this discussion of demons, Mark returns to the first story, the "bread" of the "sandwich," Jesus' relation to his family. We learn that it is Jesus' own family that is convinced of his madness—his mother and brothers and sisters. Traditional Catholic interpretation, based on a belief in Mary's perpetual virginity, has explained the siblings as half brothers and half sisters, born to

---

17. John Bunyan, *Grace Abounding to the Chief of Sinners* (Oxford: Clarendon, 1962), 55.

18. Augustine, "Sermon 71" (*NPNF*, 1st ser., 6:318–32).

19. *Catechism of the Catholic Church*, §1864.

20. Joachim Jeremias, *New Testament Theology*, trans. John Bowden (New York: Charles Scribner's Sons, 1971), 35–36.

Joseph by an earlier wife, or as cousins or even friends named brothers and sisters as a kind of courtesy title. Some Protestants are now supporting that view, even as some Catholics have come to doubt it.

Jesus' response to his family seems brutal. Notice that they are outside, and he does not even go out to speak to them. He simply asserts that those who do the will of God are his only true family. Particularly in a culture that emphasized the importance of the family as much as traditional Judaism did, this would have been a shocking remark. Jesus is here no defender of traditional family values.

## FURTHER REFLECTIONS
### *Demons and Satan*

Rudolf Bultmann famously declared that modern people who use electric lights and the radio cannot believe in the NT worldview. Demons who possess people and direct human conduct were one of his favorite examples of the sort of thing we can no longer believe. It is fascinating to speculate on the significance of the pervasiveness of demons and vampires in popular culture, especially popular culture directed toward teenagers. How much serious belief does it imply? "Modern" people at least turn out to be more complicated than Bultmann assumed.

A cautionary note seems in order at the start. There are Christians who assume that the mentally disturbed or even the chronically misbehaving must be possessed by demons. The attempted cures they pursue can do horrible damage to people, especially children, in serious need of other kinds of help. One should not give aid and comfort to such practices.

That does not mean we should feel confident about our understanding of the human mind. The philosopher René Descartes, at the beginning of the modern era, claimed that our own souls are the easiest of all things for us to understand. Other people, physical objects, God, even our own bodies—in every other case there are barriers to our understanding. But to know ourselves as "thinking things" all we need to do is look within. Sigmund Freud was perhaps the greatest of those who have taught us that this is not so. The psychoanalyst who helps me find the forgotten childhood event that explains my neurosis, the hypnotist who gets me to bark like a dog though I have forgotten his instruction to do so, the case study of multiple personality disorder—all reveal that there are things in my own mind hidden from me.

Freud, surely a modern, secular man, once observed that "obscure, unfeeling and unloving powers determine men's fate."[21] Thinking about the Holocaust and the rest of the Nazi evil, one finds it hard to imagine that this little man with a mustache, Adolf Hitler, and his sick friends could have created so much horror. It is not making excuses for them to say that forces greater than they seem to have been working through them—and those forces were not for good. But the evil need not be on so grand a scale. In Dostoevsky's *Brothers Karamazov* Ivan Karamazov tells this story:

> A little girl, five years old, is hated by her father and mother, "most honorable and official people, educated and well-bred." . . . They beat her, flogged her, kicked her, not knowing why themselves, until her whole body was nothing but bruises; finally they attained the height of finesse: in the freezing cold, they locked her all night in the outhouse, because she wouldn't ask to get up and go in the middle of the night . . . — for that they smeared her face with her excrement and made her eat the excrement.[22]

Notice that they did not know why themselves. What would one say to such people? Or to Pol Pot? Could one feel confident one was connecting with a human being?

Calvin's theory of "accommodation" explains that God could use the concepts comprehensible to people at the time to explain ideas to them, like an adult explaining to a child in baby talk.[23] We have not yet arrived at an adulthood in which we can fully understand what happens to a sick mind. Jesus' contemporaries understood

21. Sigmund Freud, *New Introductory Lectures on Psychoanalysis*, trans. and ed. James Strachey (New York: Norton, 1965), 167.
22. Feodor Dostoevsky, *The Brothers Karamazov*, trans. Richard Pevear and Larissa Volokhonsky (San Francisco: North Point Press, 1990), 241–42.
23. Calvin, *Institutes* 2.11.13.

when he drove out demons. To what extent he really did so, and to what extent that was the explanation accommodated to their understanding, we may not be able to know.

> The fact is that [demons] exist always and everywhere where the truth of God is not present and proclaimed and believed and grasped, and therefore does not speak and shine and rule.
>
> —Karl Barth
>
> *CD* III /3:529.

This much does seem clear. There is evil. Sometimes the evil seems to have cunning as if it were a *person* at work, but its force seems beyond that of any human person in the situation. There do seem to be nonhuman agents of evil in the world. Perhaps we should not go much beyond that. Barth warns, "It has never been good for anyone … to look too frequently or lengthily or seriously or systematically at demons.…It does not make the slightest impression on the demons if we do so, and there is the imminent danger that in so doing we ourselves might become just a little or more than a little demonic. The very thing which the demons are waiting for, especially in theology, is that we should find them dreadfully interesting."[24] Short of ultimately, the powers of evil can still do a great deal of damage; but, ultimately, Jesus has defeated them.

## 4:1–9
### *The Parable of the Seeds*

While Mark identified the comparison with a kingdom divided against itself as a parable in 3:23, chapter 4 begins with a parable for the first time at the center of the story. It is followed by an explanation of the purpose of parables and then two more parables. One function of all these parables is to explain why, if Satan has been defeated, as we have just been told, the world still seems so unredeemed.

Making sense of the first parable (traditionally called "the par-

24. Barth, *CD* III/3:519.

able of the sower," but it seems more about the different seeds) first requires knowing something about ancient Mediterranean agriculture. Farmers first scattered the seed and then plowed the ground to embed the seed in the earth. Planting was a serious matter—a bad harvest could easily lead to widespread starvation. This sower therefore might seem unusually careless, scattering some of his seed on a path that would not be plowed. Many interpreters, however, think of it as a temporary path, where the ground would have been beaten down very hard until it was plowed. Before the plowing can even occur, therefore, birds come and eat all this seed, scattered in plain sight on the hard ground. This seed does not even germinate. Other seed, scattered on rock covered with only a thin layer of soil ("rocky ground" seems to mean this, rather than soil with rocks scattered within it), springs up quickly but, without a strong root structure, withers and dies in the strong sun. Still other seed is surrounded by thorn plants that choke it so that it yields no grain. Finally, some seed "fell into good soil and brought forth grain, growing up and increasing and yielding thirty and sixty and a hundredfold."

Mary Ann Tolbert argues that the seed sown on the path represents the scribes and Pharisees who do not even listen to Jesus. The seed sown on rocky ground represents the disciples, "Rocky" Peter first among them, who eagerly follow Jesus at first but keep misunderstanding his message. The seed that fell among thorns stands for Herod and the rich man of Mark 10:17–22, who are distracted by their cares and pleasures from hearing the word. The seeds that land in the good soil are those who are healed or saved by their faith.[25] Whether or not one accepts these specific equations, the parable certainly makes the point that a Christian's reception of the word can go wrong in a number of different ways, from ignoring it in the first place to failing to develop in one's faith to becoming too distracted by other cares and pleasures.

One of the quarrels among modern interpreters of this parable concerns just how good the good crop was. Jeremias claimed that no ancient farmer ever got even thirty grains from one, let alone a

---

25. Tolbert, *Sowing the Gospel*, 171.

hundred, so what is described here is a miracle, "the eschatological overflowing of the divine fullness, surpassing all human measure."[26] Eta Linnemann maintained that such yields "remain entirely within the bounds of possibility."[27] Charles Hedrick researched available data from the ancient Mediterranean (though the available data did not come from Palestine itself) and concluded that a yield of fifteen times would have been very good, and a hundred times unlikely but just barely possible.[28] As best we can guess, then, a first-century audience would have heard these numbers as amazing, astonishing. Pastors with struggling congregations, incidentally (and I mean this as a serious point), may find comfort in Calvin's observation that the parable does not seem to distinguish between thirtyfold and a hundredfold—all those which "do not entirely disappoint" are found good.[29]

## 4:10–20

### *Parables as Mysteries*

Such interpretations assume that Mark's audience, then and now, could understand this parable, but that is not what Mark seems to say. When Jesus is alone with the Twelve, he says, in one of the most puzzling passages in this puzzling Gospel, that the secret of the reign of God has been given to the Twelve, "but for those outside, everything comes in parables; in order that 'they may indeed look, but not perceive, and may indeed listen, but not understand; so that they may not turn again and be forgiven.'" Our first instinct is that parables make things clearer by making ideas vivid and concrete (Luther says, in defiance of Mark's plain meaning: "As St. Mark testifies, Christ also preached in ordinary parables for the sake of simple-minded folk"[30]), but Mark has Jesus declare (quoting, more

26. Joachim Jeremias, *The Parables of Jesus*, trans. S. H. Hooke, rev. ed. (New York: Charles Scribner's Sons, 1963), 150.
27. Eta Linnemann, *Jesus of the Parables*, trans. John Sturdy (New York: Harper & Row, 1966), 181.
28. Charles W. Hedrick, *Many Things in Parables* (Louisville: Westminster John Knox, 2004), 172–73.
29. Calvin, *Harmony of the Evangelists*, 2:117.
30. Martin Luther, "Personal Prayer Book, 1522," trans. Martin H. Bertram, *Devotional Writings II*, LW 43 (Philadelphia: Fortress, 1968), 43.

or less, Isa. 6:9–10) that their purpose is to mislead and hide the truth "so that they may not turn again and be forgiven." In his classic commentary on Mark, Vincent Taylor found this statement "intolerable."[31] Albert Schweitzer thought it "repellent" and also "incomprehensible," since the parables can in fact be understood easily enough.[32] The Jewish scholar Meir Sternberg calls these the most offensive words in the Christian Bible.[33] The author of Matthew's Gospel changed the passage, saying that Jesus spoke in parables not "in order that" people would fail to understand but "because" they had failed to understand. As Frank Kermode explains, Isaiah (and Matthew) seem to say that the people's "stupidity is extremely tiresome; this seems the best way to get through to them," while Mark, in a move worthy of Kafka, asserts that "outsiders must stay outside and be damned."[34]

Where to begin? An obvious place is with the word "parable," derived from the Greek verb *ballō,* meaning "throw, place, put," and the prefix *para,* meaning "alongside of." So a parable puts something alongside something else; it makes a comparison. The Greek word, however, would translate the Hebrew *mashal,* which, like its Aramaic parallel, means a riddle, a fable, or a mysteriously dark saying. When the Lord tells Ezekiel to "propound a riddle and speak a *mashal* to the house of Israel" (Ezek. 17:2), *mashal* is presumably a synonym for "riddle." A parable then, both clarifies by its concreteness and makes things mysterious by its riddling character. As C. H. Dodd wrote, it is "a metaphor or simile drawn from nature or common life, arresting the hearer by its vividness or strangeness and leaving the mind in sufficient doubt about its precise application to tease it into active thought."[35] Paul Ricoeur identified three characteristics in parables: a narrative form, a metaphorical process, and

---

31. Vincent Taylor, *The Gospel according to Mark,* 2nd ed. (New York: St. Martin's Press, 1966), 257.
32. Albert Schweitzer, *The Quest of the Historical Jesus,* trans. W. Montgomery et al., ed. John Bowden (Minneapolis: Fortress, 2001), 216–17.
33. Meir Sternberg, *The Poetics of Biblical Narrative* (Bloomington: Indiana University Press, 1985), 48–49.
34. Frank Kermode, *The Genesis of Secrecy: On the Interpretation of Narrative* (Cambridge: Harvard University Press, 1979), 30–31.
35. C. H. Dodd, *The Parables of the Kingdom* (New York: Charles Scribner's Sons, 1961), 5.

a qualifier such as extravagance, oddness, or radicality that points it toward the reign of God.[36] John Dominic Crossan has contrasted parables with myths: "You have built a lovely home, myth assures us; but, whispers parable, you are right above an earthquake fault."[37] Myths support the status quo; parables shake it up.

Parables, in other words, are comparisons, either simple or complex, that take ordinary elements of our experience (farmers, seeds, etc.) and put them together in an odd way that challenges our ordinary ways of thinking and leads us to look at the world afresh. As Barth says, "Real men, whether peasants, rich and poor, fathers and sons, kings or others, do not normally act and speak as in these stories. . . . Strange things happen. . . . It is not intended that the hearers and readers should recognize themselves in them. . . . It is the kingdom of heaven which is likened unto them, and they to it."[38] If we are to make the world a little more like God's reign, then we must start acting and thinking differently, and parables push us in the right direction—toward faith.

> Not even the whole world itself could contain the books that might be written in relation to such parables.
> —Origen
>
> ANF 9:502.

It is in the nature of faith, however, that human argument cannot bring us to it. Philosophers of science like Thomas Kuhn tell us that even the shift from one scientific paradigm to another cannot be made purely by a series of logical steps but must involve what Kuhn is reduced to calling a kind of "conversion experience."[39] Jesus' parables seek to evoke such a radical shift in the way we see things—indeed, a more radical one, since they affect not just our understanding of some aspect of science but the way we see the whole world and live our lives. As Origen put it, "The writers of the Gospels . . . withhold any detailed exposition of the parables because the things signified by them were beyond the power of words to express."[40]

36. Paul Ricoeur, "Biblical Hermeneutics," *Semeia* 4 (1975): 30–33.
37. John Dominic Crossan, *The Dark Interval* (Niles, IL: Argos Communications, 1975), 56–57.
38. Barth, CD IV/3.1:112–13; see also Ricoeur, *Biblical Hermeneutics*, 115.
39. Thomas S. Kuhn, *The Structure of Scientific Revolutions*, 2nd ed. (Chicago: University of Chicago Press, 1970), 150.
40. Origen, *Commentary on Matthew* 14.12; Oden and Hall, *Mark*, 50.

Calvin addressed these matters in his famous, not to say notorious, doctrine of election or predestination: "We cannot gainsay the fact that, to those whom he pleases not to illumine, God transmits his doctrine wrapped in enigmas in order that they may not profit by it except to be cast into greater stupidity."[41] It is a phrase as brutal as Mark's explanation of the parables; Calvin means it as an honest account of the realities of faith. Some people read the Gospels and do not see the world in a new way. They are not captured by a new vision of things. Sometimes they desperately wish they could come to faith. It is futile to tell them just to try harder, like impatiently demanding that the color blind notice the difference between yellow and orange. In the face of such cases, Calvin maintains, Christians, who do see the world through the lens of the Gospels, cannot pridefully congratulate ourselves on our greater efforts or intelligence. We can only be grateful that we have been given what others have not: "Christ declares that there are certain elect people, on whom God specially bestows this honor of revealing to them his secrets, and that others are deprived of this grace. No other reason will be found for this distinction, except that God calls to himself those whom he has gratuitously elected."[42] Whether that is fair, and how many may be elected, are questions to which we will have to return. For now, the point is that this doctrine is meant to teach those who have faith to be grateful rather than proud.

In Mark's context, this was not an abstract question. By and large, Jews, the members of God's chosen people, were not responding positively to the gospel, while Gentiles must have been joining Mark's church in increasing numbers. We lose sight of just how astonishing this must have been to those familiar with both the Jewish Scriptures and the new news about Jesus. Jews were obviously set apart, the elect people of God, known around the Roman world for their moral rectitude, their piety, and their determined commitment to monotheism, sometimes in the face of all sorts of threats. Yet tinkers, tailors, and tentmakers from the Gentile world were coming to faith in Jesus in larger numbers. Both the coming and the rejecting must be, somehow, part of God's plan.

41. Calvin, *Institutes* 3.24.13.
42. Calvin, *Harmony of the Evangelists*, 2:104.

# 4:21–25

### A Lamp under a Basket?

Mark next almost reverses himself. The division that leaves some on the outside may not be the last word. Again, a parable begins with commonsense experience. If you have a lamp, you put it up on a lampstand so it will illuminate the room; you do not hide it under a basket or a bed. (No commentators seem to mention it, so with some reticence I note that such a practice might end up burning the house down!) Surely, then, God does not mean to keep his good news available only to a select few: "For there is nothing hidden, except to be disclosed; nor is anything secret, except to come to light." Those to whom a grace of understanding has been given had better pay attention. With gratitude should come responsibility—to nurture the faith that has come to them as a gift.

> As if I asked a common Alms,
> And in my wondering hand,
> A Stranger pressed a Kingdom,
> And I, bewildered, stand—[43]

How can there be a sharp line between insiders and outsiders if common sense tells us that a lamp is meant to be put somewhere where it will light up the whole room? The answer lies in a distinction between present and future. As Mark goes on to explain, seeds provide a good example.

# 4:26–34

### Further Parables about Seeds

As any good gardener knows, one can plant seeds carefully, water, and fertilize, but the key transformation happens mysteriously, underground, beyond our observation and control. The tiny dry seed

---

43. Emily Dickinson, no. 323, *The Complete Poems of Emily Dickinson*, ed. Thomas H. Johnson (Boston: Little, Brown, 1960), 153.

goes beneath the soil, time passes without any observable changes, and suddenly a small green plant emerges. So it is, Mark says, with the reign of God, and so it is, one might add, with faith. Pastors can preach the word, teachers can teach, Christians of all sorts can try to provide good examples of faith and upright conduct. But conversion to Christian faith does not follow neat recipes. It happens, indeed, underground. So Luther experienced the success of his Reformation: "I simply taught, preached, and wrote God's Word; otherwise I did nothing. And while I slept or drank Wittenberg beer with my friends Philip and Amsdorf, the Word so greatly weakened the papacy that no prince or emperor ever inflicted such losses on it. I did nothing; the Word did everything."[44] We live in a world divided between believers and unbelievers, full of tragedy and hatred. Two thousand years after the time of Jesus, it is hard to see clear beginnings of the reign of God. Yet, Mark says, hidden transformations are already occurring.

> **Whether people notice it or not, the kingdom has come right up to them.**
>
> **—Karl Barth**
>
> *The Christian Life*, trans. Geoffrey W. Bromiley (Grand Rapids: Eerdmans, 1981), 248.

When their results appear, they may be dramatic. Botanists tell us that orchid seeds are actually smaller than mustard seeds, but the mustard seed would have been the smallest common in Palestine. Yet it can produce a bush nine or ten feet high, a dramatic example of transformation. The image evokes similar pictures in the Hebrew Scriptures. In one of Daniel's visions,

> there was a tree at the center of the earth,
> and its height was great.
> The tree grew great and strong,
> its top reached to heaven,
> and it was visible to the ends of the whole earth.
> Its foliage was beautiful,
> its fruit abundant,
> and it provided food for all.

44. Martin Luther, "The Second Sermon, March 10, 1522," trans. John W. Doberstein, *Sermons I*, LW 51 (Philadelphia: Muhlenberg, 1959), 77.

The animals of the field found shade under it,
    the birds of the air nested in its branches,
    and from it all living beings were fed.

(Dan. 4:10–12)

Similarly, the birds make nests in the shade of the mustard bush. The image from Daniel is of all the nations, indeed all living things, finally finding comfort beneath the "tree" that represents Israel. Mark's mustard bush is likewise a symbol of welcoming.

Is it also just a bit ironic? In a passage Mark's first readers might have recalled, Ezekiel has God imagining a great cedar tree under which

every kind of bird will live;
    in the shade of its branches will nest
    winged creatures of every kind.

(Ezek. 17:23)

A ten-foot-high mustard bush is impressive, but not in comparison with a majestic cedar tree. Is Mark ironically aware of the boldness of claiming too much for the tiny new Christian community? Still, Jesus preaches and teaches and heals, and a seed gets sown. Later, Tertullian proclaimed that the blood of the martyrs was the seed of the church, and certainly Christians' courage in standing up to the threat of torture and death inspired others to learn more about this new faith. "The true victories, won in secret, sometimes look like defeats," wrote Martin Buber. "Our faith that God is the Lord of history may sometimes appear ludicrous; but there is something secret in history which confirms our faith."[45] In our time too, Christians die for their faith, or fail, or embarrass themselves. The ground looks bare. We do not know what is already germinating beneath the surface.

---

45. Martin Buber, "And If Not Now, When?" *Israel and the World: Essays in a Time of Crisis* (New York: Schocken, 1948), 238–39.

# 4:35–41
## *Even the Wind and Sea Obey Him*

Evening comes after a day of preaching, and Jesus and his disciples get in a boat to cross the Sea of Galilee. A recent archaeological discovery found an ancient fishing boat from roughly the same area, twenty-six feet long and eight feet wide, not much space for thirteen people or much protection in a storm.[46] As usual in Mark, there are puzzles. The Twelve take Jesus "just as he was," whatever that may mean. "Other boats were with him," but they disappear once the story gets going.

A great windstorm comes up—the Greek suggests something like a tornado, sudden, unexpected, and perhaps not a natural phenomenon. The scene might remind readers of the story of Jonah, where also a great wind comes up, the sailors are terrified, and the main character remains asleep (Jonah 1:4–5); even some of Mark's word choices follow the Septuagint version of Jonah. Jonah has to sacrifice himself to save the ship (and a ship would become a standard symbol of the church). Jesus here simply commands the winds and sea to be still, but he will in time sacrifice himself for others and lie three days in the tomb just as Jonah spent three days in the belly of the great fish. In this story too, we see both humanity and divinity. In the Hebrew Scriptures only God can command the sea (Job 26:11–12; Ps. 104:7, Isa. 51:9–10) as Jesus does here. Yet the story also draws parallels with Jonah, that most reluctant and thus most human of the prophets, who resisted the Lord at every step of the way. While Jesus' sleep and his outward appearance "showed man, the sea and the calm declared him God."[47]

The Twelve are panicked; Jesus is asleep. They wake him with a plea for help. Other than the brief comment that people are looking for him at 1:37, this is the first time Mark has the Twelve speaking to Jesus. The grammar of their question expects a positive answer. They may be in panic, but they do trust their teacher. He "rebukes"

---

46. John J. Rousseau and Rami Arav, *Jesus and His World: An Archaeological and Cultural Dictionary* (Minneapolis: Fortress, 1995), 25–30.
47. John Chrysostom, *Homilies on Matthew* 28.1 (*NPNF*, 1st ser., 10:190).

> Preachers . . . when they present and preach Christ . . . must suffer persecution, and nothing can prevent it; and that it is a very good sign of the preaching being truly Christian.
>
> —Martin Luther
>
> "Fourth Sunday after Epiphany."

(a strong verb) the wind with the same almost vulgar "Shut up" or "Muzzle yourself" he used in 1:25 to drive out an evil spirit. Again, this storm seems not a standard natural phenomenon. Luther suspected that those other ships mentioned in verse 36 sailed calmly; only the one with Christ in it "had to suffer distress because of Christ being in it," just as, "The world can indeed tolerate all kinds of preaching except the preaching of Christ." Preachers facing persecution should take comfort in the thought that their suffering likely means that their preaching, like that one boat, has Christ in it.[48] Indeed, Luther seems to interiorize the whole story as a matter of faith. If only the disciples had had faith, he told his congregation, "it would have driven the wind and the waves of the sea out of their minds, and pictured before their eyes in place of the wind and the tempest the power and grace of God."[49]

## FURTHER REFLECTIONS
### Miracles

Some scholars argue that stories like the calming of the sea represent a postresurrection appearance moved back into Jesus' lifetime, or, pushing Luther a step further, take it as a symbolic account of the struggles of faith. But healings and exorcisms seem central to Mark's account of Jesus' identity. Roughly half of the verses in the first ten chapters (200 out of 425) concern what we might call "miracles." Overall, Mark recounts eighteen "miracle stories": eight healings, four exorcisms, one raising from the dead, and five "nature miracles." Nearly all come in the first half of the Gospel.

48. Martin Luther, "Fourth Sunday after Epiphany," *Sermons of Martin Luther*, vol. 2, *Sermons on Gospel Texts for Epiphany, Lent, and Easter*, ed. John Nicholas Lenker, trans. Lenker et al. (repr. Grand Rapids: Baker, 1983), 2:97.
49. Ibid., 93.

I have been putting "miracle" in quotation marks, because it is not a word Mark uses. He speaks ten times of *dynamis* ("deed of power" in the NRSV), five times of *sēmeion* ("sign"), and once of *teras* ("omen")—the last two are used only negatively. The word "miracle" is defined by the contemporary philosopher Richard Swinburne as a "violation of a law of nature by a god."[50] Neither Mark nor any of his contemporaries could have made sense of that, for they had no concept of "law of nature." God does everything. God does some things rather rarely and in ways different from his usual modes of operation, and, if these lead us to faith, Augustine calls them "miracles" or "portents": "For how can an event be contrary to nature when it happens by the will of God, since the will of the great Creator assuredly is the nature of every created thing? A portent, therefore, does not occur contrary to nature, but contrary to what is known of nature."[51] As Benedicta Ward explains, "They were wonderful acts of God shown as events in this world, not in opposition to nature but as a drawing out of the hidden workings of God within a nature that was all potentially miraculous."[52] Strange things happen in the world, and if such a thing points us vividly to the workings of God, who is at work in all things, Augustine would count it a miracle.

The ancient world distinguished miracles or deeds of power from magic in roughly the way some modern anthropologists would. Magic follows a cookbook procedure. Do and say the right things in the right order (sometimes very complicated and full of mysterious words), and the right result will follow. The act teaches no lesson but the power of the magician, and the goal may seem trivial—making a love potion, punishing an enemy. Mark thus does not present Jesus as a magician, he uses no complicated spells or formulas. When he quotes an Aramaic word spoken as part of a cure, he does not leave it mysterious but translates it. Jesus does not go about seeking to do cures; people come to him, and he seems to act out of compassion.

50. Richard Swinburne, *The Concept of Miracle* (New York: St. Martin's Press, 1970), 11.
51. Augustine, *Concerning the City of God against the Pagans* 21.8, trans. Henry Bettenson (Harmondsworth, Middlesex: Penguin, 1972), 980.
52. Benedicta Ward, *Miracles and the Medieval Mind* (Philadelphia: University of Pennsylvania Press, 1982), 3.

Jesus' cures would have seemed to his contemporaries an unusual gift he had, but not a unique one. Nor were they the sort of thing only uneducated people in the backwoods believed in. Josephus, the educated, sophisticated Jewish historian, describes the omen of a star shaped like a sword that hovered over Jerusalem and that God provided during the Jewish War to warn the people of the city's destruction.[53] Tacitus, the tough-minded Roman historian, tells how the emperor Vespasian (himself a quite cynical character) cured a blind man by wetting his eyes with spittle.[54] Such events come and go in the Hebrew Scriptures in an odd way. They are regular, dramatic features of the stories of Moses and Elijah and Elisha. But the narratives of David and Solomon, for instance, contain almost nothing anyone would call a miracle. Yet the text makes nothing of the difference. It is as if including such deeds of power is one way of telling a story, and leaving them out is another—both equally valid.

So given all this, what did Jesus do? People who came to him ill in one way or another left him transformed; I have no doubt of that. In the Jewish culture of that time, that transformation meant not only that they "felt better" but that they were restored as full members of the community from which they had heretofore been excluded. The naturalistic explanations developed by eighteenth- and early-nineteenth-century theologians, which Schweitzer demolished with such glee in the early chapters of *The Quest of the Historical Jesus*, were ridiculous. Jesus did not "walk on water" by walking on the shore behind a mist. The story of the calming of the sea cannot be explained by saying that the boat moved behind a headland, out of the wind.[55] Still, even Barth thought there could be a place for something like psychosomatic explanations in the case of some of Jesus' healings.[56] Nothing Mark says would be refuted if Jesus sometimes transformed people with nothing more than a calm voice and an authoritative manner.

53. Josephus, *Jewish War* 6.288.
54. Tacitus, *Histories* 4.81.
55. Schweitzer, *Quest of the Historical Jesus*, 50–51, citing H. E. G. Paulus, *Das Leben Jesu* (Heidelberg: C. F. Winter, 1828).
56. Barth, *CD* IV/2:213.

On the other hand, Christians believe that God, the Creator of the whole universe, was present in this man Jesus of Nazareth. If one accepts that premise, it would not be surprising if some quite remarkable things happened around him. At least one thing did: Jesus was raised from the dead. If the laws of physics work quite differently in the first seconds of creation, who is to say how they might operate if the Creator were present in the midst of history? Even in ordinary times, Archbishop Rowan Williams writes, "perhaps a really intense prayer or a really holy life can open the world up that bit more to God's purpose so that unexpected things happen." How much more in the life of Jesus:

> If God's action is always at work around us, if it's always "on hand," so to speak, we shouldn't be thinking of God's action and the processes of the world as two competing sorts of things jostling for space. But what if there were times when certain bits of the world's processes came together in such a way that the whole cluster of happenings became a bit more open to God's final purposes? What if the world were sometimes a bit more "transparent" to the underlying act of God?[57]

# 5:1–20
## *The Gerasene Demoniac*

Having crossed the Sea of Galilee, Jesus enters Gentile territory for the first time. If we happen not to notice this, the presence of a herd of pigs soon makes clear that he is no longer among Jews. In Mark's longest healing story, Jesus encounters one who is an outsider in nearly every way imaginable. He is possessed by demons and lives in the local cemetery, itself an unclean space in most ancient cultures. In Isaiah God condemns those "who sit inside tombs, and spend the night in secret places; who eat swine's flesh" (Isa. 65:4). This man is guilty on all counts. He is unnaturally strong, and we have already learned that Jesus is the one who can defeat the "Strong Man." His

57. Rowan Williams, *Tokens of Trust: An Introduction to Christian Belief* (Louisville: Westminster John Knox, 2007), 44–45.

neighbors have failed in their attempts to control him; his chains and shackles are broken, so that he is a physical danger to the community. "The man here is a picture of death, of one already banished from the land of the living, from human community that makes human life possible."[58] We learn the name of the demons who inhabit him, but the man himself remains nameless.

He is in "the country of the Gerasenes," but the town of Gerasa is thirty-seven miles southeast of the Sea of Galilee, making it hardly possible for Jesus to arrive there by stepping out of the boat. (Some manuscripts read "Gadarenes" or "Gergesenes" but Gadara and Gergesa are not on the lakeshore either.) Many scholars conclude that Mark has his geography muddled, but there is a different explanation. Military language pervades this story. "Legion" (Mark uses the Latin word), the name the demons give, referred in Mark's world to a large unit of Roman soldiers. A wild boar was the symbol on the standard of the Roman legion stationed at this time in Palestine. *Agelē* at 5:11, translated "herd," was not ordinarily used of pigs but would have been commonly applied to a disorganized group of military recruits. The NRSV renders the beginning of 5:13, "So he gave them permission," but the word is a standard military command, like our "Dismissed." Later in 5:13, the swine "charge" down the steep bank and into the sea—again, the verb is commonly used in military contexts.[59] We are getting a lot of signals that this story is, among other things, about soldiers.

In an episode in the Jewish War in the late 60s, about the time Mark was written, the town of Gerasa rebelled. The Roman emperor Vespasian sent a punitive expedition that, according to Josephus, burned the town and killed a thousand of its people.[60] Simon bar Giora, who became a leader of the Jewish revolt, came from Gerasa.[61] As a place to land on the shore of the Sea of Galilee, Gerasa is all wrong, but as a symbol of Roman violence and Jewish resistance,

---

58. Boring, *Mark*, 150.
59. Ched Myers, *Binding the Strong Man: A Political Reading of Mark's Story of Jesus* (Maryknoll, NY: Orbis, 1988), 191; Boring, *Mark*, 151.
60. Josephus, *Jewish War* 4.488–89.
61. Ibid., 4.503.

it is just right. As Gerd Theissen remarks, then, for Mark's earliest readers/listeners, this story would have symbolically satisfied a desire to drive Roman legions into the sea like pigs,[62] and would have done so in a way that hid such meanings from Roman readers. But the story is not just about Roman soldiers; it really is about a demoniac. Readers who recognized themselves as oppressed victims of the Romans would also have had to come to terms with the way they isolated the outsiders of their own society. The story functioned, perhaps, as would a contemporary American story on the surface about an AIDS victim but at a symbolic level about terrorists. For most of us, our own position in the story would be a complicated one.

The demons, as usual, recognize Jesus, bow down, and yell their collective head off: "Jesus, Son of the Most High God." In the Hebrew Scriptures "Most High God" is occasionally used by non-Israelites to refer to Israel's God. Hence it is appropriate in the mouth of these Gentile-territory demons. The demons presumably think they will survive in the swine and do not anticipate their drowning; we miss a good bit of this story if we do not recognize that it is funny. A good many readers today tend to pass over the joy of the cured lunatic and worry about the farmers who lost their swine, one more case of how much our priorities can differ from those of Jesus. The Gerasenes clearly want Jesus to get out of town, not only because he is killing off their pigs but also just because of the sheer power he manifests. We modern readers are fooling ourselves if we think that we, by contrast, would have liked having Jesus around. We do not understand Mark's picture of him unless we recognize that he is terrifying.

The ex-demoniac wants to follow Jesus, but Jesus sends him home to his friends to tell how much the Lord has done for him. Has Mark forgotten the principle of the messianic secret? Or, since this is not Jewish territory, is there here no danger of a misunderstood messiahship?

---

62. Gerd Theissen, *The Miracle Stories of the Early Christian Tradition*, trans. Francis McDonagh, ed. John Riches (Edinburgh: T. & T. Clark, 1983), 255–56.

## 5:21–43

### *Jairus's Daughter and a Hemorrhaging Woman*

Here again Mark uses intercalation, the sandwich technique in which he starts telling one story, interrupts himself to tell a second, and then goes back to finish the first, forcing readers to think about the relation between the two stories. In this case, both stories are about women who are ill—a twelve-year-old girl threatened by death and a woman who has been suffering from vaginal bleeding for twelve years. Twelve was the earliest a woman was thought sexually mature and old enough for marriage; vaginal bleeding made pregnancy impossible and was grounds for divorce. So both women are at risk of being in a way cut off from sexuality, as well as facing illness and possibly death. The story does not give either of them a name.

They have much in common, but much that differs as well. The little girl is the daughter of one of the leaders of the synagogue, Jairus (his office comes before his name to define him by its importance). She has a room of her own, a sign of her family's wealth. The woman with a hemorrhage, having spent all her money on doctors, is now destitute and physically worse than ever, suffering from constant bleeding that would render her ritually unclean as well as in pain. Called in Hebrew a *zabah* (literally an "oozer"), she could not enter the temple or take part in religious rituals. Family and friends should avoid touching her, or her clothes, or a bed where she had slept, or a chair where she had sat (Lev. 15:19–27). She had "endured" or "suffered" much—a verb Mark otherwise uses of the Son of Man. She was violating all sorts of taboos by coming out in the crowd at all. It is hard to imagine anyone more marginalized by her society, more different from the beloved daughter of a wealthy community leader. One AIDS patient, in the early days of that epidemic, told about how his parents forced him to live in the garage and put his food on the floor of the back porch, insisting that he not approach until they had retreated into the house. This woman could have empathized.

She was the extreme case of an affliction Jesus' culture imposed on every woman, for every woman was thought ritually unclean during her menstrual period. These are the sorts of practices that exist in societies where men make the rules.

Jairus approaches Jesus from the front, pleading his request. The anonymous woman has to sneak up from the back, through the crowd. Indeed, as the crowd presses in, she is rendering everyone around her unclean by her touch, and they would be angry at her presence if they knew her story. But she gets healed first. Indeed, Jairus's daughter seems lost to death when Jesus, and the narrative, pause over the case of this unclean woman. Moreover, while the little girl is *Jairus's* daughter, Jesus identifies the woman as *his* daughter.  Chrysostom notes that the person society would have dismissed as less important, indeed despised, gets Jesus' first attention and a welcome into his symbolic family: "Do you see how the woman is superior to the ruler of the synagogue? She did not detain Him, she took no hold of Him, she just touched Him with the end of her fingers, and, though she came later, she went away healed first."[63] Her "superiority" lies in Jesus' attitude toward her, not in her own virtues. I have heard Gustavo Gutiérrez say that "Blessed are the poor" is a statement not about the poor, but about God. It is not that the poor  are better than anyone else, but that God has blessed them.

But Jairus's daughter gets healed too.

> It was too late for Man—
> But early, yet, for God—
> Creation—impotent to help—
> But Prayer—remained—Our Side[64]

This is not a story about how outsiders get rewarded while insiders get punished. The last may come first and the first last, but the first are not excluded. In our society, we tend to assume that one person's gain is another's loss. God's reign will be different. So Virgil explains to Dante in the *Purgatorio* the difference between earth's competitive spirit and the charity that pervades heaven:

---

63. John Chrysostom, *Homilies on the Gospel of St. Matthew* 31.2 (*NPNF*, 1st ser., 10:207, translation altered).
64. Emily Dickinson, no. 623, *Collected Poems*, 307.

You set desire where sharing with one's fellows
Means that each partner gets a smaller share,
Wherefore you sigh, and envy works the bellows.

Did but the love of the most lofty sphere
Turn your desires to take the upward way,
Your hearts were quit of all this fearful care;

Because the more there are who there can say
"Ours," the more goods each has, and charity
Burns in that cloister with a larger ray.[65]

Climbing the corporate ladder, one person's promotion means that someone else did not get the job. In our public hospitals, caring for one impoverished patient may leave no funds with which to care for another. One's gain is inevitably another's loss. It is characteristic of the reign Jesus is bringing in that Jairus and his daughter have not lost just because the hemorrhaging woman won.

What happens to this woman and this young girl? Jesus engages in no ritual or even prayer. The power to cure seems to come from him rather than from some other source and only through him. The NRSV nicely captures the fact that the same verb (*sōzein*, "made well") appears in verses 23, 28, and 34. It is what Jairus asks for his daughter, what the woman hopes for, and what Jesus tells the woman has come because of her faith. Other translations alternate between "cured" and "saved." The Greek root means something like "deliverance from danger or suffering"; it was a common term for cure from life-threatening illness but could also refer, especially in the Septuagint and later apocalyptic literature, to the rescue from all earthly dangers that will come when God reigns. ("Turn to me and be saved, all the ends of the earth! For I am God, and there is no other," Isa. 45:22.) It is the word Mark uses in 8:35 when Jesus promises that those who lose their lives for his sake will save them.[66] Jesus tells Jairus's daughter to "get up" (*egeire*), and she "got up" (*anestē*)—

65. Dante, *Purgatory* 15.49–57, trans. Dorothy L. Sayers (Harmondsworth, Middlesex: Penguin, 1955), 182, referred to by Marcus, *Mark 1–8*, 370.
66. See also Mark 10:26; 13:13, 20; Marcus, *Mark 1–8*, 357.

both verbs that Mark and the early church in general characteristically used for Jesus' resurrection. So while she will indeed grow old and die in the ordinary human way, she is already initiated into the new life Jesus brings.

At one level, then, both cases are "cures." The woman stops bleeding; Jairus's daughter gets up, walks around, and has something to eat. But Mark's choice of words invites us to think that in both instances this encounter with Jesus has meant more. The woman can now go to the temple and associate in a normal way with her neighbors—she can be part of the Jewish people. This is her salvation. The girl will presumably live to adulthood in the ordinary way and then die a normal death. But the terms used offer just a hint that in the midst of that life this girl is already somehow participating in the new kind of life that will be made known in Jesus' resurrection.

Whatever happened, in both cases it happened because of faith. Jesus tells the woman as much: "Daughter, your faith has made you well" (v. 34). Jairus and his daughter provide a start and finish within which her story is sandwiched, but the whole block of these two stories is in turn sandwiched between Jesus' cure of the Gerasene demoniac and his visit to his hometown of Nazareth. The Gerasenes beg Jesus to leave their neighborhood, and the Nazarenes treat him with such contempt that he can do little good there. What a contrast with Jairus, this important official, who comes to Jesus, falls at his feet, and begs him repeatedly, and with this unnamed woman who risks everything merely to touch him.

So both episodes are stories of faith. Neither Jairus nor the unnamed woman articulates any belief *about* Jesus. "She had heard about Jesus" (v. 27)—whatever that may mean, we lack even that much preliminary for Jairus. But he falls at Jesus' feet and begs him. In hope of touching Jesus, she risks the chance that the crowd might turn on her and drive her away. Is her faith superstition? Theodore Jennings asks. "It is. But there is something else here. She bets everything on a desperate gamble. That is faith. That is the only faith she has. It is sheer audacity."[67] Likewise, we will recall,

67. Theodore W. Jennings Jr., *The Insurrection of the Crucified* (Chicago: Imprint Books, 2003), 76.

Peter and the others simply "followed." Understanding Jesus' identity is important—Mark's central purpose, after all, is to tell us who Jesus is—but it does not come first. First, we have to trust and obey and follow.

# FURTHER REFLECTIONS
## *Clean and Unclean*

Many episodes in Mark, like the one involving this unnamed woman, make sense only in the context of first-century Jewish rules about purity, and understanding that context requires some more general reflection on human ideas about what is clean or unclean. One of the most basic of human instincts is to organize things into categories. Our very survival, after all, depended on recognizing that this plant is good to eat, that one poisonous, this dangerous animal slow and lumbering, that one too quick to outrun. We are frustrated when some things seem not to fit the proper categories. So the anthropologist Mary Douglas famously noted the special status of the scaly anteater among the Lele people of the Congo: it has scales like a fish but lives in the forest and climbs trees; it is an animal but produces one offspring at a time like human beings. So it may be either sacred or polluting, but it is surely not ordinary.[68] Similarly, the animals most familiar in ancient Israel either chewed the cud and had cloven hoofs or else swallowed their food directly and had solid hoofs. Camels, however, chew the cud but do not have divided hoofs, while the reverse is true of pigs. Something is wrong there; they do not fit; better not eat them.

Similarly, we define what is dirty or unclean in terms of whether it fits. I would not say my back yard is "dirty," though it is certainly dirt. But just a bit of that dirt dragged into the house renders the floor dirty. "Dirt" implies something where it is not supposed to be, something that, in its location, defies the categories. Few categories are more basic than the distinction between what is "me" and what is "not me." Therefore things that come out of me, like excrement

---

68. Mary Douglas, *Implicit Meanings* (London: Routledge and Kegan Paul, 1975), 33–35.

or menstrual blood, are particularly dirty. (This is not an idea con-fined to "primitive" cultures.) We can analyze the danger of infection involved, and so on, but in our disgust at "filth" there is something more pernicious. According to the philosopher Paul Ricoeur, "What resists reflection is the idea of a quasi-material something that infects us as a sort of filth, that harms by invisible properties, and that nevertheless works in the manner of a force in the field of our undividedly psychic and corporeal existence."[69]

When I was a little kid, we used to worry about "catching cooties" from the other kids. I never knew quite what "cooties" were, and it all seemed a silly game. But, looking back, I realize with horror that less attractive kids or poorer ones who were badly dressed were more likely to "have cooties," girls more than boys. In our supposed inno-cence, we were drawing painful lines of social hierarchy. Similarly, in racial, ethnic, or class bigotry, the despised group nearly always gets described as "dirty." ("Those dirty....") Those with fewer changes of clothes or less good sanitation may be physically dirty, but some-thing more than that is at work. We are implying that, like dirt on the living room carpet, these "others" in our midst are somewhere they do not belong.

Like most religious cultures, ancient Israel cared about ritual cleanliness. One did not bring a blind sheep or a bird with a broken wing to the temple as a sacrifice. God deserves our best, so anything defined as "unclean" should not be brought into the presence of God. The Pharisees were trying to spread the religious standards of the temple to ordinary Jewish people. They were a democratic group, but the form of their egalitarianism was to apply to everyone rules previously reserved mostly for the temple elite. So particularly for them in Jesus' time the "unclean," whether lepers or women with chronic menstrual bleeding or whatever, were isolated from even ordinary social affairs. Such ostracism of the physically deformed is not unique to the first century or to Judaism. Into the twentieth century, a man who was disfigured in a way that would be a distrac-tion to worshipers or who had incomplete genitalia could not be a

69. Paul Ricoeur, *The Symbolism of Evil*, trans. Emerson Buchanan (Boston: Beacon, 1967), 25–26.

Catholic priest, and ministers with a visible disfigurement can still find it hard to get a job in a Protestant church (though I concede it is a rare pastoral selection committee that would ask about genitalia!).

But Jesus will have none of it. He literally reaches out to touch those whose touch is supposed to render unclean, and power flows in the opposite direction: they do not pollute him—he cleanses them, and thereby raises the question of whether they were "polluted" in the first place. He challenges his culture's basic values and assumptions, not on behalf of a new set of rules about who is clean and unclean, but about the very appropriateness of such categories. Once such questions have been raised, the whole world looks different.

# 6:1–6a

## *Unbelief in Nazareth*

Jesus comes home, to Nazareth, a town historians think had about three hundred people in the first century, the sort of place where everyone knows everyone else. Any Jewish adult male could be invited to speak in a synagogue, and Jesus, a local boy come home, accepts such an invitation. The first reaction is one of amazement. He is a *tekton*—"construction worker" might be a better contemporary translation than "carpenter"; the term referred to anyone who worked with his hands building things. Even two hundred years later Celsus, one of Christianity's greatest early opponents, ridiculed the Christians for worshiping an ordinary laborer.[70] Yet Jesus speaks with wisdom and can do deeds of power.

Amazement, however, quickly turns to suspicion. They know who he is—a construction worker, the son of an undistinguished local family. Though it is not mentioned here, we readers know that his family think he has gone crazy. To label a first-century Jew the son of his mother rather than the son of his father was an insult, hinting in a vulgar way at illegitimacy. If we have read Matthew and Luke, we know of another possible explanation—he was

---

70. Origen, *Contra Celsum* 6.34, 36.

the son not of Mary's husband, but of God. But Mark has not mentioned any miraculous birth, and refers here to Jesus' brothers and sisters in a way that at least raises questions about any claims to Mary's virginity.

As noted earlier, Christians who believed in the virgin birth have come up with different explanations of these brothers and sisters. Tertullian thought they were Mary's children, but born after Jesus; Clement of Alexandria proposed that they had been born to Joseph by a previous marriage. Both Jerome and Augustine believed they were Jesus' cousins. Today, reversing the expected positions, the Catholic John Meier accepts that they were biological full brothers and sisters while the Protestant Richard Bauckham defends the idea that they were cousins.[71] No doubt Christians will continue to disagree. On the one hand, there are legitimate ways to make the text consistent with the claim that Jesus was Mary's only child. On the other hand, I hope Christians generally can reject the hysterical horror at sexuality characteristic of Jerome's insistence on Mary's perpetual virginity, when he says to his opponents: "You have set on fire the temple of the Lord's body, you have defiled the sanctuary of the Holy Spirit from which you are determined to make a team of four brethren and a heap of sisters come out."[72] Whatever Mary's life may have involved, it is no disgrace for a married woman to have sex and get pregnant.

In any event, the people of Nazareth dismiss Jesus with contempt. "And he could do no deed of power there, except that he laid his hands on a few sick people and cured them." To say that Jesus *could not* do any deed of power of course raises theological questions. Jesus twice tells people he has cured (the woman with a hemorrhage, 5:34; and Bartimaeus, 10:52) that their faith has made them well; and having faith or seeking Jesus out, either on the part of the person cured or by a relative or friends, is a common prelude to cures. In contrast, though, Jesus seems to cure the Gerasene demoniac while the demons are still in control of him, and at least we can

71. John P. Meier, "The Brothers and Sisters of Jesus in Ecumenical Perspective," *CBQ* 54 (1992): 1–28; Richard Bauckham, "The Brothers and Sisters of Jesus: An Epiphanian Response to John P. Meier," *CBQ* 56 (1994): 686–700.
72. Jerome, *The Perpetual Virginity of Blessed Mary* 18 (*NPNF*, 2nd ser., 6:343).

see no evidence of his faith. Writing in the fourth century, Gregory of Nazianzus declared, "For since, for healing to occur, there is need of both faith in the patient and power in the healing, when one of the two failed the other was impossible."[73] "Impossible" seems strong, and not quite in accord with this text, where Jesus finds no faith but yet cures a few people anyway. Calvin acknowledges that "unbelievers . . . bind up the hands of God by their obstinacy," yet points to the few who are healed in Nazareth as proof that God always finds a way to bestow favors upon us.[74] As is often the case, an ambiguity captures what Mark wants to say: if people have no faith, it puts an insurmountable barrier between them and God—but God can surmount insurmountable barriers.

The episode in Nazareth is a kind of turning point. His town here rejects him, just as his family has and the leaders of his people will. Cures and exorcisms after this usually come only with some sort of struggle. Jesus never enters a synagogue again.

## 6:6b–13
### *The Mission of the Twelve*

Jesus sends the Twelve out on their own for the first time—two by two, to proclaim that people should repent, to cast out demons, and to cure the sick. It is hard to know just what the gospel would have been at this point, and their proclamation may not have been much different from what John the Baptist said, though, if they were influenced by Jesus at all, it would have more love and hope and less threat in it.

They went two by two. Jewish law required two witnesses to establish a charge's truth (Deut. 19:15; cf. Num. 35:30), but Jesus' point may have been one of simple companionship. They were to wear sandals and a tunic and carry a staff—no food, no money, no bag, no extra clothes. Sandals, staff, and tunic are what people are told to wear and carry at the exodus from Egypt (Exod. 12:11), so here

---

73. Gregory Nazianzus, Oration 30:10 (*NPNF*, 2nd ser., 7:313, translation altered).
74. Calvin, *Harmony of the Evangelists*, 2:216.

again we have the Twelve as a reconstituted people of Israel. More important, they will be *radically* dependent on charity. Some traveling Buddhist monks follow the practice, as did the early Franciscans. Hope that someone will offer you food and a place to sleep; if not, go hungry and sleep outside. Such life presumes radical faith: you are doing what God has called you to do, and God will take care of you. Missionaries living in such poverty, moreover, will inevitably be critics of power structures and cannot be the agents of colonialism.[75]

The towns they visit are judged on their hospitality. The question is not whether they believe you or whether they are morally upright people, but whether they welcome you. The disciples in turn should not scout around for a fancier place or a house with something better for dinner but stay in the first house where they are welcomed; this is the proper response to hospitality. If a town is not hospitable, shake the dust from your feet as you leave. Since one of a host's first duties was to see to the washing of his guest's feet, your dusty feet themselves testify to their failure of hospitality.

So the disciples traveled, anointing the sick with oil, the first instance of a common Christian custom that is a sacrament in the Catholic Church. Prior to Vatican II, "extreme unction" was reserved for those about to die, but now Catholics and many Protestants alike, after the practice of the Twelve, anoint anyone who is sick. What does this accomplish? At the very least, it manifests to suffering people that there is a community of faith concerned for them, conscious of their difficulties, and praying for them. When Mark says that the disciples cured people, he probably implies that their anointing, at least some of the time, did more than that, but he does not need to be taken as denying that sometimes it simply provided that sort of human comfort, and that can be a good thing in itself.

75. Pheme Perkins, "Mark," *New Interpreter's Bible*, ed. Leander E. Keck (Nashville: Abingdon, 1995), 8:596.

# 6:14–8:26

# *The Inclusive Banquet*

## 6:14–29

### *Herod Kills John the Baptist*

For the only time, Mark turns his story away from Jesus, to give the terrible account of how Herod Antipas killed John the Baptist. The narrative comes in the form of a flashback. Herod hears about Jesus, who sounds like another troublemaker, and wonders who he is. Some say that this is another prophet, "like one of the prophets of old." But Herod, picking up some gossip and perhaps burdened with guilt, fears that John the Baptizer, whom he had beheaded, has been raised from the dead.

It is in this odd context that the idea of resurrection first enters Mark's story. In ancient Israel, the idea of resurrection had not first emerged out of a general conviction that there must be life after death. People were content to believe that, if you lived to a ripe old age and had many descendants to carry on your name, that added up to a good life. Some sort of shadowy existence might continue after death, but it was not the focus of their faith. Resurrection hope arose in the context of belief in God's justice. Some good people, faithful Jews, did not lead long and happy lives. They suffered and died young, and they might not have any descendants at all. Such stories seemed even more common in the tragic years of Israel's exile and subjugation. If God is just, then death cannot be the end of these people's stories. So *1 Enoch* 104:5, written a century or two before the time of Jesus, offers reassurance: "You righteous ones, do not be afraid when you see the wicked grow strong and prosper. Do not join in their ways, but keep far from their violence, for you will become companions of the hosts of heaven." Knowing better than anyone that John got a bad deal in death, Herod fears John's resurrection.

This Herod was not really a king. One of the four sons of Herod the Great, he had on his father's death been appointed by the Romans "tetrarch" ("ruler of one-fourth") of Galilee and some territory east of the Jordan. Jesus would have been one of his subjects, and John the Baptist's preaching probably also took place in his tetrarchy. He wanted to be a king like his father, and lobbied hard for the title, so hard that an annoyed Roman emperor eventually (before Mark was writing) exiled him to Gaul. We cannot be sure whether the references to him here as "king" represent the standard usage of ordinary people unaware of these fine distinctions or Mark's ironic allusion to the title Herod hoped for but destroyed his career in seeking.

The family relations among the descendants of Herod the Great are very complicated. Herod Antipas, the Herod of this story, first married the daughter of the king of Nabatea, a land east of his own territory. Then he fell in love with Herodias, his niece, who was already married to another of her uncles (he was also named Herod, but, to minimize confusion, Mark calls him Philip). Antipas's wife, understandably annoyed, left him and went back to her father, so that a potentially useful alliance turned into a threat from an angry father-in-law. In fact, the king of Nabatea did later attack Herod Antipas, and the Romans had to come and bail him out.

Herod Antipas then married Herodias, who under Jewish law could not divorce her husband (only men could initiate divorce), so she was now technically married to two brothers, both of whom were also her uncles. Herod Antipas was clearly in violation of Leviticus 18:16, which prohibits marrying your brother's wife if the brother is still alive. Salome, Herodias's daughter by her first marriage, was thus Antipas's niece on her father's side, grandniece on her mother's side, and now stepdaughter. We may gossip about scandal in high places today, but we rarely if ever have material quite this rich.

The Jewish historian Josephus tells of the results in purely political terms. Antipas was afraid of John the Baptizer, whose eloquence in criticizing corruption was so compelling that it might start a revolt, so he had him killed.[1] Mark makes the story more personal, and Antipas a more complicated character. Like Pontius Pilate later

---

1. Josephus, *Jewish Antiquities* 18.118.

on, he is the person in the story with the most power, yet he seems
in some ways the weakest character. John is bravely willing to die.
Herodias is determined to get him dead. Antipas fears him, knows
he is a righteous and holy man, and even likes to listen to him. This
corrupt king with a completely messed-up family recognizes goodness when he sees it and even finds it appealing.

Herodias, however, hates John for his attacks on her marriage.
After all, she is more vulnerable. If Antipas's guilt got the better of
him and he decided on a divorce, she could hardly go back to Philip,
and indeed she would have no place at all to go. So, as Ambrose wrote,
"a banquet of death is set out with royal luxury,"[2] and the girl Salome
dances so well that her stepfather (presumably drunk?) offers her
anything she wants, up to half his kingdom. Mark calls Salome a
*korasion*, a "little girl," the same word he used for the twelve-year-
old daughter of Jairus. Some scholars argue that the dance could
have been quite innocent, and we are imposing "Western" images of
"the oriental court" if we see sexual undertones. But it seems to me
that a twelve-year-old dancing at a party hosted by her uncle/great-
uncle/stepfather in a society where women would normally have
even eaten separately has something both sensual and odd about it.
Things certainly turn sick soon enough. Herodias tells her to ask for
the head of John the Baptizer. It is the "little girl" herself who adds
the detail of having it on a platter.

Ambrose asks, "What is more base than that a murder should be
committed in order not to displease those who sat at meat?"[3] Herod
quite clearly knows it is wrong to behead the Baptizer and does not
want to do it. But with what Calvin called "the usual vanity of kings"
he does not want to reverse a promise he has made in public, and he
fears he will fall in the estimation of his guests if he does not keep
his promise.[4] It is an odd fact that the motives of the wealthiest and
most powerful so often involve an element of fear—fear of losing
what they have, fear of embarrassment, fear that someone will see
through their mask of importance to the nervous human being they

2. Ambrose, *Concerning Virgins* 3.6.27 (*NPNF*, 2nd ser., 10:385).
3. Ibid., 3.6.28.
4. Calvin, *Harmony of the Evangelists*, 2:27.

know lies within. Reinhold Niebuhr once remarked, "There is no level of greatness and power in which the lash of fear is not at least one strand in the whip of ambition."[5] Rome famously conquered the world in self-defense—they defeated other powers because they feared attack. They were not the last great power to behave in this way. In personal relations, too, the bully in the schoolyard or the office often acts out of deep insecurity. So Herod, who is the most powerful person in the room, gives way. John, deprived of all power in his prison cell, stands firm. Chrysostom highlights the contrast, "Note well the weakness of the tyrant compared to the power of the one in prison."[6] John gets beheaded on the orders of a "king" who is not really a king, and the only food mentioned at this royal banquet is a human head on a platter.

The story ends with Mark's remark that John's disciples came and took his body and laid it in a tomb. Jesus' disciples will not even do that.

# 6:30–44

## *The Feeding of Five Thousand*

Mark takes us to a very different kind of meal. The wealthy gather in the king's court for Herod's feast, but the only food mentioned is a disgusting human head. A crowd of ordinary folks follow Jesus into a deserted place with no supplies, and everyone eats till they are filled. Being "filled" or "satisfied" (*echortasthēsan*) could not be taken for granted in a peasant society. It means that they ate as much as they wanted, and that would have been a rare experience for most people. Deuteronomy 8:10 even promises it as one of the remarkable features of the promised land.

This passage begins a portion of Mark that John Meier calls "the bread section," 6:30–8:21. Its first half, 6:30–7:37, begins with the feeding of five thousand, goes on to a crossing of the Sea of Galilee, continues with a dispute with Jewish leaders that involves the

5. Reinhold Niebuhr, *The Nature and Destiny of Man*, 2 vols. (New York: Charles Scribner's Sons, 1941–1943), 1:194.
6. John Chrysostom, "On the Providence of God," in Oden and Hall, *Mark*, 87.

word "bread," and ends with the healing of a blind man. The second half begins with feeding four thousand, followed by another crossing of the sea, another dispute with Jewish leaders involving "bread," and the healing of a deaf-mute. Mark even more pointedly connects these two healings, of one who cannot see and one who cannot hear, in that they are the only two cures where Jesus uses saliva.[7] Jesus moves back and forth between Jewish and Gentile territory, curing the sick, feeding the hungry, and redefining the way we understand what "bread" means.

To begin, the author comes back from Herod's court to Jesus, where he will stay till the end of the Gospel (to the extent that it has an end). The Twelve come back from their first missions, tired but eager to tell about their experiences, and Jesus tries to lead them off to a "deserted place," but all kinds of people follow them, and Jesus starts to teach the crowd. "He had compassion for them, because they were like sheep without a shepherd."

The phrase has many echoes in the Jewish tradition. Moses and David, Israel's greatest leaders, were both shepherds. When Moses grows old, he asks the Lord to appoint a successor "so that the congregation of the LORD may not be like sheep without a shepherd" (Num. 27:17). Under Ahab, perhaps the most corrupt of David's royal successors, the prophet Micaiah has a vision of "all Israel scattered on the mountains, like sheep that have no shepherd" (1 Kgs. 22:17). Both Jeremiah and Ezekiel promise a future ruler who will guide the people like a good shepherd (Jer. 23:4; Ezek. 34:23). People need a shepherd, and too many rulers do not take good care of their sheep.

What should a shepherd do? Sheep, as those who raise them know, are easily frightened and just stupid. The shepherd's job is not to give them whatever they want. Rather, as Karl Barth wrote, a true shepherd

> would know that He was responsible for them and would therefore act solely on their behalf. He would hear the general and foolish crying and bleating as each tried to assert their own individuality, and He would understand the basic reason

7. Meier, *Marginal Jew*, 2:691, 905–6.

for it better than the people themselves. He would not, therefore, reject or despise them. He would know what they need
and how they can be genuinely helped. He would keep them
together, bringing them both as a whole and as individuals to
the place where what they need is to be found.[8]

We certainly need such political and ecclesial shepherds today,
when too many of us pursue immediate, selfish concerns even as we
demand that selfishness come to an end. We need leaders who will
not pander to what we think we want but will have the vision and
eloquence to lead us to the place where we find what we truly need.

I do not know what happened in that deserted place. The version
of the story I learned in my liberal Sunday school was that everyone
in fact had food stashed away, but, selfishly, they were afraid to share
it until Jesus inspired them with a spirit of generosity, and it turned
out there was plenty of food to go around after all. That is not what
Mark says, though he is characteristically mysterious about just how
the multiplication of food happens. In his *Life of Jesus*, originally published in German in 1835–36 and still one of the great books on the
"historical Jesus," David Friedrich Strauss argued that, if one rejects
such stories as "miracles," one should take them as legends that grew
up about Jesus or were told to make a symbolic point rather than
looking for naturalistic explanations for them. I have already said
that, if the Creator of the universe was walking around Galilee in
the first century, it seems plausible
that some quite unusual things
might have happened in his immediate vicinity. As Chrysostom
wrote, "For although the place be
desert, yet He that feeds the world
is here."[9] One way to read this story
in Mark is as an account of something that happened, and I would
not rule out that possibility.

> Jesus' miracles "point to the
> bodily character of salvation
> and to the God who loves
> earthly life."
> —Jürgen Moltmann
>
> *The Way of Jesus Christ* (San Francisco:
> HarperSanFrancisco, 1990), 107.

8. Barth, *CD* IV/2:186.
9. John Chrysostom, *Homilies on Matthew* 49.1 (*NPNF*, 1st ser., 10:304).

On the other hand, the story does seem full of symbolic meaning. A theological commentary on Mark need not try to penetrate behind the Gospel to history, but it does need to ask how literally Mark meant his story to be taken. Luther proposed that the five loaves represent things understood by the senses, since there are five senses, and the two fish stand for the patriarchs and prophets—the fish are cooked, since so many prophets were persecuted and martyred. The twelve baskets left over represent the twelve apostles, the results of Jesus' work, which goes beyond things we can know by the senses or learn from the Hebrew Scriptures.[10] Well, perhaps. The story does seem to point back to parallels in the history of Israel, forward to the anticipated eschatological banquet, and also to the Last Supper and the Eucharist.

Exodus 16 tells how the Lord fed the people of Israel in the wilderness with quail in the evening and manna (a breadlike substance) in the morning. The story gets repeated in Numbers 11, this time even with a reference to fish (11:22). In 2 Kings 4:42–44 the prophet Elisha feeds a hundred men with twenty loaves of barley, and there is bread left over. In the time of Moses, then, God fed the people of Israel in the wilderness—now Jesus feeds this new community of his followers in the wilderness. Feeding large numbers with small quantities and then some left over is one of the things prophets do. The numbers here do seem significant: five books of the Law feed the people of Israel, just as five loaves feed these people, and there are twelve baskets left over, just as there are twelve tribes of Israel. Scholars also point out the military and eschatological imagery: only men are fed here (as opposed to the later feeding of "four thousand *people*" at 8:9), and they are arrayed in groups of hundreds and fifties, as an army might be. Several passages from the Dead Sea Scrolls, presumably written about Jesus' time, describe the eschatological community camped out in groups of hundreds and fifties and tens.[11] So this feast is a foretaste of that one, where the

10. Martin Luther, "Fourth Sunday in Lent," *Sermons of Martin Luther*, vol. 2, *Sermons on Gospel Texts for Epiphany, Lent, and Easter*, ed. John Nicholas Lenker, trans. Lenker et al. (repr. Grand Rapids: Baker, 1983), 167.

11. Florentino García Martínez and Elbert Tigchelaar, eds., *The Dead Sea Scrolls Study Edition*, 2 vols. (Grand Rapids: Eerdmans, 2000), 1:72–73, 570–71, 572–73.

gathered people of God will eat together. In all the Gospel stories and pictures of the scene in early Christian art, there are always two fish. Some have proposed that these are the sea monsters Leviathan and Behemoth, whose defeat by God is often part of eschatological stories and would presumably leave them to be eaten in the great banquet.[12] It is also connected with the Eucharist. Jesus *takes* the loaves and fishes, looks up to heaven, and then *blesses*, *breaks*, and *gives* them to his disciples—the same four verbs he will use with the bread at the Last Supper.

Jesus acts with compassion and confidence. The people, sheep without a shepherd, take him as their shepherd. The disciples worry about scarcity and want to exclude; Jesus creates plenty and includes everyone. The story's symbolism points in all sorts of directions. Mark certainly thought that Jesus *could* have multiplied bread and fish, and so do I. I am less sure that Mark focuses here on Jesus' amazing power rather than on the symbolic meanings conveyed in the course of this narrative. Nor need one choose between these interpretations. Perhaps the best guess is to say that the text presumes the amazing power but does not focus on it primarily.

## 6:45–52

### *Jesus Walks on the Sea*

The next story is multivalent in a similar manner. However one explains the stories, Jesus did help people with physical and mental sufferings. If we knew more about how Mark's mind worked, we could better determine how literally he wants us to take these stories of multiplied food and walking on the sea. It is striking how often in Mark Jesus wants to be by himself. Here he sends his disciples off in a boat and climbs a mountain to pray. Then the story gets confusing. He comes toward them "when he saw that they were straining at the oars against an adverse wind." But, "he intended to pass them by." If he came to help them against the adverse wind, why would

12. Richard H. Hiers and Charles A. Kennedy, "The Bread and Fish Eucharist in the Gospels and Early Christian Art," *Perspectives in Religious Studies* 3 (Spring 1976): 38–39.

he have intended to pass them by? In any event, they see him, think him a ghost walking on the water, and are terrified. With considerable impatience, Calvin remarks that, since they have just seen Jesus feed the five thousand, "it showed a very extraordinary stupidity" on the disciples' part not yet to understand that Jesus could do amazing things.[13]

If we try to understand "pass them by" not in the context of the literal story but symbolically, it makes much more sense. When God appears to people in the Hebrew Scriptures, he regularly "passes by." Mark uses the same word, *parerchomai*, that the Septuagint uses in such cases. So in Exodus, when Moses asks the Lord to show him his glory, the Lord responds, "I will make all my goodness pass before you. . . . and while my glory passes by I will put you in a cleft of the rock, and I will cover you with my hand until I have passed by" (Exod. 33:19, 22). But Jesus comes toward them, walking on the sea, which in the Hebrew Scriptures is one of God's attributes (Job 9:8, Ps. 77:19).

As Jesus approaches them, he says in Greek, *egō eimi*, which could mean just, "It's me," but, as "I am," is God's most dramatic formula of self-revelation in the Hebrew Scriptures. When Moses asks the voice from the burning bush to give a name he can tell to the Hebrew people, the voice replies, "I AM WHO I AM. . . . Thus you shall say to the Israelites, 'I AM has sent me to you. . . . This is my name forever" (Exod. 3:14–15). "I am" is thus Israel's central verbal formula of divine self-disclosure. Jesus then tells the disciples not to be afraid, which is the standard comment God makes after a revelation. In sum, combine passing by, walking on water, saying *egō eimi*, and telling them not to fear—everything in this passage is screaming out, "Jesus is God!" This very human human being, who at the beginning of the episode needed to be alone to pray, says and does the things God says and does.

13. Calvin, *Harmony of the Evangelists*, 2:239.

# 6:53–56
## *Crowds of the Sick in Gennesaret*

Even with the feeding of five thousand, Jesus' activity has so far seemed on a small scale. Mark has pictured just the group in Jesus' presence. Now people "rushed about that whole region." "Wherever he went, into villages or cities or farms," his reputation precedes him and crowds quickly gather. We do not know what Jesus wants to do with his popularity, but he seems to have enough support to be a threat to the powers that be if he wants.

# 7:1–23
## *Whatever Goes into*
## *a Person Cannot Defile*

Mark has already presented Jesus as rejecting traditional purity laws. He touches a leper and a corpse; he eats with tax collectors and sinners. Until now, however, he has not moved from such particular actions to a general principle. But in this episode he reformulates the very idea of purity. The conversation begins over a rather trivial point. Some Pharisees and some scribes who had come from Jerusalem notice that Jesus' disciples do not wash their hands before they eat. Mark pauses to explain that "the Pharisees, and all the Jews, do not eat unless they thoroughly wash their hands," so Jesus' disciples are violating this "tradition of the elders." This is one of the places that suggests Mark was writing primarily for a Gentile audience, who need to have Jewish customs explained to them. Puzzlingly, though, his explanation seems not to be true. Jewish priests carefully washed before eating the holy food in the temple rituals, following Numbers 18:8–13, and perhaps some strict Pharisees were trying to extend this practice to all consumption of food, but it was never the practice of "all the Jews." Is Mark misinformed or exaggerating or what? We do not know. Even the translation poses problems. The best manuscripts say that the Jews "wash their hands with the fist," but the NRSV follows a minority of manuscripts in having "thoroughly" rather than "with the fist," principally because no one has ever figured out what "wash their hands with the fist" could mean.[14]

In any event, Jesus uses the occasion, quoting Isaiah, to denounce the hypocrisy of his opponents. They follow the "traditions of the elders," the detailed application of various laws that had developed over time, but lose sight of the basic commandments God gave the people of Israel. For example, the *corban* was an oath in which one dedicated some item of one's property to the temple. One of the Ten Commandments specifies that we should honor our father and mother. So, if his (I use the male pronoun since men would ordinarily be the owners of property) parents were in financial difficulties, a pious Jew ought to sell some of his property to help them out. (In pre–Social Security days, children would be the expected support of their parents in the parents' old age.) If he wanted to get out of that obligation, however, he could dedicate his property to the temple in some vague way, perhaps to go into effect only after his death. Then he could say, "Gosh, folks, I would really like to help you, but all my property is tied up in vows to the temple, so there is nothing I can do," thus using a technical point of traditional law to avoid fulfilling a fundamental principle of the Ten Commandments. Jerome explained, "It frequently happened that while father and mother were destitute their children were offering sacrifices for priests and scribes to consume."[15] But it was worse than that: if you were smart enough, you could figure out how to keep property from your parents without giving it to the priests and scribes either. "And you do many things like this," Jesus concludes.

Then comes the punch line: "There is *nothing* outside a person that by going in can defile, but the things that come out are what defile." The challenge is not to particular details of traditional purity laws but to the whole idea that "purity" means keeping your distance from unclean persons, things, and types of food. Food does not enter the heart but the stomach, and the waste products go right out the other end. What *defiles* are fornication, theft, murder, adultery, avarice, wickedness, deceit, licentiousness, envy, slander, pride,

14. Hooker, *Gospel of Mark*, 174–75.
15. Jerome, Letter 123.6 (*NPNF*, 2nd ser., 6:232).

and folly—things that we *do* or *feel*, not things that we *touch* or *eat*. Having contrasted the human-made idea of *corban* with the commandment to honor father and mother, Jesus here too starts his definition of the truly defiling with the Ten Commandments. If we classify fornication as adultery, avarice as coveting, and deceit and slander as forms of bearing false witness, then seven of the twelve items on Jesus' list come directly from the second table of the Ten Commandments, the part that concerns our relations with other people. Worry about your own attitudes and behavior, not how you might look to others if they see you associating with the wrong people. There are no "wrong people" when it comes to those Christians should care about.

> Insofar as the second table of the Decalogue sets forth particular directives about treating the neighbor, one may not read them narrowly.
> —Patrick D. Miller
>
> *The Ten Commandments,* Interpretation (Louisville, KY: Westminster John Knox Press, 2009), 45–46.

In Flannery O'Connor's masterful short story "Revelation," a middle-aged southern white woman, Ruby Turpin, struggles to understand a strange episode where a college girl back from the north attacked her and yelled, "Go back to hell where you came from, you old wart hog." Mrs. Turpin cannot understand, for she is a respectable, grateful woman with a good disposition, fond of her husband, Claud. She is sure she is not a racist, for she would rather be a "Negro" than be "white trash." That evening, though, feeding her hogs about sunset, she has a vision, seeing

> a vast swinging bridge extending upward from the earth through a field of living fire. Upon it a vast horde of souls were rumbling toward heaven. There were whole companies of white-trash, clean for the first time in their lives, and bands of black niggers in white robes, and battalions of freaks and lunatics shouting and clapping and leaping like frogs. And bringing up the end of the procession was a tribe of people whom she recognized at once as those who, like herself and Claud, had always had a little of everything and the God-given wit to use it right. She leaned forward to observe them closer. They were marching behind the others with great dignity, accountable as

they had always been for good order and common sense and respectable behavior. They alone were on key. Yet she could see by their shocked and altered faces that even their virtues were being burned away.[16]

Jesus invites us to let all our respectability be burned away so that nothing will distinguish us from the freaks and lunatics, and only thus to enter his reign.

## 7:24–30

### *The Syrophoenician Woman*

Having challenged all barriers to welcome, all distinctions between clean and unclean, Jesus is now himself challenged, in a story in which, as Sharon Ringe puts it, it seems that even Jesus "was caught with his compassion down."[17] Jesus has gone into Gentile territory again, up to the north of Galilee. Again he seeks solitude, but a Gentile woman "whose little daughter had an unclean spirit" comes to ask him for a cure. She hears about him immediately; she bows at his feet and begs. Unlike Jairus, she seems to take for granted that Jesus can work cures at a distance. Before a word is exchanged, she is already presented as a woman of deep faith.

Jesus gives her a brutal answer. He has come to the Jews; she is a Gentile: "Let the children be fed first, for it is not fair to take the children's food and throw it to the dogs." What he says is harsh enough in our culture, but even harsher then, in a culture where dogs were not beloved house pets but disgusting scavengers who skulked about living on garbage. Calling someone a "dog" was a real insult (see for instance 2 Kgs. 8:13). With some justice, the Jewish scholar Joseph Klausner remarks, "If any other Jewish teacher of the time had said such a thing Christians would never have forgiven Judaism for it."[18]

16. Flannery O'Connor, "Revelation," in *Collected Works* (New York: The Library of America, 1988), 654.
17. Sharon H. Ringe, "A Gentile Woman's Story," in *Feminist Interpretation of the Bible*, ed. Letty Russell (Philadelphia: Westminster, 1984), 69.
18. Joseph Klausner, *Jesus of Nazareth: His Life, Times, and Teaching*, trans. Herbert Danby (New York: Macmillan, 1929), 294.

Christians have used a variety of strategies to try to explain away Jesus' answer. Some claim Jesus' manner made clear that he did not really mean what he said. The normally sensible William Barclay writes, "We can be quite sure that the smile on Jesus' face and the compassion in his eyes robbed the words of all insult and bitterness."[19] A. E. J. Rawlinson assures us, "The words are probably spoken half whimsically."[20] Nothing in the text justifies such interpretations. The Nicaraguan peasants in Ernesto Cardenal's parish of Solentiname thought Jesus must have been so harsh to the woman because she was rich and had taken advantage of the poor: "She must have been an oppressor."[21] This analysis has at least some historical support—Tyre was a rich city whose merchants did often make large profits by taking advantage of farmers in the Galilean hinterland.[22] Unfortunately, this passage is clearly primarily about the relation of Jews and Gentiles, not of rich and poor.

The woman responds, "Sir, even the dogs under the table eat the children's crumbs," and Jesus, admiring her answer, tells her that her daughter is cured. John Chrysostom proposed that Jesus, who knew all things, knew how brilliantly the woman would respond to his harsh remark and wanted to give her the chance so that he could respond by not just acceding to her wishes but also praising her for her faith and insight.[23] At least this does not conflict with the text, but, for all its intent to honor the woman, it makes her just an actor in the performance Jesus has all-knowingly staged. Luther was bolder. He recognized that the woman won the exchange: "She catches Christ with his own words. He compares her to a dog, she concedes it, and asks nothing more than that he let her be a dog. . . . Where will Christ now take refuge? He is caught."[24] For Luther, the woman is the hero of the story, and faith is her heroic virtue: she clings "in her confidence to the good news she had

19. William Barclay, *The Gospel of Mark*, 2nd ed. (Philadelphia: Westminster, 1956), 122.

20. A. E. J. Rawlinson, *St. Mark*, Westminster Commentaries (London: Methuen, 1960), 99.

21. Ernesto Cardenal, *The Gospel in Solentiname*, trans. Donald D. Walsh, 4 vols. (Maryknoll, NY: Orbis, 1976–1982), 2:215.

22. Susan Miller, *Women in Mark's Gospel* (London: T. & T. Clark, 2004), 92.

23. John Chrysostom, *Homilies on Matthew* 52.3 (*NPNF*, 1st ser., 10:322–23).

24. Martin Luther, "Second Sunday in Lent," *Luther's Sermons*, 2:152.

heard and embraced concerning him, and never gives up." The story reminds us how deeply God can conceal grace from us, but in the midst of such hiddenness the Syrophoenician woman "still firmly believes his goodness is yet concealed in that answer, and still she will not pass judgment that Christ is or may be ungracious."[25] Jesus' attitude to Gentiles will never again be the same.

If Mark did not show us Jesus' initial harsh remark, we could not see the grace with which Jesus concedes defeat in an argument. That the woman does win the argument is a point any valid interpretation needs to acknowledge. To say that that could not happen is to deny Jesus' full humanity. Here yet again humanity and divinity come together in a single narrative of a single agent—the same Jesus who loses the argument can cure her daughter. It is her faith, though, that lies at the center of the story. Sometimes God responds brutally to our faith too. We put our trust in God, and one disaster follows another. Our faith needs to be, as Luther said, such that even when God's goodness is concealed, we will not imagine that the God we know in Jesus Christ ultimately "is or may be ungracious."

> But, oh, how painful it is to nature and reason, that this woman should strip herself of self and forsake all that she experienced, and cling alone to God's bare Word, until she experienced the contrary. May God help us in time of need and of death to possess like courage and faith!
>
> —Martin Luther
>
> "Second Sunday in Lent," *Luther's Sermons*, 2:150.

## 7:31–37

### *Curing a Deaf Man*

The literal geography gets confused, but the symbolic geography is clear enough. One would not go due north from Tyre to Sidon in order to get southeast to the Decapolis area east of the Sea of Galilee. It is as if Mark is mentioning every Gentile city or territory his audience might know in order to make clear that Jesus is now among

25. Ibid., 150–51.

the Gentiles. The issues raised by his encounter with the Syrophoenician woman remain important, and her argument has carried the day. Jesus heals a deaf man and feeds a multitude. What he had done for Jews he now does for Gentiles too.

"They brought to him a deaf man who had an impediment in his speech; and they begged him to lay his hand on him." Mark offers no explanation of who "they" are, but Luther notes that they must be good people: "They do not need this work themselves, nor do they look to themselves, but to the poor man, and think how they may help him; they seek no reward, but act independently and freely. Thus you should by right do likewise; if not, you are no Christians."[26] Here among the Gentiles there are good folks disinterestedly seeking help for their disadvantaged neighbor. Jesus quickly provides the help; no more arguments about who gets help first. He puts his fingers in the man's ears and a bit of spittle on his tongue, looks up to heaven, sighs or groans, and says, "*Ephphatha*," which, as Mark explains, means, "Be opened."

Jesus' action erases distinctions between clean and unclean. In a culture where spittle was thought as disgusting as excrement, Jesus is bold to use it to cure. As usual when Mark quotes Jesus in Aramaic, he makes clear that this is no secret magical formula by promptly translating it. Jesus "sighs"—the word could also mean "groans." Is he reacting in compassion to the man's suffering? Does this cure involve some sort of struggle, in contrast to apparently effortless earlier ones? It happens, in any event, "immediately." Jesus is fulfilling what Isaiah promised when God's reign comes:

> Then the eyes of the blind shall be opened,
>   and the ears of the deaf unstopped;
> then the lame shall leap like a deer,
>   and the tongue of the speechless sing for joy.
>                                                (Isa. 35:5–6)

---

26. Martin Luther, "Twelfth Sunday after Trinity," *Sermons of Martin Luther*, vol. 4, *Sermons on Gospel Texts for the First to Twelfth Sundays after Trinity* (repr. Grand Rapids: Baker, 1983), 372–73.

Or in Charles Wesley's paraphrase,

> Hear Him, ye deaf; His praise, ye dumb,
> Your loosen'd tongues employ;
> Ye blind, behold your Savior come;
> And leap, ye lame, for joy.[27]

Then we face the "messianic secret" again, this time in its most paradoxical form: "Jesus ordered them to tell no one; but the more he ordered them, the more zealously they proclaimed it." Is Jesus just incompetent at giving instructions? What has happened to his authority? The pattern is a common one in Mark, though this passage is a particularly dramatic instance of it. Jesus orders silence, and everybody talks. To be sure, here in Gentile territory, the danger that Jesus will be misunderstood as a political-military Messiah and generate a rebellion is far less, but a puzzle remains. Mark wants to insist on two things: Jesus does not want to be known in his true identity until it will be clear that suffering rather than power lies at the core of that identity, but Jesus' charismatic accomplishments are so great that they cannot be hidden. There is an inevitable tension between those two claims, and it is Mark's style just to say both, lay them beside each other, and not worry very much about explanations. Karl Barth says that this is often a good way to do theology; it is what he calls theology's inevitable brokenness. If we know X and we know Y, but X and Y seem inconsistent, better to say them both and leave a mystery than to try to make a coherent system and in the process lose sight of one of the things we knew in the first place. The "ultimate word, however, is not a further thesis, not a synthesis, but just the name Jesus Christ."[28]

---

27. Charles Wesley, "For the Anniversary Day of One's Conversion" ("O, For a Thousand Tongues to Sing"), in *Charles Wesley: A Reader*, ed. John R. Tyson (Oxford: Oxford University Press, 1989), 109.
28. Barth, CD I/2:24.

# 8:1–10

## *The Feeding of Four Thousand*

Studies of the relation of this passage to the feeding of five thousand people in 6:30–44 illustrate some important changes in NT scholarship. Why are there these two feeding stories in Mark? A generation or two ago, most scholars focused on historical questions about sources. Did Mark inherit two different stories about the feeding of a multitude? Could those two sources be traced back to the same origin? More recently, the emphasis often shifts to literary and theological questions: How do these two stories function in Mark's narrative?

Location provides a first obvious difference between the two stories. Jesus has crossed the Sea of Galilee; he is now on the predominantly Gentile side. In the earlier feeding, the key numbers related to the history of Israel—five loaves, like the five books of the Law, fed them; twelve baskets, like the twelve tribes, were left over. Jesus laments that the people are sheep without a shepherd, regretting the lack of the sort of great leader Israel once had. Those fed are all identified as men, and they are arrayed in a kind of battle formation, evoking eschatological calls to gather the troops of Israel.

In this second feeding, *four* thousand are fed with *seven* loaves, and there are *seven* baskets left over. Four, representing the four corners of the universe or the four directions, was a common symbol for the whole world. Jewish law also specified four basic laws that Gentiles living among Jews should be required to obey (Lev. 17:8, 10–13; 18:26), and the book of Acts reports that these four rules, but not the rest of Jewish law, were required of Gentile converts to Christianity (Acts 15:19–20), so these ideas were being considered in the early church. In Genesis 9:4–7 God gives Noah seven laws; these presumably apply to the whole world, Noah's descendants, in contrast to the five books of Jewish law. Deuteronomy 7:1 contrasts the Hebrew people with the seven nations of Canaan. For first-century readers, fascinated by number symbolism, this passage would have cried out, "This time Jesus is feeding *Gentiles.*"

Jesus mentions, moreover, that some of these people have come from a great distance, as Gentiles might have. They are "people" rather than "men" and there is no quasi-military ordering—no calling of eschatological Israel is represented here. The regret that they have no shepherd is not mentioned, thereby avoiding reference to Israel's tradition of divinely anointed shepherd-kings. In the earlier story, the "baskets" filled with leftovers (6:43) are of a type associated with Jews; here they are just generic baskets. The earlier story has Jesus follow the Jewish custom of reciting a blessing before eating; here he gives thanks, as would have been more common among Gentiles.[29]

The first theme of the story, then, is that Jesus has come to feed Gentiles as well as Jews. The Syrophoenician woman was right. What Jesus has to give is available to all the world's people. In the early church Mark was addressing, the central debate about inclusion and exclusion concerned the relation of Jewish and Gentile Christians. In reading Mark for our time, we have to think about what our central issues about inclusion and exclusion may be, and whether Mark's good news that Jesus reaches out to everyone applies to them as well.

This is also a story about failure to understand, a theme that will become more explicit in the next episode Mark tells. Jesus had shortly before fed a multitude, and here is another multitude, and the disciples ask, "How can one feed these people with bread here in the desert?" Calvin remarks, "The disciples manifest excessive stupidity in not remembering, at least, that earlier proof of the power and grace of Christ, which they might have applied to the case at hand."[30] It apparently does not occur to them to say, "You know, that thing you did to feed a lot of people back on the other side of the Sea of Galilee—could you do it again?" Mark pushes the disciples' failure to understand to comic levels; no chance his audience will miss it. What they fail to understand is above all who Jesus is. If, as we readers learned at the beginning of the Gospel, Jesus really is the Messiah, the Son of God, then they have nothing to worry about—ever. But they have not yet learned that.

29. For most of the above, see Boring, Mark, 220–21; also Theodore W. Jennings, The Insurrection of the Crucified (Chicago: Imprint Books, 2003), 113.
30. Calvin, Harmony of the Evangelists, 2:274.

This feeding points back to the earlier feeding of five thousand, but it also points forward to the Last Supper and the Eucharist. Jesus takes the loaves, blesses them, breaks them, and gives them to his disciples. Mark's original audience would have recognized the pattern of the most central of Christian rituals. Just as Jesus fed both Jews and Gentiles in the lands around Galilee, so he still feeds Christian people. At the beginning of this story, Jesus says he has compassion for these people (the same phrase used in the earlier feeding), for they have been with him "for three days." Here too it is hard to imagine that early Christians could hear "three days" and not think of the time between crucifixion and resurrection. This story, then, reminds us of the Last Supper and the Eucharist, and of Jesus' death and resurrection. The disciples at that time do not understand who he is, but we as later Christians know the story that is coming.

> While they were eating, he took a loaf of bread, and after blessing it he broke it, gave it to them, and said, "Take; this is my body."
>
> —Mark 14:22

# 8:11–21
## *"Do You Not Yet Understand?"*

Jesus now talks first with Pharisees and then with his disciples. The Pharisees come to *argue* with him. They want to *test* him. They have not come to learn or to have an interesting conversation; they are by now, in Mark's story, Jesus' opponents—whether or not this was true of some or all Pharisees historically. They want him to give a sign, and he replies, "No sign will be given to this generation." As a linguistic point, in Mark Jesus does "mighty deeds" or "deeds of power" (*dynameis*) but never "signs" (*sēmeia*). Jesus acts out of compassion, to cure people or feed them, and, undeniably, in so doing, he shows his remarkable powers. But the point is not to offer evidence of his identity; indeed, he keeps telling people not to report what he has done. J. B. Gibson comments, "Mark has Jesus refuse the demand because for Jesus to do otherwise would be nothing less than to advocate, initiate, and engage in triumphalism—a type of activity that, according to Mark, was forbidden to Jesus if he wished to remain faithful to the exigencies of his divine commission."[31] Jesus' call is to be suffering in love, not to triumph in power. Love cannot resist the impulse to do good, but doing good must not become the vehicle for powerful triumph.

Jesus next gets in a boat again, to cross the Sea of Galilee. In both previous crossings there was a storm. This time there is no external storm, but certainly an inner one, his most dramatic confrontation yet with his own disciples. The disciples are apparently complaining that they have only one loaf of bread. One understands Jesus' impatience. Have they not yet realized that a shortage of bread is no problem when he is with them? Indeed, Mark may be identifying the "one loaf with them in the boat" with Jesus himself. We have been hearing about bread constantly for the last several chapters. Now the word suddenly disappears, and Mark does not use it again until 14:22, when Jesus takes bread, blesses and breaks it, and gives it to his disciples, saying, "This is my body." Is it already Jesus' body that is that one loaf with them in the boat?

Jesus warns his disciples against the "yeast" or "leaven" of the Pharisees and of Herod. Yeast is ordinarily a good thing, something added to the dough to make bread rise. At the time of the exodus, however, the Lord instructed the Hebrews to eat only unleavened bread, so that they could be ready to depart Egypt on a moment's notice, without having to wait for bread to rise. The prohibition on leavened bread remains part of the Passover ritual, and Jews search the house just before Passover, to make sure they have cleaned out every bit of yeast. As a game, some even gets hidden for children to find, like Christian children hunting for Easter eggs. Thus yeast becomes, in connection with Passover (remember when Jesus will die!) an impurity that needs to be cleaned out. Paul picks up the image:

> Do you not know that a little yeast leavens the whole batch of dough? Clean out the old yeast so that you may be a new batch,

31. J. B. Gibson, "Jesus' Refusal to Produce a 'Sign,'" *Journal for the Study of the New Testament* 38 (1990): 55.

Parables shake you up

70 "you have built a lovely home!
    But you are right above an earthquake fault"
    ( Crossman )

71 Election ? ?

76 - 9 Parables    79 Rowan W. Tokens

05 - 110 Jesus feeds a gentile +
    then feeds 4,000 of them !

as you really are unleavened. For our paschal lamb, Christ, has been sacrificed. Therefore, let us celebrate the festival, not with the old yeast, the yeast of malice and evil, but with the unleavened bread of sincerity and truth. (1 Cor. 5:6–8)

"Watch out," Jesus warns his disciples, "beware of the yeast of the Pharisees and the yeast of Herod."

So what is the "yeast" of the Pharisees and of Herod? We know (3:6) that the Pharisees and the followers of Herod are conspiring to destroy Jesus. Herod is (under Rome's ultimate authority) the secular ruler of Galilee; the Pharisees are probably the most respected religious leaders. The Pharisees have just asked Jesus for a sign. Jesus has refused to give a sign, it seems reasonable to infer, because that would lead to triumphalism, to basing his authority on power. So their yeast somehow represents the power of this world, and it works to destroy Jesus.

But the disciples do not understand. Jesus can enable the blind to see and the deaf to hear, but he cannot bring understanding to his own disciples. "Understanding," here, incidentally, means something more like accepting something or getting hold of it than our more intellectualistic sense of the word.

## 8:22–26

### *Healing a Blind Man*

When they have come to Bethsaida, "people brought a blind man to him and begged him to touch him." Jesus cannot ignore the begging of the needy, but, as we might expect from the previous dialogue, he is more concerned than ever that his curative powers remain relatively secret. For the first time in a healing he takes the extra precaution of leading the man out of the village before he does anything, and at the end he tells him not even to go back to the village.

Uniquely, Jesus cures this man in two stages. After he has put saliva on his eyes, the man can see things but apparently in a fuzzy or incoherent way: "I can see people, but they look like trees, walking." Then Jesus lays his hands on the man's eyes again, and his sight is fully restored. Calvin says Jesus cured this man gradually instead of all at once just to show that he was not limited to one way of curing.[32] I have wondered if there might be some recollection of a historical reality behind this story. People who regain or gain sight often take some time to sort out and understand the realities they are seeing. The contemporary scholar Ira Driggers suggests that Mark is anticipating his own theme: the healing of the blind man requires two stages just as, we shortly learn, the disciples need first to realize that Jesus is the Messiah and then understand that he must suffer.[33] Certainly Driggers's interpretation best focuses on this passage's place in the text as a whole, for Mark is leading his readers to the first human confession of Jesus' identity.

32. Calvin, *Harmony of the Evangelists*, 2:285.
33. Ira Brent Driggers, *Following God through Mark: Theological Tension in the Second Gospel* (Louisville: Westminster John Knox, 2007), 63.

# 8:27–10:52

# On the Way to Jerusalem

## 8:27–9:1

### A Suffering Messiah

Mark's Gospel comes to a turning point. Peter confesses that Jesus is the Messiah. Jesus begins to teach that he must suffer and die. He and his disciples have been traveling around Galilee and surrounding territories, sometimes by boat back and forth across the Sea of Galilee. Now, in the first verse of this passage, Mark describes them as "on the way." "The way" is, from here on, the road one takes to follow Jesus. It has a direction: it leads to Jerusalem and the cross.

First, though, they go to Caesarea Philippi, a thoroughly Hellenistic city newly named after the Roman emperor and Herod Antipas's brother (and Herodias's first husband) Philip. It had long been a center of the worship of various pagan gods, and was now a prominent site for emperor worship. Jesus and his disciples are, in short, headed straight to a city that stands for political rulers and the worship of deities other than the God of Israel. The very geography signals he is preparing to make a challenge.

Jesus asks his disciples about what has increasingly become the central question of Mark's story: who he is. Some, they report, say he is John the Baptist (as we have already heard Herod Antipas fears), others that he is Elijah or another of the prophets. To the more direct question, "But who do *you* say that I am?" Peter replies, "You are the Christ." (Whereas *christos* is normally translated as "Christ," here the NRSV oddly switches to a translation to Hebrew, "Messiah" or *mashiach*. Mark knows how to switch to Hebrew or Aramaic, nevertheless, here he uses *christos*.) The word has not appeared in Mark since the very first verse. It has never been part of Jesus' teaching. Mark does not make explicit what Matthew says—"Flesh and

115

blood has not revealed this to you, but my Father in heaven" (Matt. 16:17)—but the implication is there. Peter's confession comes out of the blue, not directly prepared for by Jesus' previous teaching. As always in Mark, faith is a gift from God.

Jesus tells the disciples not to tell anyone about what Peter has said. "Then he began to teach them that the Son of Man must undergo great suffering, and be rejected by the elders, the chief priests, and the scribes, and be killed, and after three days rise again. He said all this quite openly." This is the first of three predictions Jesus makes concerning his fate (8:31; 9:31; 10:33–34). Notice the contrast between the secrecy about being the Messiah and the quite open teaching about suffering and death. Jesus could not allow himself to be proclaimed Messiah, Wolfhart Pannenberg explains, until the term had been redefined: "The meaning of the title first had to be revised by linking it to the Crucified, so that instead of a political liberator, a messianic king, there would be seen a suffering Messiah."[1]

Peter begins to "rebuke" (*epitimaō*) him. The verb is a strong one, the same word Jesus uses against the demons in his exorcisms, as if Peter thought Jesus was possessed. Hence perhaps Jesus' almost violent answer: "Get behind me, Satan!" Peter jumps in four verses from proclaiming that Jesus is the Messiah to forcefully correcting him. This first tells us something about impatient, volatile, rocky-soil Peter. It also indicates the extent of the paradigm shift Jesus is demanding. For all the differences in the pictures of the Messiah anticipated by various first-century Jews, they shared a hope of triumph. Somehow the Messiah would win victories, defeat Israel's enemies, restore Israel's greatness. The idea of a *suffering* Messiah was radically new. Thus as soon as one of his disciples recognizes him as Messiah, Jesus has to begin a second stage in his teaching: "but not at all the kind of Messiah you expect." ("Son of Man" just here seems to mean no more than "I.") He *must* undergo suffering and rejection, death and resurrection; this is not a good guess about what will happen or an indication simply of the path Jesus is choosing, but the affirmation that this way of suffering is God's plan for him.

1. Wolfhart Pannenberg, *Systematic Theology*, trans. Geoffrey W. Bromiley, 3 vols. (Grand Rapids: Eerdmans, 1991–1998), 2:312.

He calls the crowd to follow him in taking up their cross. Is the calling of the crowd at just this point one more indication that the disciples themselves do not seem the most promising raw material? What follows are tough words: take up your cross, lose your life. We react against them in part simply because we would rather be comfortable, rather be safe. But these words also inspire legitimate concerns. Women particularly, and other groups that have suffered oppression, have too often had these words used to keep them suffering. Does your husband mistreat you? Does your father sexually abuse you? Does your slaveowner beat you? Put up with it! Jesus wants you to take up your cross and lose your life for his sake. As Joanne Carlson Brown and Rebecca Parker have written,

> If the best person who ever lived gave his life for others, then, to be of value we should likewise sacrifice ourselves. Any sense that we have to care for our own needs is in conflict with being a faithful follower of Jesus.... The message is complicated further by the theology that says Christ suffered in obedience to the Father's will. Divine child abuse is paraded as salvific and the child who suffers "without even raising his voice" is lauded as the hope of the world.[2]

Too often, Christian calls for those who are suffering to suffer some more indeed merit this critique.

But Jesus calls those who would follow him to pick up their *cross*. A cross was not a random form of suffering; it was the punishment those in power in his time imposed on rebels and troublemakers who challenged things as they were. As John Howard Yoder wrote, "The cross of Calvary was not a difficult family situation, not a frustration of visions of personal fulfillment, a crushing debt, or a nagging in-law; it was the political logically-to-be-expected result of a moral clash with the powers ruling his society."[3] Risking that particular kind of suffering is not a form of accepting an oppressive order, but a way of challenging it.

2. Joanne Carlson Brown and Rebecca Parker, "For God So Loved the World," in *Christianity, Patriarchy, and Abuse: A Feminist Critique*, ed. Joanne Carlson Brown and Carole R. Bohn (New York: Pilgrim Press, 1989), 2.
3. John Howard Yoder, *The Politics of Jesus* (Grand Rapids: Eerdmans, 1972), 129.

"One cannot try to be a martyr," Karl Barth remarked. "One can only be ready to be made a martyr."[4] Seeking to be persecuted is a form of pathology, not a way of following Jesus. One simply does what is right, helps those who need help, stands up for the truth even when it is unpopular. Occasionally such witness simply succeeds. Sometimes success comes only after a rock through a window, an arrest, or a cross burned on the lawn. Quite ordinary American pastors and laypeople have experienced such things in uncounted numbers over the years, in conflicts over civil rights, immigrants, or a host of other issues. One might lose a job. One might get killed. It is not possible to know in advance where standing up for the right will lead.

Such uncertainty about the end of the path makes taking even a modest first step frightening. But much in the Christian tradition assures us that we should not worry quite so much. Listen, for instance, to Augustine:

> What the Lord enjoins does seem hard and grievous: that "whosoever will come after him must deny himself." But what he enjoins is not hard or grievous, since he aids us so that what he enjoins may be done. . . . For whatsoever is hard in what is enjoined us, charity makes easy. . . . Consider what labor all lovers undergo, and are not conscious of their labors; such people most feel labor when they are hindered from labor.[5]

We do all sorts of difficult things when we are in love, and we count them as joy. Indeed, as Augustine says, we are frustrated only when we are prevented from acting out of our love. Similarly, those who have given themselves to following Jesus—think of St. Francis, think of Dorothy Day—manifest joy in the midst of what looks to the outsider like suffering. Those who lose their lives for his sake and for the sake of the gospel, Jesus says, will save their lives. "Save" (*sōzein*), like *shalom* in Hebrew, means to have wholeness, health, integrity. It is not an external reward, whether present or future, but the good life one experiences in the very following of Jesus, like the joy of being in love.

4. Barth, *CD* III/4:79.
5. Augustine, *Sermons on New Testament Texts* 46.1 (*NPNF*, 1st ser., 6:408, translation revised).

Yet so often we are willing to turn aside from the path that follows Jesus for such trivial things. In Robert Bolt's play about Thomas More, *A Man for All Seasons*, young Richard Rich has betrayed More and given the dishonest evidence that makes it possible to execute him. Rich enters More's prison cell wearing the chain of office of the attorney general for Wales, and More says, with sad irony, "Why, Richard, it profits a man nothing to give his soul for the whole world . . . but for Wales!"[6] (Apologies to all proud Welsh! Older translations translated *psychē* here as "soul," but the NRSV, seeking to capture its meaning of something like "whole self," without any intent of distinguishing soul from body, translates it as "life.") We are called to be faithful and assured, in words Tertullian wrote amid persecutions in the late second century, "I am safe, if I am not ashamed of my Lord."[7] A generation later, Cyprian, himself eventually a martyr, wondered at the cowardice of Christians who had sacrificed to the emperor to avoid persecution: "And does he think that he is a Christian, who is either ashamed or afraid to be a Christian? How can he be one with Christ, who either blushes or fears to belong to Christ?"[8]

> God is "the source of our life and our strength; from him we gain vitality."
> —Tertullian
>
> *Ad Donatum*, 4 in *The Early Christian Fathers*, ed. and trans. Henry Bettenson (New York: Oxford, 1969), 273.

In an earlier section ("Further Reflections: Reign of God," on pp. 31–35) I discussed the possible meanings of the verse with which this section ends. Some standing there "will not taste death until they see that the reign of God has come with power" (my trans.). Perhaps Mark, or Jesus, thought that the present age of the world was about to come to a banging end, and he was wrong. Perhaps the meaning is that the reign of God is already coming in Jesus' ministry (but "with power"?). Perhaps the emphasis should be on "they see"—the reign is already here, and what will happen before some people die is that they will recognize the fact; as Barth puts it, "This

6. Robert Bolt, *A Man for All Seasons* (New York: Random House, 1962), 158.
7. Tertullian, *On the Flesh of Christ* 5 (*ANF* 3:525).
8. Cyprian, *On the Lapsed* 28 (*ANF* 5:445).

passage assumes that the kingdom of God has already come. What has still to happen is that it should be seen."[9] Calvin concludes that, by "coming of the kingdom," Jesus here means "the manifestation of heavenly glory" that begins in Jesus' resurrection and continues in the coming of the Holy Spirit.[10] As Mark has placed the verse, it seems natural to take one step further back than Calvin's interpretation and interpret this anticipation of Jesus' heavenly glory as an introduction to the transfiguration story, which follows. So far in Mark's story, no one has seen Jesus in his divinity; even walking on the water he could be mistaken for a ghost, and the vision at his baptism, in this Gospel, comes only to Jesus himself. Six days later, everything would be different.

# FURTHER REFLECTIONS
## Messiah

As already noted, "anointed one" (Hebrew *mashiach*, Greek *christos*) could mean many different things to first-century Jews. The discovery of the Dead Sea Scrolls has complicated an already complex picture. Some Jews did not think very much about a messiah at all. Some hoped for a military leader who would drive out the Romans, some for a new high priest who would restore the Law. Some expected an ordinary human being accomplishing things in an ordinary human way; others imagined that the messiah would have all sorts of God-given powers. Some thought there would be more than one messiah.

When Mark has Peter say to Jesus, "You are the Christ," therefore, we cannot give any simple answer as to what that meant. At least it meant this: "You are God's anointed, who will somehow make things better than they are now, better than they have been for a long time." In ancient Israel, kings, priests, and prophets were all anointed—they had oil poured on them as a symbol that they were

---

9. Barth, *CD* III/2:499; see also C. H. Dodd, *Parables of the Kingdom* (New York: Charles Scribner's Sons, 1961), 53.
10. Calvin, *Harmony of the Evangelists*, 2:307.

ordained by God for some special service for the people of Israel. So Samuel says to Saul, "The Lord sent me to anoint you king over his people Israel" (1 Sam. 15:1). So the Lord tells Moses to take the special priestly tunics and sashes and headdresses and "put them on your brother Aaron, and on his sons with him, and . . . anoint them and ordain them and consecrate them, so that they may serve me as priests" (Exod. 28:41). So that anonymous prophet Second Isaiah declares, "The spirit of the Lord God is upon me, because the Lord has anointed me" (Isa. 61:1).

As early as the fourth century, the church historian Eusebius saw Christ, *the* anointed one, as the fulfillment of all three of these earlier offices: "No one of those symbolically anointed of old, either of priests or of kings or indeed of Prophets, possessed so great a power of divine virtue as was displayed by our Savior and Lord Jesus, the only true Christ."[11] John Chrysostom spoke of Christ's "threefold dignity" as king, prophet, and priest.[12] But it was in Protestant theology, first in Andreas Osiander and Martin Bucer but especially in John Calvin, that the "threefold office" became a key way of explaining Christ's person and work. As prophet, Calvin explains, Christ provides the perfect teaching on what we should believe and how we should live: "He was anointed by the Spirit to be the herald and witness of the Father's grace."[13] He is a spiritual king, not a temporal one. Hence those who follow him "must fight throughout life under the cross, our condition is harsh and wretched." Yet, "we may patiently pass through this life with its misery, hunger, cold, contempt, reproaches, and other troubles—content with this one thing: that our King will never leave us destitute, but will provide for our needs until, our warfare ended, we are called to triumph."[14] Finally, "The priestly office belongs to Christ alone because by the sacrifice of his death he blotted out our own guilt and made satisfaction for our sins."[15]

11. Eusebius, *Ecclesiastical History* 1.3, trans. Roy J. Deferrari, FC 19 (Washington, DC: Catholic University Press of America, 1953), 48.
12. Chrysostom quoted in Thomas Aquinas, *Catena Aurea: St. Matthew*, trans. J. H. Parker (Oxford: J. G. F. and J. Rivington, 1842), 11.
13. Calvin, *Institutes* 2.15.2.
14. Ibid., 2.15.4.
15. Ibid., 2.15.6.

As a prophet, Christ is a teacher who shows us what to believe and how to live in what he says and does. His kingship is more paradoxical, for the one who can calm the winds and walk on the sea, who has power beyond the imaginings of even the most powerful of Roman emperors, is also the one who travels around Galilee among ordinary folk and will in the end be tortured and crucified. His reign has begun, but it remains hidden in this world. I will need to return to the theme of his priesthood when Mark's story comes to the cross; for now, the obvious point is that he is both priest and sacrifice. The greatest of Reformed hymn writers, Isaac Watts, ties Christ's three offices together:

> We bless the prophet of the Lord,
> That comes with truth and grace;
> Jesus, thy Spirit and thy word
> Shall lead us in thy ways.
> We reverence our High-Priest above,
> Who offered up his blood;
> And lives to carry on his love,
> By pleading with our God.
> We honour our exalted King;
> How sweet are his commands!
> He guards our souls from hell and sin
> By his almighty hands.
> Hosanna to his glorious name,
> Who saves by different ways;
> His mercies lay a sovereign claim
> To our immortal praise.[16]

---

16. Isaac Watts, "Hymn 132," *The Psalms, Hymns, and Spiritual Songs of the Rev. Isaac Watts*, ed. Samuel Worcester (Boston: Crocker & Brewster, 1855), 452.

# 9:2–8

## *The Transfiguration*

At the beginning of the first half of Mark's Gospel, the heavens were ripped apart and a voice declared (in this Gospel only to Jesus himself) that Jesus was his Son, the Beloved. Now the second half of the Gospel begins. Trips around Galilee and across its sea have ended; Jesus is about to begin on the way to Jerusalem. Again a voice from the heavens declares, "This is my Son, the Beloved," this time to the three most privileged disciples. No ripping of the heavens on this occasion. Is it because God is already loose in the world? Or is it that Jesus, Peter, James, and John climb into what is already a heavenly realm?

Mountains are of course symbolic, holy places, away from the ordinary and closer to heaven. The Venerable Bede writes, "When he was about to show his glory to the disciples, he led them up a lofty mountain in order to teach everyone desiring to see this [glory] not to rest in base pleasures, not to serve fleshly allurements, not to become attached to earthly avarice, but to be always raised by the love of what is eternal toward the things of heaven."[17] In the midst of our hectic lives, people today are looking more than ever for such mountains, places where we can escape life's daily busyness and perhaps catch a glimpse of something more profound. This mountain also evokes that other mountain where Moses received the law, where Moses took three followers (Aaron, Nadab, and Abihu) and seventy of the elders, "and they saw the God of Israel. Under his feet there was something like a pavement of sapphire stone, like the very heaven for clearness" (Exod. 24:9–10). There a cloud descended on the mountain, and Moses waited six days to ascend. Here there is likewise a cloud, and Mark notes (such time indications are unusual in this Gospel) that they climb the mountain six days after the earlier conversation.

Jesus was "transfigured" before them—the word denotes a change of appearance or form. Writing to the Philippians, Paul declares that Christ Jesus

---

17. Bede, the Venerable, *Homilies on the Gospels* 1.24, trans. Lawrence T. Martin and David Hurst (Kalamazoo, MI: Cistercian Publishing, 1991), 236.

> though he was in the form of God,
>      did not regard equality with God
>      as something to be exploited,
> but emptied himself,
>      taking the form of a slave,
>      being born in human likeness.
>                              (Phil. 2:6–7)

Now, these three disciples see something of the form of God of which Jesus has emptied himself. As Chrysostom puts it, "What does 'transfigured' mean? It means that he opened out a little of the godhead and showed them the indwelling deity."[18] Such a claim is full of paradox. The Hebrew Scriptures regularly insist that God cannot be seen, that any approach to seeing God would result in death, so overwhelming would it be.

Leo the Great avoided the issue by claiming that what the disciples see is the "royal splendor, which, in a special manner pertaining to the nature of the manhood he had taken up, he wished to be visible to these three men. For, encompassed up to now in mortal flesh, in no way were they able to look at and see that ineffable and inaccessible vision of divinity itself."[19] Who can penetrate these mysteries with confidence? Still, it seems to me that Christ's humanity has the form of a servant; it is not overwhelmingly radiant. Just as Moses and his companions in Exodus 24, the passage from Hebrew Scripture this story most evokes, see the God of Israel, so here the three disciples somehow see something of Christ's divinity. In Exodus 33, the Lord puts Moses in a cleft of a rock and covers him until God has passed by. When Moses' eyes are uncovered, Moses sees God's back but not God's face. The flesh of Christ, Irenaeus says, is that cleft in the rock where Moses stood while he saw God.[20]

Such issues became important in the eighth and ninth centuries, when several Byzantine emperors, convinced that Scripture forbids

18. John Chrysostom, Homily 21, cited in John Anthony McGuckin, *The Transfiguration of Christ in Scripture and Tradition* (Lewiston, NY: Edwin Mellen, 1986), 112.
19. Leo the Great, Sermon 51.2, *Sermons*, trans. Jane Patricia Freeland and Agnes Josephine Conway, FC 93 (Washington, DC: Catholic University of America Press, 1995), 220.
20. Irenaeus, *Against Heresies* 4.20.9 (*ANF* 1:490).

any images of God, imposed iconoclasm (image breaking) on their empire. In 2001 the Taliban rulers of Afghanistan destroyed two huge ancient Buddhist images in their territory on the same principles. Among Christians the iconoclasts did not finally carry the day, and the key argument against them was that Jesus was fully God and that Jesus, as also fully human, most definitely had an appearance that could be represented. John of Damascus wrote in the early eighth century, "In former times, God, who is without form or body, could never be depicted. But now, when God is seen in the flesh conversing with men, I make an image after the God I see."[21] Without that conclusion, the role of icons in Orthodox faith and the whole history of European art would have been different.

As Irenaeus said, Jesus was thus "revealing God indeed to men . . . and preserving at the same time the invisibility of the Father."[22] Jesus is God's self-revelation; seeing him, we see God. What about those "appearances of God" in ancient Israel, then? Reflecting on the matter, John Calvin concluded that "the God who of old appeared to the patriarchs was no other than Christ."[23] If Christ is God's self-revelation, then, whenever people encounter God, they must be, knowingly or unknowingly, encountering God in Christ. Gregory Palamas, the great Byzantine theologian, took things one step further. What happened on that mountain, he said, was not that Jesus was transformed into something he ordinarily was not: "Christ was transfigured not by receiving something he did not have before, nor by being changed into something he previously was not, but as manifesting to his disciples what he really was, opening their eyes and from blind men making them see again."[24] Christ never stopped being fully God. At the transfiguration, the three disciples finally caught a glimpse of it.

Mark's account is full of symbolism and references to various parts of the Hebrew Scriptures. As Hans Urs von Balthasar remarks, "The attempt to disentangle from this husk the event that has been

---

21. John of Damascus, *On the Divine Images* 1.16, trans. David Anderson (Crestwood, NY: St. Vladimir's Seminary Press, 1980), 23.
22. Irenaeus, *Against Heresies*, 4.20.7 (ANF 1:489).
23. Calvin, *Institutes* 1.13.27.
24. Gregory Palamas, "Homily 34," cited in McGuckin, *Transfiguration*, 113.

formulated in this way, with reference to the whole of the Bible, and to explain it on its own—as an historical psychological experience of Jesus, or as a visionary experience of the disciples—leads nowhere."[25] This is one of the places where, preeminently, we need to read Mark's story as it is and see what it tells us, not try to penetrate to some historical kernel behind the textual husk. The poet Edwin Muir imagines the disciples asking unanswerable questions:

> Was it a vision?
> Or did we see that day the unseeable?
> ....................................
> Was the change in us alone
> And the enormous earth still left forlorn,
> An exile or a prisoner?[26]

The story tells us that Jesus' clothes became dazzling white. Such whiteness is like the radiance of Moses' face when he had been talking with God, so bright that he had to cover it with a veil when he spoke to the Israelites (Exod. 34:29–35). It is like the color of the Ancient One Daniel sees on a throne: "his clothing was white as snow, and the hair of his head like pure wool" (Dan. 7:9), or like the one like the Son of Man in John's vision in Revelation: "His head and his hair were white as white wool, white as snow; his eyes were like a flame of fire" (Rev. 1:14). It is the color of purity and of light without darkness. Mys-

> Jesus recognizes as disciples those who have the courage to march open eyed into the terra incognita of Jesus' glory, to get sucked into the vortex of really Real Kingdom coming, so as never to come out on the other side.
> —Marilyn McCord Adams

"Mark 9:2–9," in David L. Bartlett and Barbara Brown Taylor, eds., *Feasting on the Word: Preaching the Revised Common Lectionary*, Year B, Volume 1 (Louisville, KY: Westminster John Knox Press, 2008), 456.

25. Hans Urs von Balthasar, *The Glory of the Lord: A Theological Aesthetics*, vol. 7, *Theology: The New Covenant*, trans. Brian McNeil (San Francisco: Ignatius Press, 1989), 342.
26. Edwin Muir, "The Transfiguration," in *Collected Poems, 1921–1958* (London: Faber and Faber, 1960), 173–75.

tics down the centuries describe their experience of such light, and the Hesychast mystics of the Orthodox tradition particularly claim the experience of the Uncreated Light that the disciples saw on the Mountain of the Transfiguration. Simeon the New Theologian, writing a bit after 1000, insists, "Those who have not seen this light, have not seen God: for God is Light."[27]

Elijah and Moses appear, talking with Jesus. Both were associated with mountains—on a mountain, Moses receives the Law; and, in a time of despair, Elijah goes back to that mountain and, after wind, earthquake, and fire, encounters God in "a sound of sheer silence" (1 Kgs. 19:12). Both Moses and Elijah turned away from the luxury of a royal court to take the role of outsiders standing up against tyrants. Of Moses uniquely it is written that "the LORD used to speak to Moses face to face, as one speaks to a friend" (Exod. 33:11). Elijah uniquely (except possibly for the odd case of Enoch) did not die but "ascended in a whirlwind into heaven" (2 Kgs. 2:11).

When the disciples climbed the mountain of the transfiguration, they caught a glimpse of a different realm. Scholars continue to debate, to put it crudely, where they went. Kathryn Tanner, developing ideas in Aquinas, believes they went into eternity. She accepts the scientific conclusion that some day the world will blow up, burn out, or otherwise be destroyed. Therefore, she seeks to understand "what a Christian eschatology would be like if scientists are right that the world does not have a future."[28] She concludes, "Such an eschatology would not center on the world of the future but on the world as a whole and on an ongoing redemptive (rather than simply creative) relation to God that holds for the world of the past, present and future."[29] At every moment we are in relation with a God who is not in time, at least time as we know it, so that, even when our time comes to an end, we are still in that relation: "There is a life in the triune God that we possess now and after death, in Christ through the power of the Holy Spirit. Ante and post mortem do not mark any

27. Simeon the New Theologian, Homily 79.2, cited in Vladimir Lossky, *The Mystical Theology of the Eastern Church* (London: J. Clarke, 1957), 218.
28. Kathryn Tanner, *Jesus, Humanity and the Trinity: A Brief Systematic Theology* (Minneapolis: Fortress, 2001), 100.
29. Ibid., 102.

crucial difference with respect to it."[30] It is that life that Peter, James, and John presumably become aware of on the mountain.

Jürgen Moltmann, in contrast, thinks the disciples saw into the eschatological future. He would think Tanner's view too based on a Greek metaphysics of eternity and not enough on biblical eschatology, in which, as Moltmann puts it, God's "eternity is not timeless simultaneity; it is the power of his future over every historical time."[31] For Moltmann, the biblical hope is for a radical future transformation of the world, and any appearance of God is a glimpse of that future. In the transfiguration story, one might take Moses, giver of God's eternal law, as a symbol of Tanner's view, and Elijah, forerunner of the Messiah who is to come, as representative of Moltmann's. The problem with Moltmann's view is how, in a world where science teaches us that our planet circles a minor star on the edge of one of many galaxies, to make anything like the eschatological vision of the New Testament seem plausible. Tanner creates a theology that fits better with science, but is it really faithful to the views of the New Testament?

In his more recent work, Wolfhart Pannenberg has been struggling toward a compromise. He would agree with Tanner that we need to focus on eternity: "The future of consummation is the entry of eternity into time."[32] Yet, following some ideas in Karl Barth's later theology, he thinks we cannot treat eternity as simply the opposite of time. Eternity is not the central point of the circle, to which every point on the circumference is equally related. Rather, eternity has its own kind of duration, so that creatures in their temporality can participate in God's eternity. Something like that is presumably what Mark wants to convey in his account of the transfiguration.

Peter proposes to Jesus that they "make three tents [or dwellings], one for you, one for Moses, and one for Elijah." All interpreters seem to agree that this was the wrong thing to do, since the next sentence states that Peter did not know what to say. Exactly why it is wrong is

---

30. Ibid., 108.
31. Jürgen Moltmann, *The Coming of God: Christian Eschatology*, trans. Margaret Kohl (Minneapolis: Fortress, 1996), 24.
32. Pannenberg, *Systematic Theology*, 3:603.

less clear. Origen proposed that Peter, who had already heard Jesus' warning of the suffering to come, is trying to preserve the glory of this "mountaintop experience" and forestall the return to the plain and the journey to Jerusalem that will follow.[33] Others argue that the problem is that Peter wants to build *three* dwellings or tents, thereby treating Jesus as the equal of Moses and Elijah. He is persuaded that Jesus is the equal of the other two but does not yet fully grasp how superior to them he is. The voice from heaven does not say, "These are my beloved sons." As Augustine notes, "*This is my beloved Son*; this was to make sure they didn't compare Moses and Elijah with him, and suppose that the Lord was to be taken just as one of the prophets."[34] As Bede says, Peter was right to say, "It is good that we are here," however, "for in reality the sole good of a human being is to enter into the joy of his Lord and to attend upon him by contemplating him forever."[35] At the end of the story, Moses and Elijah have disappeared, and only Jesus remains. At Jesus' baptism, "Son" might still have meant a human chosen one, a messianic king, but this radiant figure, greater than Moses or Elijah, is something far more than that—truly divine. As Rudolf Bultmann wrote, the title "Son of God," "which originally denoted the messianic king, now takes on a new meaning which was self-evident to Gentile hearers. Now it comes to mean the *divinity of Christ, his divine nature*, by virtue of which he is differentiated from the human sphere; it makes the claim that Christ is of divine origin and is filled with divine 'power.'"[36]

Before the voice speaks, a cloud overshadows the mountain. Those of us who live in well-watered lands often forget that, in semi-desert territory, clouds are symbols of life and hope. One good rain can make the difference between a good year and near starvation. So God is the one "who rides upon the clouds" (Ps. 68:4), and at crucial moments (Exod. 40:34–38; 1 Kgs. 8:10–11) it is the descent of a cloud that affirms God's presence. Out of the cloud a voice speaks,

---

33. See H. A. Kelly, "The Devil in the Desert," *CBQ* 26 (1964): 217.
34. Augustine, "Sermon 79A," *The Works of St. Augustine: A Translation for the 21st Century*, part 3, vol. 3: *Sermons*, trans. Edmund Hill, ed. John E. Rotelle (Brooklyn: New City Press, 1991), 348.
35. Bede, the Venerable, *Homilies on the Gospels* 1.24 (240).
36. Rudolf Bultmann, *Theology of the New Testament*, trans. Kendrick Grobel, 2 vols. in 1 (repr. Waco, TX: Baylor University Press, 2007), 128–29.

reaffirming the baptismal declaration, "This is my Son, the Beloved," but now adding, "Listen to him." It is the kind of paradox characteristic of Mark that the voice does not say, "Listen to me," or "Look at him," transformed as Jesus is in radiance, but rather, "Listen to him," though at the moment Jesus does not speak. Talk of a beloved son on a mountain evokes the story of Abraham's near sacrifice of Isaac (Gen. 22), and Jesus' previous warnings of the fate that awaits him indicate that this divine Father is indeed willing to sacrifice his Son.

The first military use of a nuclear weapon, the atomic bomb the United States dropped on Hiroshima, hit its target on the Feast of the Transfiguration, August 6, 1945. At the first testing of the bomb, J. Robert Oppenheimer, seeing the explosion, quoted the moment in the Bhagavad Gita where the god Krishna reveals himself to Arjuna in his full, terrible glory: "I am become Death, destroyer of worlds." Oppenheimer saw in the explosion a kind of transfiguration of scientific expertise into horror and death, just as the disciples saw the transfiguration of a human teacher into the radiance of divine glory. Humankind may still face a choice between those two transfigurations.

## 9:9–13

### A Question about Elijah

Moses and Elijah disappear, the radiance fades, and "they saw no one with them any more, but only Jesus." As they come down the mountain, the disciples are thoroughly confused. Jesus tells them not to speak of what they have seen "until after the Son of Man had risen from the dead," but they do not understand "what this rising from the dead could mean." Yet Mark wants us to think of something as remaining in their memories. In the dark times of the fifth century, as the Roman Empire was collapsing, Pope Leo the Great wrote, "The Transfiguration chiefly occurred for this end that the scandal of the cross should be taken away from the hearts of the disciples, and so that, since they had been given the revelation of his secret majesty, the abasement of the Passion might not confound their faith."[37] In terms of Mark's view of the disciples, that hope may be too optimistic, but still they have caught a glimpse of something beyond all present suffering, something to sustain them in the days ahead.

They now accept what Peter confessed, that Jesus is the Messiah. They do not speak of it directly, but raise the question of whether Elijah was not supposed to return before the Messiah comes. Jesus replies that Elijah has already come—presumably in the person of John the Baptizer. No more preliminaries are needed.

# 9:14–27
## *Healing a Boy with a Spirit*

Another healing story, a rather long one, is distinguished by clinical details about the disease and a particularly famous statement about faith. Jesus, Peter, James, and John return to the rest of the disciples and see a whole crowd gathered. The crowd is "overcome with awe"—does something of the radiance of the transfiguration remain? Among them is a man with a sick son, whom the disciples have been unable to help. The father gives an account of all his son's symptoms, and on that basis Calvin reasonably assumed that the boy must have had epilepsy, though he added that Satan must have "availed himself of this for aggravating the disease."[38] Jesus asks questions about the course of the disease, the sorts of questions a doctor might ask, but Mark tells how the spirit within the boy convulses him when it sees Jesus and how Jesus cures the boy by commanding the spirit to come out. It is a story that poses for modern readers in a particularly vivid way the question of whether Jesus is working cures in battles with demons or by the psychological force of a charismatic personality.

Mark clearly assumes, as most of his contemporaries would have, that evil spirits are at work in such cases. Yet Calvin was surely right to read the story and conclude that the boy was an epileptic. It is fair

---

37. Leo the Great, Homily 51.3, cited in McGuckin, *Transfiguration*, 116.
38. Calvin, *Harmony of the Evangelists*, 2:322.

to say that we still do not know nearly enough about how psychological forces can cure physical illnesses. My own former doctor used to
look firmly at patients with warts and tell them that removing one
wart would make all the others go away. There is no known medical
reason why this should be so, but it nearly always worked. Warts can
also be cured by hypnosis. I think a modern reader can meet a story
like this one halfway: we can admit that there are many things we do
not know about how cures work, and the story itself simply tells us
what Jesus did and what resulted, without making any claims about
the mechanism through which his action succeeded.

The father has the best line in the story. When he urges Jesus to
work a cure, "if you are able," Jesus quotes impatiently back at him
and insists, "If you are able!—All things can be done for the one who
believes." The father cries out, "I believe; help my unbelief." Calvin
rightly says, "These two statements may appear to contradict each
other, but there is none of us that does not experience both of them
in himself."[39] Faith is not the same as certainty, the twentieth-century
theologian Paul Tillich kept insisting. I *trust* in the object of my faith
with passion and commitment, but, "If doubt appears, it should not
be considered as the negation of faith, but as an element which was
always and will always be present in the act of faith."[40] Take even my
faith in a friend. I loan him the money to get him through some hard
times. I really do trust him. Yet I recognize that someone who has
gotten into financial trouble could get into deeper financial trouble.
I have to take a risk; my faith needs courage.

Søren Kierkegaard's name is often associated with the idea of a
"leap of faith," a phrase taken somewhat out of context. Notice that
in this story, the father does not say, "I believe, I have doubts, but
I am going to try all the harder to believe." "Help my unbelief" is
not an announcement of what he is going to do; it is a prayer. We
cannot find our way to hope just by leaping; we need to be carried.
Luther writes of this father, "Giving up all other hope, despairing of
himself, he comes to hope exclusively in the grace of God and clings

39. Ibid., 325.
40. Paul Tillich, *Dynamics of Faith* (New York: Harper & Row, 1957), 25.

to it without ceasing."[41] Not our own strength, but only God's grace, like the wings of an eagle, sustains our leaps of faith. And God grants us such grace. In our story Jesus does not say to the father, "Well, you'll have to try harder." The father having begged for faith, Jesus simply cures his son. In Augustine's words, "He did not find fault with him on the ground of his want of belief, but really encouraged him to a yet stronger faith."[42] So we take our fragile, half-broken faith to God, and in God's grace it suffices.

> Not by might, nor by power, but by my spirit, says the LORD of hosts.
>
> —Zechariah 4:6

# 9:28–32
## *Failures of the Disciples*

The unnamed father gets it, and throws himself on Jesus' mercy. The disciples still fail to understand. They had not been able to cure the boy, and, when they ask why, Jesus explains, "This kind can come out only through prayer." But the story includes no account that Jesus prayed. Others need to pray, need to throw themselves on God's mercy in difficult situations, but Jesus *is* God. His cures generally come *from* him, not *through* him.

The father of the sick boy gets it and throws himself on Jesus' mercy, but the disciples still do not understand. A second time Jesus foretells his death and resurrection, "But they did not understand what he was saying and were afraid to ask him." In contrast to the courage of faith, we see the cowardice of people who are lost. Mark says that Jesus will be "handed over," "delivered up," or "betrayed" (*paradidōmi*) into human hands. Mark uses this verb once of John the Baptizer (1:14), now three times of Jesus (9:31; 10:33; 14:41), as well as three times of Christians who will suffer persecution (13:9–13). It always appears in the passive voice, so that its subject

41. Martin Luther, "The Sacrament of Penance," trans. E. Theodore Bachmann, *Word and Sacrament I*, LW 35 (Philadelphia: Muhlenberg, 1960), 19.
42. Augustine, *Harmony of the Gospels* 2.28.66 (*NPNF*, 1st ser., 6:135).

remains ambiguous. Who is handing Jesus over? Judas? Some Jewish leaders in Jerusalem? God? "Yes" seems the right answer to all
those questions. Mark has already said that the Son of Man *must*
undergo suffering, be rejected, be killed, and rise again. This is all
part of a divine plan. Yet it is also the action of bad people acting out
of bad motives. Mark will try in the account ahead to show through
his narration how it can be both.

## 9:33–37

### A Little Child

The disciples not only fail to understand the fate that awaits Jesus;
they fail to understand what it means to follow him. The Twelve
have been arguing about which of them is the greatest, and, when
he asks what they have been discussing, they will not tell him. They
do deserve some sympathy. The faults they are manifesting lie deep
in flawed human nature. In the Genesis story of Adam and Eve in
the garden, which I take to be a profound account of basic features
of human nature, Adam and Eve pridefully put their own judgment
in the place of God's. Whereas God told them not to eat the fruit of
a particular tree, they concluded that it was good for food, a delight
to the eyes, and would make them wise, and so they ate. Here the
disciples have been told that following Jesus means picking up their
crosses, and Jesus now insists that "whoever wants to be first must be
last of all and servant of all." They show again that human instinct to
insist they can figure things out for themselves and that they should
be competing for wisdom or status. Adam and Eve try to hide from
God in shame after they have disobeyed God's command. The disciples are ashamed and refuse to answer when Jesus asks what they
have been arguing about.

Jesus puts a little child before them—welcome a child, he says,
and you welcome me, welcome me and you welcome God. It is
easy to misread the text, drawing from a later passage and one's own
cultural assumptions. Jesus does not say here that we should be *like*
children; he says we should *welcome* them. In the ancient world, children were not considered primarily as models of innocence. Augus-

tine cites the case of a baby who had had plenty of milk but screamed its head off out of sheer envy when watching another baby being fed. No innocence there. The distinctive thing about children was their lack of any rights. A father could put a newborn outside to starve to death if he had wanted a boy and got a girl or if the baby seemed weak or handicapped. Children existed for the benefit of their parents—really of their fathers. In the Aramaic that Jesus was presumably speaking, the same word (*talya*) can mean either "child" or "servant." Welcoming children means helping the most vulnerable. Jesus is thus not urging childishness in any form on his disciples but telling them to stop competing about who will make the top and make sure they care for those on the bottom.

> Jesus' welcoming of the children takes them from the bottom of the family hierarchy and makes them persons in their own right.
> —L. William Countryman
>
> *Dirt, Greed, and Sex: Sexual Ethics in the New Testament and Their Implications for Today*, rev. ed. (Minneapolis: Fortress, 2007), 80.

## 9:38–41
### *An Unknown Exorcist*

The Twelve make one mistake after another. They encounter an exorcist they have never seen before who is casting out demons in Jesus' name, and "we tried to stop him, because he was not following us." Notice that they do not say the person was not following *Jesus* but rather "he was not following *us*." They are, it turns out, not making a new mistake but the same prideful, competitive one. If someone is not part of their group, their gang, their tribe, then how dare he claim to do anything in the name of Jesus.[43]

The basic direction of Jesus' response is clear enough—if people are doing good in Jesus' name, leave them alone. His particular arguments are more complex. The first seems to be a pragmatic one: anyone who has been acting in Jesus' name will not be able "soon afterward" to speak evil of Jesus or his cause. Take support where

43. Calvin, *Harmony of the Evangelists*, 2:373.

you can find it. His last argument has more the character of a promise—those who help anyone "because you bear the name of Christ"
will receive a reward. Even from outsiders, even cynical passersby—
any help in Jesus' name will not be forgotten. In our time political campaigns have grown very nervous about their contributors,
afraid of being embarrassed by a scandalous supporter. Churches,
too, want to be careful of their associations. Not Jesus! Give to help
a good cause, and he will thank you. And why not? Is it not better
to take the money of someone who would otherwise spend it on
gambling, sex, and tobacco than from those who would feed their
children?

Between his first and last arguments, however, Jesus makes a
more sweeping statement: "Whoever is not against us is for us."
What does it mean not to be against Jesus? Dante gives some of the
worst punishments of his Hell to those who could never bring themselves to choose a side. Jesus seems eager to give neutrals the benefit of the doubt. But what does it mean to be neutral with respect
to Jesus? Around 400 at the Council of Carthage, one of the del-
egates, Pusillus of Lamasba, condemned all those outside the
Catholic Church. Augustine replied, "But there may be something
Catholic outside the Catholic Church, just as the name of Christ
could exist outside the congregation of Christ, in which name he
who did not follow with the disciples was casting out devils."[44] Even
if people had left the church, if they wanted to return, he urged that
they "should rather by recognized with approbation than wounded
by condemnation."[45]

Augustine, in short, generally favored giving just about everyone
the benefit of the doubt. When he later angrily modified that view, it
led him to some of his least attractive actions. In the fourth century
or the twenty-first, however, tolerance leads to its own paradoxes.
A friend of mine once confessed she is a bigot about bigotry; she
despises people who despise people. Similarly, Augustine declared
that, even when people do the right thing, if "they had not charity,

44. Augustine, *On Baptism, Against the Donatists* 7.39.77 (*NPNF*, 1st ser., 4:508).
45. Ibid., 1.7.9 (4:416).

they cannot attain to eternal salvation."[46] So some of us today, in debates about tolerance, are eager to condemn those who seem too intolerant in the most vituperative terms. Even there, Jesus might remind us that the "intolerant" may be doing more than we are to feed the hungry and spread the gospel; they may even convert people to a Christian faith more tolerant than their own. It is not for the self-consciously tolerant to judge them.

## 9:42–50

### *Unquenchable Fire*

Mark does not describe Jesus as talking much about punishment after death; there is this passage and a passing reference at 12:40. Certainly the Jesus we have just been hearing seemed in favor of giving everyone the benefit of the doubt. These verses thus come as a surprise, for they offer very dire warnings indeed. If your hand or foot or eye causes you to stumble, cut it off—better to be without a hand or foot or eye than "to be thrown into Gehenna, where the worm never dies, and the fire is never quenched" (my trans.).

Gehenna was a valley south of Jerusalem where in ancient times babies were sacrificed to the Canaanite god Moloch. In the reforms under King Josiah (7th century BCE) such practices were brought to an end, and the area became a garbage dump, where refuse was continually smoldering. Gehenna was a horrible place, full of fire, smells, maggots, rats, and things in decay. Its history as a locus of child sacrifice further evokes the context here, where Jesus is singling out for condemnation those who "put a stumbling block before" or "trip up" any of the "little ones who believe in me." ("Little ones" may suggest the poor, the rejected, or other groups, but, in the light of verses 36–37, children are its immediate reference.)

In case Gehenna should seem a purely historical reference, it is worth remembering the number of third-world cities today where thousands of families and especially orphaned or abandoned children struggle for survival by foraging on garbage dumps far vaster

46. Ibid., 1.9.12 (4:417).

than anything around ancient Jerusalem. Are all of us who do nothing about this causing them to stumble?

A few recent scholars have tried to interpret each of Jesus' meta-
phors as referring to a specific sexual sin. Thus putting "a stumbling
block before these little ones" means child abuse, stumbling caused
by the hand refers to masturbation, stumbling caused by the foot
to adultery (one walks from home to elsewhere), and stumbling
caused by the eye to lustful glances.[47] They base their arguments on
a similar passage in the Talmud that offers this interpretation. That
seems to me to overread Mark's text. What is clear is that this is the
one point in the Gospel where Mark looks at specifically sexual sins,
and the opening framework is that it is wrong to injure vulnerable
ones. It is protecting the vulnerable rather than preserving purity
that sets the context.

It is customary to react to the hypothetical statements in this passage with horror, but they seem to me, as hypotheticals, true enough.
*If* you could stop being a sinner by cutting off one foot or one hand
or poking out one eye, should you not do it? Anyone who says no to
that has failed to grasp the horror of sin. But the hypotheticals, while
true in themselves, rest on faulty premises. Our hands and feet and
eyes do not cause us to sin. We ourselves, our minds, our souls, our
wills—whatever language one wants to use, the source of our sin
is not a part of us that can be removed with a sharp enough knife.
The point of the passage, then, is to say, "This is how serious sin is: it
would be worth cutting off part of your body to cure it. If only it were
that easy. So we have to think even more deeply about sin."

Punishment, it seems, will follow, if we do not stop sinning,
though the form of the punishment here can be misinterpreted. It
is, I think, annihilation. The great English evangelical preacher John
Stott has made the argument that the NT view is that those who
are ultimately condemned cease to exist rather than suffering eternal punishment. In this text, at least, it is the fire that lasts forever,
not the punishment, and the most natural reading is that one gets

47. Will Deming, "Mark 9:42–10:12, Matthew 5:27–32, and *B. Nid.* 13b: A First Century
    Discussion of Male Sexuality," *New Testament Studies* 36 (1990): 130–41; Raymond F.
    Collins, *Sexual Ethics and the New Testament* (New York: Crossroads, 2000), 62–72.

burned up, terminally. Gehenna as a place of eternal punishment (an assumption the NRSV helps by translating Greek *geennan* as "hell") is an assumption we bring to the text.

The *Apocalypse of Elijah*, a Jewish text from roughly the time of Jesus, declares at the time of the Last Judgment that God "will move the temple a great distance away from the destruction of the age, so that the righteous will not hear the voice of the crying of the wicked and seek mercy for them. They will be as though they never existed."[48] In contrast to a good many texts in Christian history, where watching the suffering of the wicked is one of the eternal pleasures of the righteous,[49] the *Apocalypse of Elijah* does imagine that the righteous, if only they knew, would seek mercy for those who suffer, even if their suffering is deserved. As a result, though, it pictures an outcome in which the righteous human beings are more merciful than God.

These are hard questions. On the one hand, as the twentieth-century Russian philosopher Nicholas Berdyaev put it, doing away with hell "makes life too easy, superficial and irresponsible."[50] Can we look forward to introducing six million Jews to Chancellor Hitler in heaven? Dostoevsky's Ivan Karamazov captures something true when he describes the suffering of little children at the hands of human monsters and says that, if everything is forgiven in a final reconciliation, then he turns in his ticket.[51]

> Even God's judgment is sustained and surrounded by God's mercy, even His severity by His kindness, even His wrath by His love.
> —Karl Barth
> CD II /2:211.

On the other hand, God is merciful, more loving than we can imagine. If we imagine ourselves among the righteous observing

48. Cited in Dale C. Allison Jr., *Resurrecting Jesus: The Earliest Christian Tradition and Its Interpreters* (New York: T. & T. Clark, 2005), 79.
49. See ibid., 94–95, for vivid examples.
50. Nicholas Berdyaev, *The Destiny of Man*, trans. Natalie Duddington, 4th ed. (New York: Harper & Row, 1960), 266.
51. Feodor Dostoevsky, *The Brothers Karamazov*, trans. Richard Pevear and Larissa Volokhonsk (San Francisco: North Point Press, 1990), 245.

eternal punishment, we think we would hope for mercy for the wicked. Can we think that God is less merciful than we are? Looking at Peter Paul Rubens's astonishing painting of St. Francis trying to protect the globe of the earth as Jesus prepares to throw thunderbolts at it, it is hard not to think that something had gone badly wrong here. Moreover, if we are honest, we are not among the righteous. Any hope that we ourselves have lies in mercy. Can we not wish for mercy for others if we so depend on it for ourselves? Thus a long tradition of Christian theologians, from Origen, Gregory of Nyssa, and Diodore of Tarsus to Karl Barth and Hans Urs von Balthasar, *hopes* that everyone gets saved in the end. Even John Calvin says that we should pray for the salvation of all.

Heinrich Heine once remarked, "Dieu pardonnera; c'est son métier"—God will forgive; that's his job. Christians cannot face divine justice with such casual reassurance. Human beings, ourselves very much included, deserve punishment. On the other hand, we cannot set limits in advance to God's mercy. There is no sin that God cannot forgive. Thus we must live in hope rather than in either confidence or despair.

Moreover, God is holy. Sin cannot exist in the presence of holiness; it self-combusts. We do not know how we may have to change in order to be saved. It may not be a pretty process. Mark has Jesus say, "Everyone will be salted with fire." When we have failed to be what we ought to be, we lose our "saltiness," and it may well be that only fire can restore it.

# 10:1–12

## *Divorce*

The first half of Mark 10 discusses three important areas of human action: marriage, children, and possessions. Marriage comes first. Most Jews in Jesus' time took a man's right to divorce a woman for granted. Women could not divorce their husbands. Deuteronomy 24:1 declares that, if a man "finds something objectionable about" his wife, he can write a certificate of divorce, put it in her hand, and "she then leaves his house." Rabbi Shammai said that the "something objectionable" could only be sexual misconduct, but Rabbi Hillel allowed for divorce "even if she spoiled cooking a dish for him," and Rabbi Aqiba permitted it "even if he found another more beautiful than she is."[52] (Note that Hillel, normally considered "more liberal" than Shammai, gives the man more freedom in a way that strikes us as deeply unfair to the wife.) These options were not just theoretical. The Jewish historian Josephus remarks rather casually and without apology at one point in his autobiography, "At this period I divorced my wife, being displeased at her behavior."[53]

Jesus acknowledges that this is what the law says but insists that God allowed divorce at all only "because of your hardness of heart." The way God created things to be, a man and a woman are joined together in marriage "and the two shall become one flesh," so that either one, if remarrying after divorce, is committing adultery. Divorce is necessary, Elizabeth Schüssler Fiorenza explains, "because of the male's hardness of heart; that is, because of men's patriarchal mind-set. . . . However, Jesus insists, God did not intend patriarchy."[54] Jesus rejects a social system that treats wives and children as men's property. As Donald Juel explains, "Forbidding of divorce is clearly a statement about the status of women in society. . . . Crucial to their survival has always been economic support. Easy divorce of women with young children means abrogating responsibility for caring for the most important members of society at a time of maximum vulnerability."[55]

A society in which men can divorce their wives on a whim but women cannot divorce their husbands at all is obviously unfair. It would not end the injustice if Jesus were to allow women equal rights to divorce their husbands since, given the economic realities of the time, virtually all married women were too dependent on their husbands to be able to exercise such a right even if they had it. It is not quite clear what Jesus offers as an alternative. He seems to recognize

52. Cited in John R. Donahue and Daniel J. Harrington, *The Gospel of Mark*, SP (Collegeville, MN: Liturgical Press, 2002), 296.
53. Josephus, *Life*, 426.
54. Elizabeth Schüssler Fiorenza, *In Memory of Her: A Feminist Theological Reconstruction of Christian Origins* (New York: Crossroad, 1985), 143.
55. Juel, *Gospel of Mark*, 131–32.

that, given human "hardness of heart," divorce will still sometimes be necessary while insisting that it should always be acknowledged as a failure, a result of human sin. When he calls remarriage after divorce "adultery," does he then imagine that within the community of his own followers divorced people would, in repentance, remain unmarried? Or does the realistic rule about hardness of heart apply to his followers as well? It is hard to be sure.

The Catholic Church solves the problem with annulments: some people can remarry because they are declared not to have been really married the first time. Karl Barth similarly proposed that there have been cases where a couple has never really been married in the eyes of God, and in such cases human permissions "can, and perhaps in certain situations must, dissolve it, because without the divine foundation which alone could make it indissoluble it lacks genuine and essential permanence, because it is not in the judgment of God a tenable marriage."[56] But this solution too is subject to abuse, forcing as it does the difficult human decision that a marriage was never real when the more honest thing might be to say that, initially real or not, it is simply no longer viable.

We have as a society fallen into the habit of considering divorce a rather ordinary event to which children generally adjust easily. This is a lie. We need to admit that divorce is always a tragedy. Sometimes, most clearly but not only in cases of abuse, it is the tragedy of the evil one partner does to the other. Often it is a tragedy where two parties (and maybe relatives and friends and employers as well) are to blame. Things can have come to a point where a divorce is better than any alternative, but they have reached that point because of sin. One of the responsibilities of a Christian community is to try to prevent marriages within it from reaching such a point. Indeed, a Christian community in which divorce is routine is either granting it too easily, not giving its married members enough help and support, or allowing marriages without enough prior counseling. Those who divorce, unless they are simply victims of their partners, should undertake a time of serious repentance. The children of a divorce know that they have undergone a tragedy (allowing the possibility

56. Barth, CD III/4:211.

that the continuation of the marriage might have been a greater trag-edy), and they will be healthier if they are part of a community that acknowledges that tragedy. Such a community will be listening to Jesus' teachings in Mark 10.

# 10:13–16
## *Children*

People are bringing little children to Jesus so he might touch them. This is something new. The children are presumably not sick and in need of a healing touch. People just feel that Jesus has some kind of power such that they would like him to touch their children. Here as earlier, children represent not primarily innocence but vulnerabil-ity. In this society they have no legal protections. Their parents want Jesus to touch them. Yet once more the disciples miss the point. These are just nameless children, perhaps the children of the poor—the disciples sternly order them away.

In our society, legislation gives children far more legal rights. If the children are poor or otherwise disadvantaged, all those laws often do them little good. Runaway kids would rather live on the street and make money by prostitution than return to the homes they have fled. Some street kids, we learn, are not "runaways" but "throwaways." They did not choose to leave their families; they were abandoned or expelled. An abortion may sometimes be the best solution for everyone involved; I do not want to tackle that question. But when abortion becomes a common means of birth control and we cast the moral issue as one in which the concerns of the child-that-is-to-be play no role at all, are we too treating as property what we ought to consider as at least the potentially human? Sometimes, cynically, it seems that in our political debates no one is much con-cerned about both the potentially human and actual children. Those most concerned about the not yet born seem sometimes indifferent to the already born, and vice versa. It is hard to find a political posi-tion that really represents what Jesus taught.

## 10:17–31
### Wealth

A man in most ancient cultures would have thought of wife, children, and wealth as all his property. So Mark turns now to wealth. A man runs up to Jesus with a question. Theologians have long debated about this man. Those who believe we humans are all sunk in sin and can be saved by grace alone regard his claims to have kept all the commandments since his youth with considerable suspicion. He should have been humble, Calvin says, "But, intoxicated with foolish confidence, he fearlessly boasts that he has discharged his duty properly since childhood."[57]

Luther demands, "Where is he who keeps the Decalogue? Or who can fulfill the commandments? . . . After the Fall of Adam no one . . . has fulfilled the law."[58] Yet "Jesus, looking at him, loved him"—the only time in Mark that Jesus is described as loving a particular individual. Should we be so quick to condemn the boastfulness of someone whom Jesus loved? Still, it is a concern that the man's question is, "What must I do to inherit eternal life?" Not who can give it to him, or how he can attain it, but what *he* can *do*. Calvin insists, "He therefore dreams of merits."[59]

Mark again presents a text with a subtext. The man addresses Jesus as "Good Teacher," and Jesus replies, "No one is good but God alone." Hilary of Poitiers says, "The question was put to him as if he were merely a teacher of the law."[60] At the surface level, Jesus is saying that he does not deserve the title "good." But we readers, who know by now that Jesus is God, recognize that Jesus is not really saying, "I am not good," but "I am not just a teacher."

Jesus more or less reviews the second table (the commandments referring to our relations with other people rather than with God) of the Ten Commandments, though without explanation he sub-

---

57. Calvin, *Harmony of the Evangelists*, 2:396.
58. Martin Luther, "The Disputation Concerning Justification, 1536," argument 27, trans. Lewis W. Spitz, *Career of the Reformer IV*, LW 34 (Philadelphia: Muhlenberg, 1960), 187.
59. Calvin, *Harmony of the Evangelists*, 2:393.
60. Hilary of Poitiers, *On the Trinity* 9.16, trans. Stephen McKenna, FC 25 (Washington, DC: Catholic University Press of America, 1954), 337.

stitutes "You shall not defraud" for "You shall not covet." This does have the effect of making all the commandments mentioned refer to external actions, thereby rendering the man's claim to have kept them all since his youth more plausible. It is surely easier to say that one has never defrauded than that one has never coveted. After the man claims to have done all this, and Jesus looks on him and loves him, Jesus continues, "You lack one thing: go, sell what you own, and give the money to the poor, and you will have treasure in heaven; then come, follow me." The man is shocked, and goes away grieving, "for he had many possessions." Mark shows his literary skill by saving a central part of the story till the very end. We learn that the man (till then just "a man") is wealthy only as he is walking away.

The man had good reason to be shocked. Traditional Jewish piety would usually have said that wealth was a blessing from God, a sign of divine favor. If you obey all the commandments, Moses tells the people of Israel in his final address to them, "the LORD will make you abound in prosperity" (Deut. 28:11). Proverbs declares, "The blessing of the LORD makes rich, and he adds no sorrow with it" (Prov. 10:22). The rich were expected to be generous and pious, but, if they were, it would not have occurred to anyone to criticize their wealth. As Tevye dreams in *Fiddler on the Roof,*

> If I were rich, I'd have the time that I lack
> To sit in the synagogue and pray.
> . . . . . . . . . . . . . . . . . . . . . . . . . . . . .
> And I'd discuss the holy books with the learned men,
> . . . . . . . . . . . . . . . . . . . . . . . . . . . . . . . . . . . . . . . . . .
> That would be the sweetest thing of all.[61]

But Jesus proclaims, "How hard it will be for those who have wealth to enter the kingdom of God!"—harder than for a camel to go through the eye of a needle, or, in Frederick Buechner's wonderful twentieth-century paraphrase, harder "than for Nelson Rockefeller to get through the night deposit slot of the First National City Bank."[61]

61. Stanley Richards, *Ten Great Musicals of the American Theatre* (Radnor, PA: Chilton Book Co., 1973), 502.
62. Frederick Buechner, *Telling the Truth* (San Francisco: Harper & Row, 1977), 63.

A few clarifications may be in order. Some report that there was a small gate in Jerusalem, called "the eye of the needle," which a camel could just barely pass through. There was no such gate, and the first reference to this way out of the problem does not appear until the ninth century.[63] Another claim is that the word translated "camel" here actually means "rope," but this is dubious and dodges the problem that a rope cannot get through the eye of a needle either. The reality is that for most of Jesus' or Mark's audience a camel was the largest animal they would ever see, a needle's eye the smallest aperture they knew about, and one going through the other was impossible.

Are the rich then without hope? Clement of Alexandria, writing in second-century Egypt, declared that even the rich can be saved "if one is able in the midst of wealth to turn from its power, to entertain moderate sentiments and to exercise self-command and to seek God alone, and to breathe God and walk with God."[64] John Chrysostom, preaching in Constantinople several centuries later, argued that, just as a brass worker or a weaver or a carpenter has a particular art, so there is an art in using wealth, and let the rich person "learn then to use his wealth aright, and to pity the poor; so shall he know a better art than all these."[65] These and other Christians maintain that the problem lies not in wealth itself, but in one's attitude toward it. If one can find wealth a heavy responsibility, then one's task may be to cultivate the difficult art of being wealthy that Chrysostom describes. To those of us who know wealthy people who work hard and imaginatively to make good use of their wealth, this is far from a silly idea.

But is it quite what Jesus says here? When the rich man goes away, Jesus does not say, "That particular man was too caught up in wealth." He turns to his disciples and says, "How hard it will be for those who have wealth to enter the kingdom of God." Think of the tremendous difference we could make in the condition of the world's poor if those of us with comfortable means shared more of what we have. So why do we not do it? Moreover, we do not acquire riches by accident; we work to get them. Some people provide a ser-

63. Boring, *Mark*, 292.
64. Clement of Alexandria, *Who Is the Rich Man that Shall Be Saved?* (*ANF* 2:598).
65. Chrysostom, *Homilies on Matthew* 49.4 (*NPNF*, 1st ser., 10:307).

vice, do a job, follow a vocation, even play the stock market for the sheer satisfaction of winning at the game of it. That doing so accumulates wealth is nearly an afterthought. But it is hard not to get captured by the money side of things, to think of the less fulfilling job that would make more money, the less useful product that might sell better, and so on. John Wesley wrote that it is hard for the rich to be good Christians, since it becomes too easy for them to trust in their wealth and not think they need to trust in God, too easy to love the world when surrounded by all its allurements, and too hard to escape pride in a society that so values wealth: "The whole city of London uses the words *rich* and *good* as equivalent terms. 'Yes,' they say, 'he is a good man; he is worth a hundred thousand pounds.' . . . How is it possible that a rich man should escape pride?"[66]

The book of Acts tells how, in the first Christian community in Jerusalem, "All who believed were together and had all things in common; they would sell their possessions and goods and distribute the proceeds to all, as any had need" (Acts 2:44–45). As Barth remarks, "It is worth pondering that the venture was at least made. And it will always be inevitable that there should be impulses in this direction whenever the Gospel of Jesus is proclaimed and heard."[67] Sharing all that we have does at some level seem to be what Jesus invites us to do. If we do not see that there is any problem at all about there being wealthy Christians, then we are not reading the New Testament seriously enough. Jesus' message about

> The good is distributed by God and is to be distributed by us in imitation of God, in an indiscriminate, profligate fashion.
>
> —Kathryn Tanner
>
> *Economy of Grace* (Minneapolis: Augsburg Fortress, 2005), 25.

wealth is a *radical* one. To quote Barth again, "We do not really know Jesus (the Jesus of the New Testament) if we do not know Him as this poor man, as this (if we may risk the dangerous word) partisan of the poor, and finally as this revolutionary."[68]

---

66. John Wesley, "Sermon 108: On Riches," *The Works of John Wesley* (repr. Grand Rapids: Baker, 1979), 7:216, 219.
67. Barth, *CD* IV/2:178.
68. Ibid., 180.

Nevertheless, we recognize the remarkable good that some rich people do in the world (even as we remember that other rich people hold on to every last penny). We recognize that some of the poor can fall into their own set of characteristic sins—bitterness, and a mixture of despair and laziness (even as we remember that other poor people struggle heroically or are in situations where we too cannot see how their efforts could help them). Caesarius of Arles, one of the theologians earliest influenced by Augustine, preached to his poor congregation, "Beware of pride, lest the humble rich surpass you. Beware of wickedness, lest the pious rich confound you."[69]

When his disciples wonder, "Who can be saved?" Jesus replies, "For mortals it is impossible, but not for God; for God all things are possible." Every station in life has temptations. None of us is free from sin. We are saved only by grace. On this matter, let Augustine have the last word:

> Riches . . . are gained with toil and kept with fear. They are enjoyed with danger and lost with grief. It is hard to be saved if we have them; and impossible if we love them; and scarcely can we have them but we shall love them inordinately. Teach us, O Lord, this difficult lesson: to manage conscientiously the goods we possess.[70]

Having heard the fate that apparently awaits the wealthy, Peter protests, "Look, we have left everything and followed you." Jesus assures him that those who have left "house or brothers or sisters or mother or father or children or fields" for his sake will "receive a hundredfold now in this age—houses, brothers and sisters, mothers and children, and fields, with persecutions—and in the age to come eternal life." This sounds at first like a proclamation of the "gospel of wealth"—"Send your check in to my ministry, and I guarantee that within three months you will receive a hundredfold in return." But Mark is more subtle. He never mentions money. Why would one want a hundredfold return in houses and siblings? He is not referring

---

69. Caesarius of Arles, Sermon 153.2, *St. Caesarius of Arles: Sermons*, trans. Mary Magdeleine Mueller (Washington, DC: Catholic University of America Press, 1963), 2:338.
70. Augustine, "Sermon 133," cited in Oden and Hall, *Mark*, 144.

to some sort of super–hedge fund but to the community of those who follow Jesus. Peter left his wife and mother-in-law; James and John left their father. But they will find a new family among Jesus' followers (remember that in 3:31–35 Jesus identified these followers as his true family), and this will be a more rewarding, more inclusive family than any they have previously experienced.

Careful reading of a carefully written text suggests it will be a different kind of family, in at least three ways. First, people will leave "brothers or sisters or mother or father or children" and will receive "brothers and sisters, mothers and children"—but no fathers. They will have one father, God. Given the patriarchal society of the time, where fathers thought of themselves as owning their wives and children, there is no place for human fathers in the family of Jesus' followers. Second, they will leave fields and receive a hundredfold "fields and persecutions." Mark slips that last word in so casually one can almost miss it, but it is central to Jesus' promise here. Following Jesus will be tough. One will be supported by the community of a new family, but one will suffer persecution. No promise simply of a life of rewards. Third, "Many who are first will be last, and the last will be first." The hierarchies of current society will be radically overturned. Anyone who enters the community of Jesus' followers confident of retaining their status and social position is likely in for a rude shock. "God chose what is foolish in the world to shame the wise; God chose what is weak in the world to shame the strong; God chose what is low and despised in the world, things that are not, to reduce to nothing things that are, so that no one might boast in the presence of God" (1 Cor. 1:27–29).

"And in the age to come eternal life." The rich man began this particular story by seeking eternal life. This is one of the few times in the Gospel where Jesus uses the apocalyptic language of the "two ages." It returns us to the question (discussed above in relation to the transfiguration) of whether "eternal life" is a timeless, always accessible eternity or the inbreaking of the eschatological future, or some combination of the two. Just here, in any event, Jesus seems to be combining his promises for the two ages. The kind of egalitarian, inclusive community his followers will form in this age will not be lost in the age to come.

# 10:32–45
### On the Way to Jerusalem

They are on the "way" or "road," going up to Jerusalem. Mark has already established "way" as the word for how one follows Jesus. Physically, one does go "up" to Jerusalem, which is located on high ground. But the cross raised high on the hill of Golgotha seems somewhere in the background here too. Jesus is going to his fate. He explains it once more to the Twelve. In Mark, as in folktales, things tend to come in threes, and this is his third anticipation of his death and resurrection. This account is the most vivid and detailed, the first to mention mocking and spitting and flogging. Is Jesus trying to make an impression on his rather dense disciples? Or is the reality of what is to come growing more vivid in his own mind?

Now, shortly before they reach Jerusalem itself, two of the disciples manifest the last and perhaps most dramatic of Mark's many cases of disciple misunderstandings. They still think that Jesus is headed for glory and triumph, and they want the positions of greatest prominence, at his right and left hand. They have understood neither the egalitarian character of the new community nor the suffering that awaits Jesus. He challenges them on both counts. Are they ready to suffer what he will suffer? He uses two images—to be baptized, and to drink the cup. "Baptized" in Greek can also mean "flooded with calamities," and the image is of an immersion that is partway toward drowning. The cup, as Jesus will soon explain to them, is the cup of his blood. Thus the images are both symbols of sacraments and symbols of threats, and this was appropriate to the church of Mark's time, where joining the Christian community or participating in Christian worship did risk torture and death.

James and John say they are able to face what awaits them, and we know that James was in fact one of the first Christian martyrs. Do they know what they are promising? Probably not. It is a common human experience to discover we have signed on for more than we realized or intended. Sometimes that discovery comes with panic and the need to escape, but sometimes we are grateful in retrospect for the veil that hid from us a destination we would not have had the courage for at the time, though we are now glad to have undertaken the voyage.

The others among the Twelve hear that James and John have been lobbying for privileged positions, and they are angry. Again, Jesus explains the nature of the new community he is creating. Great ones will not be tyrants, rulers will not lord it over others, "but whoever wishes to become great among you must be your servant, and whoever wishes to be first among you must be slave of all. For the Son of Man came not to be served but to serve, and to give his life a ransom for many."

## FURTHER REFLECTIONS
### *Ransom*

In Mark Jesus' death is part of God's plan; it is Jesus' destiny and somehow for the good of the world. But Mark's genre is narrative rather than theological treatise. He tells his story, but he rarely offers explanations about *why* it is necessary that Jesus die or *how* his death accomplishes some good end. This brief passage—that he will give his life as a ransom for many—is one of the few that can at all be considered an explanation, and the danger of overinterpreting it is therefore considerable.

A ransom (*lytron*) involved paying a sum of money to "redeem" animals or property in the possession of someone else or to buy a person out of slavery. The pawn shop offers a simple contemporary example. Temporarily short of money, I give the pawnbroker my mother's diamond ring in exchange for some cash, with the expectation that on my next payday I will be able to go back and "redeem" it. In explaining the duties of the next of kin, Leviticus specifies, "If anyone of your kin falls into difficulty and sells a piece of property, then the next of kin shall come and redeem what the relative has sold" (Lev. 25:25). If Uncle Ross had to sell his farm to pay his bills, as his next of kin I should buy back the farm and return it to him.

Later, when many of the people of Israel were in exile in Babylonia, they turned to the Lord as a surrogate next of kin, in hopes that he would ransom or redeem them (Jer. 31:11). Since the prophets taught them that exile was a punishment for their sins, they were hoping to be redeemed not only from the power of the Babylonians but also from the consequences of their own sins:

> Our transgressions indeed are with us,
>     and we know our iniquities. . . .
> The Lord saw . . . that there was no one to intervene;
> so his own arm brought him victory,
>     and his righteousness upheld him. . . .
> And he will come to Zion as Redeemer.
>
> (Isa. 59:12, 15, 20)

Later still, the matriarch of the Maccabee family and seven of her sons were tortured and killed, and their deaths were described as, "as it were, a ransom for the sin of our nation" (4 Macc. 17:21). Since the nation's conquest by various empires had been a punishment for its sins, a ransom needed to be paid before the nation could achieve its liberation.

By the time Mark wrote, Paul had already used the language of redemption in several of his letters to describe Christ's saving work: "Christ redeemed us from the curse of the law" (Gal. 3:13); "God sent his Son . . . in order to redeem those who were under the law" (Gal. 4:4–5); "all have sinned and fall short of the glory of God; they are now justified by his grace as a gift, through the redemption that is in Christ Jesus" (Rom. 3:23–24). Mark was using language already widespread in the Christian community when he said that the Son of Man came to give his life as a ransom for many.

But to whom does the ransom get paid? Mark offers no clear answer, and Christian theologians down the centuries have taken very different points of view. In perhaps the most famous account of Christ's saving work, Anselm of Canterbury, writing around 1100, affirmed that, since human sins were committed against God, it was God to whom a ransom was due. Anselm lived under the feudal system, where vassals owed honor to their lords in exchange for protection in those often dangerous medieval times. We humans, who have received everything we have from God, owe God all the honor we can offer in return. When we sin we betray God's honor; and, since we owe God everything we could give, once we fall behind in our account, we can never catch back up again. Since "the price paid to God for the sin of man" must "be something greater than all the universe besides God," it follows that "none but God can make this satisfaction.... But none but a man ought to do this, otherwise man does not make the satisfaction.... Therefore ... it is necessary that the same being should be perfect god and perfect man, in order to make this atonement."[71]

In 1931 the Swedish theologian Gustaf Aulén published *Christus Victor,* a now classic work arguing that Christ's saving work consisted in freeing humankind by defeating Satan, and that this was the dominant view in most of the early church and the writings of Luther. According to Aulén's theory, human beings had voluntarily submitted themselves to the power of Satan. A just God could not simply ignore Satan's claim on humankind, but a merciful God could not simply allow all human beings to remain under this evil power. Aulén quotes Gregory of Nyssa: "Now that we had voluntarily bartered away our freedom, it was requisite that no arbitrary method of recovery but the one consonant with justice should be devised by Him Who in His goodness had undertaken our rescue."[72] The life of Christ is paid to Satan as a ransom for humankind.[73]

Both these theories have been criticized ever since they were written. Anselm risks too much dividing the Trinity and its work, so that a compassionate Son pays off a just but unforgiving Father. As Anselm's near contemporary Peter Abelard put it, "In what way does the apostle declare that we are justified or reconciled to go through the death of his Son, when God ought to have been the more angered against man, inasmuch as men acted more criminally by crucifying his Son.... How did the death of his innocent Son so please God the Father that through it he should be reconciled to us?"[74] On the other hand, the *Christus Victor* model implies that

71. Anselm, *Cur Deus Homo* 1:6–7, *St. Anselm: Basic Writings,* trans. S. N. Deane (LaSalle, IL: Open Court, 1966), 244–46.
72. Gregory of Nyssa, *The Great Catechism* 22 (*NPNF*, 2nd ser., 5:493).
73. Gustaf Aulén, *Christus Victor,* trans. A. G. Hebert (New York: Macmillan, 1969), 49.
74. Peter Abelard, *Exposition of the Epistle to the Romans,* in *A Scholastic Miscellany: Anselm to Ockham,* ed. and trans. Eugene R. Fairweather, LCC 10 (Philadelphia: Westminster, 1956), 282–83.

Satan has us under his power, fair and square, when Satan is in fact a trickster and a liar and can have no real rights over any part of God's creation.[75]

Mark avoids the problem by introducing the idea of ransom without saying to whom the ransom is paid. Moreover, Mark's approach makes both Anselm and Aulén seem indifferent to the specifics of Jesus' story. In Mark, Jesus does not just suffer and die in the abstract—he does so at the hands of the political and religious leaders of his time, whom he has challenged by his efforts to welcome those whom society rejected and to challenge the rules that dominated his culture. Any adequate account of what "ransom" means in Mark has to take those particulars into consideration.

## 10:46–52

### *Healing Bartimaeus*

Jericho lies only a few miles from Jerusalem, down in the Jordan Valley. This whole section has been about taking the way to Jerusalem and all it represents, but as Jesus and his followers leave Jericho they are in the most literal sense on the way up to Jerusalem. There they meet Bartimaeus, a blind man who sits begging by the roadside. He is the last person Jesus will heal in Mark's Gospel, the only one who follows Jesus after his healing. The Hebrew prefix *bar-* means "son of," so the explanation, "Bartimaeus son of Timaeus," seems oddly redundant. Its only obvious function is to call our attention sharply to this name, something that might have happened anyway, since he is the only person seeking to be healed whose name is given. "Timaeus" could mean "one who was purchased or bought," so here, just after learning that Jesus has come to be our ransom, we encounter a son of one who was purchased or bought who needs his help.

He cries out, "Jesus, Son of David, have mercy on me." "Son of David" was a messianic title, so Bartimaeus becomes, after Peter, the second human being in the story to address Jesus by such a title. This blind man sees who Jesus really is. "Call" quickly becomes a key

---

75. So Gregory of Nazianzus argued. See Aulén, *Christus Victor*, 50.

word in the story: Jesus tells people to call Bartimaeus to him. They call him, telling him that Jesus is calling him. Not since the calling of the Twelve and Levi early in the Gospel has Jesus called anyone. Bartimaeus throws off his cloak and moves toward Jesus—a bold action indeed. A cloak might have been a beggar's only possession, and a blind man who tosses something aside in a crowd may never find it again. He is doing completely what the rich man could not bring himself to do—casting aside everything he possesses to come to Jesus.

Jesus asks him, "What do you want me to do for you?" It is the same question he just asked James and John. They wanted places of honor at his right and left; Bartimaeus simply wants to be able to see again. He calls Jesus "my teacher," a form of address used elsewhere in Mark only by the disciples when they fail to understand Jesus (9:5 and 11:21) and by Judas as he betrays Jesus (14:45). Jesus tells him, "Your faith has made you well." Since *sōzein* can mean either physical or spiritual health, the sentence could equally be translated, "Your faith has saved you." "Immediately" (yet once again Mark's favorite word) Bartimaeus regains his sight "and followed him on the way"—a "way" that by this time clearly means not just the highway but the path of following Jesus to the cross.

> In the New Testament world, the Greek terms associated with "salvation"... related generally to rescue from misfortune of all kinds: shipwreck, the ravages of a journey, enemies in times of conflict, and so on. By far, however, the most common usage of these terms... was medical. "To save" was "to heal."
> —Joel B. Green
>
> *Salvation*, Understanding Biblical Themes (St. Louis: Chalice, 2003), 36.

In sum, after a whole series of episodes in which the Twelve do not get it, here, just before Jesus' entry into Jerusalem, is someone who gets everything right. He recognizes Jesus as the Messiah, gives up everything, asks only for his sight, and follows Jesus on the way. And who is this perfect disciple? A blind beggar, sitting by the roadside, yelling his head off for Jesus.

# 11:1–13:37

# *Challenge to Authority*

## 11:1–11

### *Entry into Jerusalem*

It is all a little ridiculous, John Calvin observed. Jesus is riding not on a royal steed but on a little donkey.[1] It is not even his own but had to be borrowed. He has no saddle, so that the people have to throw their cloaks on the donkey's back. Those following him must have been a rag-tag, miscellaneous group of the poor.[2] Hard to imagine anything less like a triumphant royal procession. As Luther says,

> He sits not upon a proud steed, an animal of war, nor does he come in great pomp and power, but sitting upon an ass, an animal of peace fit only for burden and labor and a help to man. He indicates by this that he comes not to frighten man, nor to drive or crush him, but to help him and to carry his burden for man.[3]

Nevertheless, those who follow him cry out in the language of fulfilled messianic prophecies. Just as in the previous section Bartimaeus (is he among these followers?) called Jesus "Son of David," so now these people are shouting "Hosanna" (literally "Save us now"— so he is one who can save them) and proclaiming "the coming reign of our ancestor David" (my trans.), presumably to be inaugurated by Jesus, "the one who comes in the name of the Lord." The animal

---

1. I follow Adela Yarbro Collins and others in translating "young donkey" rather than "colt." See Adela Yarbro Collins, *Mark*, Hermeneia (Minneapolis: Fortress, 2007), 512.
2. Calvin, *Harmony of the Evangelists*, 2:447.
3. Martin Luther, "First Sunday in Advent," *Sermons of Martin Luther*, vol. 1, *Sermons on Gospel Texts for Advent, Christmas, and Epiphany*, ed. John Nicholas Lenker, trans. Lenker et al. (repr. Grand Rapids: Baker, 1983), 19.

that has never been ridden before was traditionally reserved for the king. Moreover, Mark alludes for the first of several times to the later chapters of Zechariah, passages not written by Zechariah himself but by an anonymous prophet of uncertain date, perhaps in the fifth or fourth century BCE. This "Second Zechariah" despaired of the idea that any human leader would come to restore Israel's power and hoped instead that the Lord himself

> will appear over them,
> and his arrow go forth like lightning;
> the Lord GOD will sound the trumpet
> and march forth in the whirlwinds of the south. . . .
> On that day the LORD their God will save them
> for they are the flock of his people.
> (Zech. 9:14, 16)

And how does the prophet describe the triumphant arrival?

> Rejoice greatly, O daughter Zion!
> Shout aloud, O daughter Jerusalem!
> Lo, your king comes to you;
> triumphant and victorious is he,
> humble and riding on a donkey,
> on a colt, the foal of a donkey.
> (Zech. 9:9)

To describe this somewhat ridiculous and utterly unwarlike procession, Mark evokes some of the most triumphant and military language in Hebrew prophecy, language moreover originally used not to describe one more human king but the arrival of the Lord himself.

Another allusion seems to be to an earlier story out of Israel's history. When Jehoram became king of Israel around 850 BCE, the Lord recognized his evil potential and decided that he must be destroyed. On the Lord's instructions, the prophet Elisha sent a secret message to Jehu, the commander of the royal army, anointing him as king. Jehu's officers "all took their cloaks and spread them for him on the bare steps; and they blew the trumpet, and proclaimed,

'Jehu is king" (2 Kgs. 9:13). The spreading of cloaks gives Jesus the honor due a king, but, beyond that, it recalls a divinely ordained coup d'état. (They also spread "leafy branches"; only John mentions palms, and there were apparently no palm trees near Jerusalem at the time.) Once again, Mark is telling its readers, "Jesus may be an altogether different kind of king, but he is nevertheless a king, indeed God come among us to challenge the powers that be."

The story contains not only the tension between this guy looking rather foolish on his donkey and the astonishingly bold claims implicitly made for him but also an air of mystery. Jesus gives two of his disciples instructions on how to obtain a donkey, and, sure enough, everything happens as he had said. Here and elsewhere a historian may wonder if Jesus had some group of followers in Jerusalem, unknown to those who had come with him from Galilee. Perhaps. But by including these elements in the story without explanation, Mark develops a sense that Jesus has power in ways mysterious to the disciples whose point of view we are following. They cannot understand everything; they must have faith. Luther, indeed, saw this whole story as importantly about faith:

> If Christ had entered in splendor like a king of earth, the appearance and the words would have been according to nature and reason and would have seemed to the eye according to the words, but then there would have been no room for faith. He who believes in Christ must find riches in poverty, honor in dishonor, joy in sorrow, life in death, and hold fast to them in that faith which clings to the Word and expects such things.[4]

Having entered the city, Jesus went to the temple and "looked around at everything." Then, in an odd anticlimax, he turns around and goes back to Bethany for the night. Why this initial visit to the temple where nothing happens? On the next day's trip, he will dramatically drive out those who are buying and selling in the temple. It may be that Mark wants that episode to start at once and with high drama, but does not want it to seem as if Jesus is condemning without evidence. Hence an earlier trip of inspection. Then too, as in

4. Ibid., 23.

good folktales, things in Mark tend to come in threes, and this first trip to the temple is followed by two more.

# 11:12–25
## *The Fig Tree and the Temple*

A man who had read one of my books once telephoned me out of the blue to announce that he was not a Christian because of the story of the cursing of the fig tree. He could not follow a Jesus who had cursed an innocent tree, when it was not even the season for figs. So—what did I think of that?

Biblical literalism is not confined to believers. Some of those who reject the Bible's message altogether nevertheless assume that odd bits of it, at least, accurately describe literal events. My friend on the telephone was not the first to find this story an ethical puzzle. Calvin wonders of Jesus, "Why was he so fiercely enraged against a harmless tree?"[5] Augustine asks, "What fault in the tree was it that it had no fruit?"[6] He concludes, "Unless this action be regarded as a figure, there is no good meaning in it."[7] The "good meaning" of the story must be symbolic.

To explore such meaning, it helps to notice that Mark has once again created a sandwich. On the way to the temple, Jesus curses the fig tree. Then he drives the money changers and other business people out of the temple and goes back to Bethany. The next day he enters the city again, and Peter sees that the fig tree has withered away to its roots. By inserting the temple story in the middle of the two halves of the account of the fig tree, Mark presses us to consider temple and fig tree together.

Fig trees play a prominent role in the Hebrew Scriptures. In Jewish legend, the "tree of the knowledge of good and evil" from which Adam and Eve ate was not an apple but a fig. Figs represented agricultural plenty. In the wilderness, the Hebrews wished for the figs of Egypt (Num. 20:5), and Moses assured them of figs in the promised

5. Calvin, *Harmony of the Evangelists*, 3:18.
6. Augustine, *Sermons on New Testament Lessons* 39.2 (*NPNF*, 1st ser., 6:389).
7. Ibid., 28.7 (*NPNF*, 1st ser., 6:344).

land (Deut. 8:8). Sitting under one's own fig tree and eating of its fruit was such an appealing idea (2 Kgs. 18:31; Isa. 36:16) that it came to be part of eschatological promises (Mic. 4:4; Zech. 3:10). Thus having fig trees wither was one of the forms God's punishment could take (Jer. 5:17; Hos. 2:12; Amos 4:9). In contrast, the fig tree could represent the people of Israel, where God looked for fruit and found none:

> Woe is me! For I have become like one who,
>     after the summer fruit has been gathered,
>     after the vintage has been gleaned,
> finds no cluster to eat;
>     there is no first-ripe fig for which I hunger.
> The faithful have disappeared from the land,
>     and there is no one left who is upright.
>                                     (Mic. 7:1–2)

The Jesus who curses the fig tree acts in the role of God, condemning Israel for its faithlessness. The withered tree can symbolize both the nation's failure and the divine punishment.

"Then they came to Jerusalem. And he entered the temple. . . ." Mark connects the fig tree story closely with what Jesus does in the temple. Here too Jesus is enacting divine judgment. Like Micah, Jeremiah has the Lord angry at a withered fig tree:

> When I wanted to gather them, says the LORD,
>     there are no grapes on the vine,
>         nor figs on the fig tree;
> even the leaves are withered.
>                                     (Jer. 8:13)

And what does this mean in less symbolic language?

>         everyone is greedy for unjust gain;
>     from prophet to priest,
>     everyone deals falsely.
>                                     (Jer. 8:10)

So now Jesus drives out those who are selling and buying in the temple, overturning the tables of the money changers and the seats of those who sold doves, then quoting Isaiah (56:7), with allusions to Jeremiah (7:11) and Zechariah (14:21), pulling together the whole tradition of prophetic condemnation of the temple ritual and its corruption.

Was the issue the temple or its corruption? We can work our way up to indignation that people were selling doves and changing money in the courtyard of the holy temple. But a central part of what one did at the temple was to sacrifice birds or animals, and carrying a live dove through the streets of Jerusalem would have involved a considerable nuisance. Gifts to the temple could hardly be paid with coins that had, say, the picture of a pagan god on them, so money changers were more or less a practical necessity. As Karl Barth says, no doubt with an element of irony, "'A den of thieves' is rather a harsh description for the honest, small-scale financial and commercial activities which had established themselves there."[8] Were the money changers and sellers of doves cheating the poor? Maybe—but Mark does not claim that. His concern seems more far reaching than keeping the business honest: Jesus "would not allow anyone to carry anything through the temple." No use of any profane containers in the temple court, no using the temple court as a shortcut while on an ordinary errand. One could interpret this as a passionate concern for the purity of the temple courtyard—but what has Jesus done in his earlier ministry to lead us to expect him to care all that much about ritual purity?

Mark's point, then, is not about keeping transactions in the temple courtyard honest or preserving the courtyard's purity. He is challenging the central place of the temple in Jewish religion. In chapter 13 Jesus will predict the utter destruction of the temple, an event that took place about the time (we would love to know whether just before or just after!) Mark was writing. What Solomon had built and Nehemiah had begun rebuilding and Herod the Great had reconstructed on a grander scale was demolished by the Romans and has never been rebuilt. Now that Israel controls the Temple Mount, it is

---

8. Barth, *CD* IV/2:176.

probably a relief to many Jews that the presence of a famous mosque on the site where the temple would have to be rebuilt makes such construction politically impossible, for Judaism too, around Mark's time, became a religion of prayer and study rather than animal sacrifice, of synagogues rather than a temple. What began as a necessity has become so natural that it is virtually impossible to imagine a return to the days of Jewish temple sacrifices.

Even in Jesus' time, others, like the Essenes, had abandoned the temple as hopelessly corrupt, and prophets like Jeremiah had long before threatened its destruction (Jer. 7:13–14). What sets Jesus apart is not that he criticizes the temple, but that he proposes himself as a replacement for it. Even Mark's odd grammar makes the point, when he uses *autos* (he, she, or it) in a series of ambiguous ways. First Jesus criticizes those who have corrupted the temple: "You have made *auton* a den of robbers." But then the chief priests and scribes seek how they might kill *auton* because they feared *auton*, since the whole crowd was spellbound by the teaching *autou* (of him). The first use refers to the temple, the other three to Jesus, but there is no signal of the shift of references.[9] The very grammar of the sentence slides from the temple to Jesus.

The temple was the place where God was present. When the Roman army finally captured it, their general broke into the temple's Holy of Holies and was astonished to find only emptiness at its center. No image of God, no incredibly valuable gold or silver. In Jacques Derrida's words, "Hence the ingenuous surprise of a non-Jew when he . . . violates the tabernacle, when he enters the dwelling or the temple, and after so many ritual detours to gain access to the secret center, he discovers nothing—only nothingness. No center, no heart, an empty space, nothing."[10] Yet in some sense God was present in that emptiness.

Prophets had long warned, however, that that presence could not be taken for granted. Jeremiah had God acknowledge, "if you truly amend your ways and your doings, if you truly act justly one

9. Robert M. Fowler, *Let the Reader Understand: Reader-Response Criticism and the Gospel of Mark* (Minneapolis: Fortress, 1991), 201–2.
10. Jacques Derrida, *Glas*, trans. John P. Leavey Jr. and Richard Rand (Lincoln: University of Nebraska Press, 1986), 49.

with another, if you do not oppress the alien, the orphan, and the widow, or shed innocent blood in this place, and if you do not go after other gods to your own hurt, then I will dwell with you in this place" (Jer. 7:5–7). *But,* he warned, "Do not trust in these deceptive words: 'This is the temple of the LORD, the temple of the LORD, the temple of the LORD'" (Jer. 7:4). No building or place or institution can guarantee God's presence.

Now, moreover, the temple had become irrelevant, since God was present *in Jesus.* The unknown author of Hebrews writes of Christ coming as a new high priest "through the greater and perfect tent (not made with hands, that is, not of this creation)"—the tent that is Jesus' own bodily presence (Heb. 9:11). Just as Jesus' word can destroy the fig tree, so God can now allow the temple made by human hands to be destroyed.

Indeed, when Jesus and the disciples return to Jerusalem the next day, they see the fig tree "withered away to its roots." The tree is not itself being punished, but functions as a symbol for the fate that awaits the temple. Peter says, "Rabbi, look! The fig tree that you cursed has withered." The only other time Peter addressed Jesus as "rabbi" was at the transfiguration, where the term seemed a mistake, a sign of his failure to understand that Jesus is not just a teacher but the Son of God. "Rabbi" is also the way Judas addresses Jesus when he betrays him. Peter is focused on the withering of the fig tree; he has missed the lesson about the temple.

Jesus replies with a lesson about the power of faith and prayer: "If you say to this mountain, 'Be taken up and thrown into the sea,' and if you do not doubt in your heart, but believe that what you say will come to pass, it will be done for you." Prominent rabbis were known as "uprooters of mountains" because they could solve complex questions of biblical interpretation,[11] so that allusion may hover in the background here. Jesus, moreover, is not discussing just any mountain but "this mountain," the Temple Mount that presumably stands before them. Peter having focused on the fig tree, Jesus turns things back to the temple. "The temple is the mountainous

---

11. William R. Telford, *The Barren Temple and the Withered Tree,* Journal for the Study of the New Testament Supplement 1 (Sheffield: JSOT Press, 1980), 95, 111–12.

obstacle which is to vanish before the faith of the gospel movement. The temple system, with its corrupt clericalism and vested interests, is to be removed in the eschatological era, which is now being experienced."[12] The general point is that faith can do amazing things, but the specific point is that the faith of Jesus' followers ought to be in him and not in the temple.

We normally think, as Barth points out, that we know we are praying but are uncertain whether God hears us. Here Jesus reverses things: it is certain that God hears but uncertain that we are really praying.[13] Prayer requires faith and the willingness to forgive others if it is to be authentic. Jesus here refers to God, for the only time in Mark, as "your Father." In this Gospel he never says "our Father." The Father to whom he prays is *Jesus'* Father. Perhaps it is only the person engaged in authentic prayer, who has faith and manifests forgiveness, who can also use the term.

In a contemporary context, of course, the male character of "Father" language has also become an important issue. Mark has already made clear that Jesus is no defender of patriarchy. He repudiates divorce laws that favor men. He imagines an ideal family in which there are mothers and brothers and sisters, but no fathers. Jesus nevertheless prays to one he calls "Father." In part this obviously follows tradition. At the beginning of the Hebrew monarchy, Nathan speaks, according to 2 Samuel, the word of the Lord to David about his son Solomon: "He shall build a house for my name, and I will establish the throne of his kingdom forever. I will be a father to him, and he shall be a son to me" (2 Sam. 7:13–14). To speak of God as "Father" can mean two things. First, it can indicate that, if God is a bit like a human father, then human fathers are a bit like God—the classic patriarchal interpretation. Alternatively, it can be a term that emphasizes intimacy: the Creator of the whole universe, the Holy One that even Moses could not see face to face without being destroyed, is someone to whom we can relate like one of our own parents. Mark's understanding of the family has ruled the first of these meanings out, and we are left with the second.

12. R. E. Dowda, "The Cleansing of the Temple in the Synoptic Gospels" (Ph.D. diss., Duke University, 1972), 250.
13. Barth, *CD* III/4:107.

# 11:27–33
## *First Question: Jesus' Authority*

As Jesus continues to teach in Jerusalem, he is asked a series of questions. The first concerns his authority. Back at the beginning of his ministry in Galilee, one of the first things people noticed about him was that he taught "with authority" (Mark 1:27). Now his opponents in the Jerusalem power structure ask him where that authority has its origin. The time has not yet come—though it is now very near—for Jesus fully to reveal his identity. And his authority comes not from some external source but from who he is. Therefore he does not want to answer their question.

He avoids it by posing a clever counterquestion. John the Baptizer had no inherited or official authority for his vocation of baptizing for repentance. As readers of Mark, we know that John's authority came from his role as forerunner to Jesus, the Elijah figure of this Messiah, but people in the story do not know that secret. When Jesus asks where John got his authority, then, he is really throwing back at his opponents the same question, for John's authority comes from his relation to Jesus' authority. We learn, what we would otherwise not know, that John still has many supporters in Jerusalem. "The chief priests, the scribes, and the elders" are afraid to criticize him, but dare not admit that his authority came from God, since they did not undertake the repentance he demanded. Stumped, they have to admit that they do not know.

# 12:1–12
## *Parable of the Wicked Tenants*

The prophet Isaiah sang a love song for his beloved. The song told how his beloved had planted a vineyard, carefully tended, on fertile soil, with a watchtower in its midst. "He expected it to yield grapes, but it yielded wild grapes" (Isa. 5:2). He had done everything for the vineyard, but it had betrayed his efforts, so now he will abandon it and make it a waste.

In ancient Hebrew poetry, a vineyard could symbolize a lover. So at the end of the Song of Solomon, one of the lovers in the poem recalls how Solomon had a vineyard at Baal-hamon, so rich that each of its fruits would be sold for a thousand pieces of silver, but

> My vineyard, my very own, is for myself;
> You, O Solomon, may have the thousand.
> (Song 8:12)

Isaiah's love song, however, is a song of unrequited love. The vineyard produced only wild grapes. At another level, Isaiah's beloved is God, and God's vineyard is the people of Israel.

> For the vineyard of the LORD of hosts
>     is the house of Israel,
> and the people of Judah
>     are his pleasant planting;
> he expected justice,
>     but saw bloodshed;
> righteousness,
>     but heard a cry!
> (Isa. 5:7)

The prophet laments the people's failure to respond faithfully to God's love.

In Mark Jesus tells a parable like Isaiah's love song, but far more violent. The owner of this vineyard has rented it out to tenants and gone off to another country. When he sends slaves to collect the rent, the tenants kill them or beat them and drive them away, time after time. "He had still one other, a beloved son. Finally he sent him to them, saying, 'They will respect my son.' But those tenants said to one another, 'This is the heir; come, let us kill him, and the inheritance will be ours.' So they seized him, killed him, and threw him out of the vineyard" (12:6–8). Notice Mark's dramatic skill (particularly if one imagines the text read aloud): "He had still one other" leads us to expect one more servant, and thus "a beloved son" comes as a shock.

Christians have been too apt to read this simply as a story about Israel. We thus avoid thinking about the ways in which it is also a story about us. Even worse, such readings can begin attitudes that may turn into anti-Semitism. In the great arc of the biblical narratives, it is a story about all of humankind, beginning with the first sin in the garden. God has made us all stewards of a vineyard called earth, and we have turned to violence.

The strangest part of the story is the father's climactic action. After a whole series of servants has been killed, he sends his beloved son. Scholars debate the exact interpretation of Hebrew law, and whether tenants inherited land in the event of the only heir's death. However one resolves such questions, though, the central puzzle remains. Is this father out of his mind? How could he send his son off to likely death in the midst of these vicious tenants? As Mary Ann Tolbert has written, "For modern readers, centuries of familiarity with the image have diluted the absurd charity of endangering a relative in order to give murderers a final chance to turn around."[14] But "absurd charity" is of course what we will be reading about concerning God as Mark continues.

So what will the owner of the vineyard do? Jesus asks, "Have you not read this scripture: 'The stone that the builders rejected has become the cornerstone; this was the Lord's doing, and it is amazing in our eyes'?" The reference to the stone plays on the Hebrew words for "son" (*ben*) and "stone" (*'eben*). The quotation comes from Psalm 118:22–23, a psalm of thanksgiving recited at Passover and especially during the Feast of Booths. The Feast of Booths, probably originally a fall harvest festival and later a festival when good Jews lived outside in tents or booths in memory of their time in the wilderness after the exodus, had come to be identified as celebrating the day when Solomon completed building the first temple. Zechariah marks it as the time when, eschatologically, the nations will come to Jerusalem "year after year to worship the King, the Lord of hosts, and to keep the festival of booths" (Zech. 14:16). In the midst of a critique of what the temple has become, Jesus celebrates what it was at its foundation and what it might have become.

14. Tolbert, *Sowing the Gospel*, 236.

This talk of cornerstones further alludes to Isaiah 28:16:

> Therefore thus says the Lord GOD, ·
> "See, I am laying in Zion a foundation stone,
>     a tested stone,
> a precious cornerstone, a sure foundation."

The prophet is condemning the corrupt rulers and priests of his time who hope to save the nation through military alliances rather than trust in the Lord. They have "made a covenant with death,"

> for we have made lies our refuge,
>     and in falsehood we have taken shelter.
>                                         (Isa. 28:15)

But God will destroy their illusions:

> And I will make justice the line,
>     and righteousness the plummet;
> hail will sweep away the refuge of lies,
>     and waters will overwhelm the shelter.
> Then your covenant with death will be annulled,
>     and your agreement with Sheol will not stand.
>                                         (Isa. 28:17–18)

Standing in a temple built by Herod (corrupt and only half-Jewish, his power secured by alliance with Rome), Jesus recalls how one of Israel's greatest prophets saw that political and military alliances cannot in the end guarantee security—only trust in God can. Little wonder that those in power "realized that he had told this parable against them."

John Donahue and Daniel Harrington argue that the first twelve verses of Mark 12 encapsulate a whole Bible in miniature.[15] The reference to Isaiah's Song of the Vineyard speaks to the covenant

---

15. John R. Donahue and Daniel J. Harrington, *The Gospel of Mark*, SP (Collegeville, MN: Liturgical Press, 2002), 341–42.

between God and Israel. The allusion to one remaining beloved son recalls two key patriarchal stories: Abraham's near sacrifice of Isaac (Gen. 22) and his brothers' sale of Joseph (Gen. 37). The cornerstone passage, with its allusions to Psalm 118 and Isaiah, evokes both the greatness of the temple and the corruption that has long shamed it. The choice of the stone that the builders rejected touches on Jesus' teaching favoring outsiders and now the place of Jesus himself, rejected by his hometown and his family and soon by the leaders of the temple, as the cornerstone of a new covenant, with an amazing vindication in resurrection.

# 12:13–17
## *Second Question: Paying Taxes*

Mark turns next from the holy temple to imperial power. Jesus' opponents have shifted from specifically named groups to an anonymous "they," maneuvering behind the scenes to send Pharisees and Herodians to trap him. (The chief priests would have been Sadducees, and unlikely to get their opponents the Pharisees to run their errands. For that matter, the Pharisees, passionate about ritual purity, make for an odd alliance with Herodians. Everyone in power is ganging up on Jesus.) Earlier questions were straightforwardly antagonistic; this one is prefaced with hypocritical flattery: "We know that you are sincere, and show deference to no one; for you do not regard people with partiality, but teach the way of God in accordance with truth."

They pose a hard question. Should Jewish people pay taxes to the Roman emperor? The word translated "taxes" (*kēnsos*) referred specifically to the Roman "head tax" due for each inhabitant, which had long been controversial. Efforts to impose it in 6 CE led to the revolt of Judas the Galilean.[16] Judas's followers continued to work underground, and in the revolt of 66–70 the Zealots saw whether one paid the *kēnsos* as a crucial litmus test of faithful Judaism. Paying taxes to a foreign power was itself a bad thing, but it is also worth remembering a traditional Israelite suspicion of censuses. When God was angry

16. See Josephus, *Jewish Antiquities* 18.1–25; *Jewish War* 2.117–18.

with Israel, he incited King David to count the people (2 Sam. 24). After David had done it, he realized how greatly he had sinned, and indeed the Lord sent three days of pestilence over the nation. What was wrong with taking a census? Presumably it manifests a lack of faith. God will provide the nation's necessary strength. Finding out exactly how many people there are in the nation turns from trust in God to human accounting. And, of course, when one is doing it for the Romans, that makes it all the worse.

Jesus asks for a coin, a denarius, roughly the value of an ordinary workman's daily wage. Is it worth noting that Jesus has to ask—he does not have that kind of money? The coin would have had an image of the current Roman emperor, Tiberius, and an inscription reading "Son of the Divine Augustus." It would thus make reference to the imperial cult, with its claim that previous emperors became divine at their deaths. "Inscription" (*epigraphia*—the NRSV has "title") otherwise appears only once in Mark—in the "inscription" on Jesus' cross, "The King of the Jews." Jesus is declared (ironically, of course) to be king; the emperors claim to be God. One has to make choices. The coin, though, has the emperor's picture on it: "Give to the emperor the things that are the emperor's, and to God the things that are God's."

The Pharisees and Herodians "were utterly amazed at him," and Jesus had presumably won the day. But what did his retort mean? As a specific answer to the question, he seems to say, "Pay your taxes." Some pious Jews refused to touch Roman coins, and one might take Jesus to be saying, "If you have bought into the Roman system and use imperial coins, you are in no position to pull out when tax time comes." Interestingly, whereas the question in verse 14 is, "Should we give/pay taxes or not?" Jesus' reply in verse 17 is, "Give/pay *back* to the emperor the things that are the emperor's," as if to say, "Get rid of all this imperial coinage; send it back where it came from." It is worth mentioning again that Jesus himself did not have a denarius. His advice, then, is that those involved in the imperial political economic system should pay their taxes, with just a hint that maybe a life outside that system could be possible. "Give to God the things that are God's"—does that not include everything?

## 12:18–27
### *Third Question: Marriage and the Resurrection*

The Sadducees (appearing here for the only time in Mark) come with another question. Their name literally meant "sons of Zadok," who was high priest under David and Solomon, though they did not claim any literal lineage. Their party did center on the temple as a kind of priestly aristocracy, and the high priest was usually a Sadducee. As Josephus writes, the Sadducees had "the confidence of the wealthy alone, but no following among the populace."[17] Since they were mostly confined to Jerusalem, it is no surprise that Jesus never encountered them in Galilee.

In contrast to the Pharisees, they accepted the authority of the written law only, not oral additions to the law. Thus they rejected newfangled beliefs appearing in Judaism like the existence of angels or the resurrection of the dead.[18] They presumably held to the ancient Jewish idea that a good fate involved living to a ripe old age and having lots of descendants—no need to think of anything beyond some very shadowy existence, if existence at all, after we die.

Hence their question. The written law ("Moses wrote for us") required the custom of levirate marriage. If a married man died without a son, his brother was to marry his widow, and treat their first child as the child of the deceased "so that his name may not be blotted out of Israel" (Deut. 25:6). It seems the custom was not much followed by Jesus' time. Still, Jesus' questioners imagine a woman who has gone through seven brothers in this way, each marrying her after the death of another. "In the resurrection whose wife will she be? For the seven had married her." An unlikely story. Indeed, Chrysostom remarks that he does not believe this could have happened, "For the third would not have taken her, when he saw the two bridegrooms dead; or if the third, yet not the fourth or the fifth; and if even these, much more the sixth or the seventh would not have come to the woman, but have shrunk from her."[19]

---

17. Josephus, *Jewish Antiquities* 13.298, *Josephus* 7, trans. Ralph Marcus, LCL (Cambridge: Harvard University Press, 1943), 377.
18. Acts 23:8; Josephus, *Jewish Antiquities* 18.16–17.
19. Chrysostom, *Homilies on Matthew* 70.2 (*NPNF*, 1st ser., 10:428).

The Sadducees' point is that the idea of resurrection is incompatible with the Deuteronomic law. Levirate marriage would create too much chaos in the afterlife. Moreover, if the dead are raised, then even the childless can have continued existence. The sense that dying without a child deprives one of any future fades away, and therefore the need for levirate marriage. Jesus rejects their argument on two counts. First they have a wrong understanding of the afterlife, "for when they rise from the dead, they neither marry nor are given in marriage, but are like angels in heaven." Similarly the Talmud quotes Rav (from the third century CE): "The world to come is not like this world. In the world to come there is no eating, or drinking, or procreation, or business, or jealousy or hatred or competition; but the righteous sit with crowns on their heads feasting on the radiance of the divine presence."[20]

Nothing indicates that Jesus was an enemy of marriage. Of the Twelve, at least Peter was married. Jesus welcomes children and makes the rules about divorce even stricter. He never holds the unmarried or celibate up as better or special. Yet he is a critic of marriage as it exists in his society, where the woman is treated as the man's property. (Significantly, the Sadducees' question takes for granted that one man might, in levirate marriage, have several wives, but cannot accept the idea that, in the afterlife, one woman might have several husbands.) His criticism of divorce practices rejects the idea that men can divorce their wives on trivial grounds while women cannot divorce their husbands. He imagines an ideal family without a patriarchal father. A remarkable number of the women with whom he comes into special relation seem to be without husbands. Marriage as it existed in his culture could not be part of an eternal human state.

Second, Jesus argues in favor of resurrection by citing the story of Moses and the burning bush, where God said to Moses, "'I am the God of Abraham, the God of Isaac, and the God of Jacob'" (Exod. 3:6). Abraham, Isaac, and Jacob had died, but God "is God not of the dead but of the living," therefore the patriarchs must have ongo

20. *Berakhot* 17a, in *The Talmud: Selected Writings*, trans. Ben Zion Bokser (New York: Paulist Press, 1989), 72.

ing life beyond their deaths. Jesus' argument beats the Sadducees at their own game, since he bases it on a text from the written law, but it persuades few if any readers today of the reality of resurrection. Even in Mark, it may function like the arguments early in some of Plato's dialogues, where Socrates is simply showing his interlocutor that he has not thought through his own position very well.

Jesus tells the Sadducees that they do not know the power of God. Even death is not too great an opponent for that power. The Sadducees may not worry overmuch about such things. They hold high positions of honor; when death comes, they can look back on a good life and perhaps be satisfied. Jesus speaks for the outsiders, life's disenfranchised, whom life has often broken through poverty or tragedy. If God is to be their God too, then death cannot be the end of their stories.

## 12:28–34
### *Fourth Question: The First Commandment*

The first thing to note about this question, from a scribe, is Jesus' respect for the questioner. The question is sincere, the scribe's response to Jesus is wise, and Jesus tells him, "You are not far from the kingdom of God." Mark may have been writing at a time of tension between church and synagogue, but he goes out of his way to indicate that not all Jewish scholars were corrupt or were Jesus' opponents.

The scribe asks which commandment is first of all, and Jesus answers, again citing the written law, quoting Deuteronomy 6:5 on loving God and Leviticus 19:18 on loving one's neighbor. Such summaries can be found in the rabbis. The Babylonian Talmud tells how, when a Gentile asked Shammai to "teach me the whole Torah while I stand on one foot," Shammai drove him off with a stick; but, given the same challenge, Hillel replied, "That which is hateful to you, do not do to others, the rest is commentary."[21] Philo cited as a well-known principle that the first five of the Ten Commandments

---

21. *Shabbat* 31a, in ibid., 87.

concern love of God, while the last five address love of neighbor.[22] Just as it is important to note that Mark portrays this scribe in a sympathetic light, so it is worth remembering that Jesus was not saying anything radically new or at odds with the Jewish tradition.

He does modify his sources a bit. Deuteronomy says that we should love God with all our heart, soul, and might. Jesus adds "with all your mind." He wants us to *think*. As Thomas More declares in Robert Bolt's *A Man for All Seasons*, "God made the angels to show him splendor—as he made the animals for innocence and plants for their simplicity. But Man he made to serve him wittily, in the tangle of his mind."[23] And *all* our mind. Christian faith does not imply there are thoughts we should not explore, questions we should not ask, or subjects we should not investigate. To have faith in God with all our mind is precisely to believe that nothing we can learn or discover could ever be a threat to belief in God.

Further, we should love our neighbors, and there should be no limits on who counts as a neighbor. No one has made the point better than John Wesley:

> *Thy neighbor*—that is, not only thy friend, thy kinsman, or thy acquaintance; not only the virtuous, the friendly, him that loves thee, that prevents or returns thy kindness; but every child of man, every human creature, every soul which God hath made; not excepting him whom thou never hast seen in the flesh, whom thou knowest not either by face or by name; not excepting him whom thou knowest to be evil and unthankful, him that still despitefully uses and persecutes thee: Him thou shalt love *as thyself*.[24]

Karl Barth points out the place of "hidden neighbors" in the Hebrew Scripture—those like Melchizedek, Balaam, Rahab, Ruth, Hiram of Tyre, and Cyrus (and later the magi), who are not part of the Hebrew people, not in any explicit covenant with God, and who sometimes appear in the story quite mysteriously, yet who are clearly presented

22. Philo, *Decalogue* 22.
23. Robert Bolt, *A Man for All Seasons* (New York: Vintage, 1990), 126.
24. John Wesley, "Sermon 7: The Way to the Kingdom," *The Works of John Wesley*, 3rd ed. (repr. Grand Rapids: Baker, 1979), 5:79.

as good people doing God's will.[25] So, he continues, Christians should be open to see unexpected folk outside the church as cooperating in God's plans.

> Love does no wrong to a neighbor; therefore, love is the fulfilling of the law.
> —Romans 13:10

Leviticus does not rest with the abstraction that we ought to love our neighbors. The verses leading up to that statement specify a series of specific applications. Farmers should leave some crops around the edge of the field and some of the grapes in the vineyard "for the poor and the alien" (Lev. 19:10). People should neither steal nor defraud. Laborers should be paid promptly, and no one should take advantage of the handicapped (Lev. 19:13–14). Maximizing profit at all costs and cutting corners are contrary to love of neighbor.

## FURTHER REFLECTIONS
### *Love*

Like Leviticus, Jesus says you should love your neighbor *as yourself*. Does that assume that you should love yourself? A long Christian tradition said yes. "A man who loves God is not wrong in loving himself," Augustine affirmed.[26] Aquinas elaborated. As he put it, love is a unitive force, and human beings ought to be one with themselves.[27] We might say that physical, mental, and spiritual health involve putting a positive value on ourselves. Quoting Aristotle, Aquinas notes that "the origin of friendly relations with others lies in our relations to ourselves."[28] We cannot help others as well as we should if we are not healthy within ourselves, and therefore we need to concern ourselves with our own health.

The Reformers broke radically with this tradition. With characteristic bluntness, Luther wrote:

---

25. Barth, *CD* I/2:425.

26. Augustine, *The City of God* 19.14, trans. Henry Bettenson (Harmondsworth, Middlesex: Penguin, 1972), 873.

27. Thomas Aquinas, *Summa theologica* 2a2ae.25.4, trans. Fathers of the English Dominican Province (Westminster, MD: Christian Classics, 1981), 1282.

28. Ibid., quoting Aristotle, *Nicomachean Ethics* 9.4.8.

Charity is love not for oneself but for another. . . . Therefore to please our neighbor means not to please oneself. . . . For as long as we must use each good for ourselves, we are not concerned about our neighbor. But true love for yourself is hatred for yourself. . . . Therefore he who hates himself and loves his neighbor, this person truly loves himself. For he loves himself outside of himself.[29]

Calvin took much the same line, seeing self-love as something that needs to be overcome if we are truly to love our neighbors:

We shall never love our neighbors with sincerity . . . till we have corrected the love of ourselves. The two affections are opposite and contradictory; for the love of ourselves leads us to neglect and despise others—produces cruelty, covetousness, violence, deceit, and all kindred vices. . . . Our Lord therefore enjoins that it be changed into the love of our neighbor.[30]

Such defenses of self-hatred or at least overcoming self-love are problematic at several levels. First, they do not seem quite in accord with Scripture. Jesus tells us to love our neighbors *as* ourselves, not *instead* of ourselves. Second, they presuppose a faulty psychology. The Reformers assumed that everyone has too much self-love—we need to cure ourselves of it. As Barth put it, "God will never think of blowing on this fire, which is bright enough already."[31] But some people *do* need to be encouraged in self-love. Abused wives, abandoned children, the severely depressed, and others need to hear that they are of value, they are among the elements of God's good creation.

We can clarify these matters if we understand a bit more what it means to love. The old joke states: "Do not do unto others what you would have them do unto you. Their tastes may be different." Indeed. Just because you love ice fishing, you do not manifest love to me by arranging a full day out on the lake. I do not show my love

---

29. Martin Luther, *Lectures on Romans*, Scholia on Rom. 15:2, trans. Jacob A. O. Preus, LW 25 (St. Louis: Concordia Publishing House, 1972), 512.

30. John Calvin, *Commentary on Galatians* (on Gal. 5:14), trans. William Pringle, Calvin's Commentaries (repr. Grand Rapids: Baker, 1979), 161.

31. Barth, *CD* I/2:388.

to an ascetic by providing her with a banquet. On the other hand, I do not necessarily show my love to you by giving you whatever your tastes lead you most to desire. I should not let you stuff yourself with sweets in spite of the doctor's warnings about the onset of diabetes. I certainly do not show love to a pedophile by arranging sex tourism to Thailand. Rather, we manifest our love for others by helping them move toward what is good for them—even if they now resist that good. Similarly, then, we should love ourselves, moving ourselves toward what is good for us. Just as I do not help you move toward what is good for you by indulging your every whim, so self-love is not about indulging my own whims. You and I are both creatures of God. There is a way we are made by God to be, and that is our final good. We should help each other toward that good—and help ourselves as well.

When the scribe asks Jesus what the first commandment is, Jesus does not exactly answer. He gives two rather than one. One can take "The first is . . ." and "The second is . . ." as offering a rank ordering, but these phrases might also simply distinguish items in a list of equals. Not surprisingly, Christian thinkers have debated the relation between these two commandments. Augustine was clear on the priority of loving God. We should love either ourselves or others not on our own account but on account of God.[32] He distinguishes between things to be enjoyed, that make us happy (what modern philosophers would call "intrinsic goods"), and things to be used, that "assist us and give us a boost, so to speak, as we press on toward happiness" (what modern philosophers would call "instrumental goods").[33] We should endeavor, he says, to enjoy only God and merely use other things: "So in this mortal life we are like travelers away from the Lord: if we wish to return to the homeland where we can be happy, we must use this world, not enjoy it."[34]

Calvin agreed that love of God "ranks higher," but he pointed out that the character of our love of God is hidden from human eyes.

---

32. Augustine, *On Christian Teaching* 1.22, trans. R. P. H. Green (Oxford: Oxford University Press, 1997), 17.
33. Ibid., 1.4, 9.
34. Ibid., 10.

We cannot observe someone else's inward piety, and hypocrites may well go through the outward motions as faithfully as the truly pious. "God therefore chooses to make trial of our love of himself by that love of our brother, which he enjoins us to cultivate."[35] We can observe whether people are helping their brothers and sisters, and thereby we can judge their love of God (see Matt. 25:31–46). The twentieth-century Catholic theologian Karl Rahner pushed this interpretation one step further. For him, it was not just that love of neighbor *shows* love of God but that it *is* love of God: "We accomplish what is the love of God in Christ when we allow the love of our neighbor to attain its own nature and perfection."[36] "The categorized explicit love of neighbor is the primary act of the love of God. . . . Whoever does not love the brother whom he 'sees' also cannot love God whom he does not see, and . . . one can love God whom one does not see only *by* loving one's brother lovingly."[37]

Jesus, however, lists *two* commandments, and I think we should honor his answer to the scribe's question. To be sure, the two are related. As the Venerable Bede wrote, "Neither of these [two kinds of love] is capable of being perfect without the other, because God cannot be loved apart from our neighbor, nor our neighbor apart from God."[38] But, if related, they are different. In a wonder and awe at nature that then goes beyond nature to its holy Creator, we are loving God in a way that has little if anything to do with love of neighbor. At the same time (though this is a more ambiguous case) I think there can be moments of immediate compassion for another human being that do not get to their end by way of God. I do not always have to say, "Maria, who is drowning, is a child of God, and therefore I will rescue her." I can rescue her simply because she is a human being, or simply because she is Maria.

Still, the first commandment does have a kind of priority, just as Christ's divinity has a kind of priority over his humanity. To love any

35. Calvin, *Commentary on Galatians* (on Gal. 5:14), 159–60.

36. Karl Rahner, *Theological Investigations* 6, trans. Karl-H. and Boniface Kruger (New York: Crossroad, 1982), 247.

37. Ibid.

38. Bede, the Venerable, *Homilies on the Gospels* 2.22, trans. Lawrence T. Martin and David Hurst (Kalamazoo, MI: Cistercian Publishing, 1991), 220.

creature as unconditionally as we should love God is a form of idolatry. I should not wish your good without any reflection on your relation to other people or the rest of creation. (If it involved too much harm to others, it would not really be your good.) I can immediately love another person without reflection on that person's relation to

> The love of God is the beginning of religion, for God will not have the forced obedience of [humans], but wishes their service to be free and spontaneous.
>
> —John Calvin
>
> *Commentary on Matthew*, 22:37.

God, but, on reflection, I will always recognize that anyone deserves love as a creature of God. I can think of cases like mystic contemplation where love of God, even on reflection, is simply love of God; love of neighbor always connects with the neighbor's status as creature of God if I think about it long enough.

## 12:35–40

### *Fifth Question: How Can the Scribes Say the Christ Is the Son of David?*

After Jesus has answered four questions so effectively, "no one dared to ask him any question." Jesus poses his own question, coming back indirectly to the central issue of his identity: "How can the scribes say that the Christ is the son of David?" (Here again I diverge from the NRSV in saying "Christ" rather than "Messiah" on the principle that when Mark wants to switch from Greek to Hebrew he does, and here he stays in Greek.) The anointed one ("Messiah" or "Christ") is the one many Jews were hoping for, in various and sometimes inconsistent ways, to bring an end to the evils of the present age and bring in God's reign. Looking back to the greatest of their kings, some referred to the Messiah as "son of David," meaning either literally a descendant of David or more loosely a leader who would be like David—a great political and military figure who would make Israel a great nation once again. It is that picture of messianic hope that Jesus wants to challenge.

Jesus and his audience and Mark and his audience would all probably have assumed that David was the author of all the Psalms, so it
would have seemed natural to quote Psalm 110:1 (the single text
from the Hebrew Scriptures most often quoted in the New Testament) as the voice of David. David wrote, we are told, "by the Holy
Spirit"—Mark's clearest reference to the inspiration of Scripture (by
which he would have meant the Hebrew Scriptures). In that text
"the Lord" (God) speaks to someone David calls "my Lord," whom
he puts at his right hand until his enemies shall be defeated. "At my
right hand," Calvin notes, "is used metaphorically for the second
or next rank, which is occupied by God's deputy. . . . This mode of
expression, therefore, does not denote any particular place."[39] This
deputy of God must be the Messiah, Jesus here argues; he cannot
be David's descendant if he is David's "Lord." "Lord" (*kyrios*), rather
than "son of David," is thus the more appropriate term to apply to
the Messiah.

*Kyrios* is a tricky word, since it can be used to mean "God" or any
human superior. Commenting on the text, the anonymous author of
the second-century work called the *Epistle of Barnabas* (which was
sometimes included in early editions of the New Testament) proclaims, "Behold how David calls him Lord and Son of God."[40] For
that author the passage clearly affirms Jesus' full divinity, and Mark
seems to mean something of the sort as well (without necessarily
having thought through the categories for saying it). What would be
the point, after all, of denying that the Messiah is David's son only to
say that he is some sort of human lord?

In Jesus' first public teaching (Mark 1:27) the people recognize
that he has authority and wonder who he is. Here at the end of his
public teaching, we get an answer—really a summary of answers
already given. Yes, he is the one you have been waiting for, the Messiah, the one who will change the world in its present form; but, no,
he is not going to be a political or military leader. Rather, he is God
come among us.

39. Calvin, *Harmony of the Evangelists*, 3:70.
40. *Epistle of Barnabas* 12 (ANF 1:145).

God comes as a servant, not a commander. Jesus makes the point by condemning those who put themselves in places of importance. Ancient NT manuscripts come without punctuation, and here that creates an ambiguity. One can read verse 38 as, "Beware of the scribes who like to walk around in long robes . . ." (that is, do not necessarily beware of all the scribes, but just those who . . .); or as, "Beware of the scribes, who like to walk around in long robes . . ." (that is, beware of all the scribes, for they are all people who . . .). Neither is obviously the correct interpretation, but, given that we have just met a scribe who "answered wisely" and is "not far from the reign of God," it seems appropriately generous to assume that not all scribes are here being condemned. Beware of those who hold the chief seats, Augustine writes, "Not because they hold them, but because they love them."[41] Those who are condemned put on a good appearance of piety, praying long prayers, but what they seek is honor and wealth.

Here once again it is wrong to infer from the text simply that some religious leaders in first-century Judaism were corrupt. Some religious leaders have sought fame and wealth in every place and time. Twenty-first-century widows can be as vulnerable to a smooth-talking preacher as first-century widows were to smooth-talking scribes. Even when religion is not in obvious ways corrupt, it can still manifest, as Reinhold Niebuhr says, the worst kind of pride:

> Religion is not simply as is generally supposed an inherently virtuous human quest for God. It is merely the final battle-ground between God and man's self-esteem. In that battle even the most pious practices may be instruments of human pride. . . . The worst form of intolerance is religious intolerance, in which the particular interests of the contestants hide behind religious absolutes. The worst form of self-assertion is religious self-assertion in which under the guise of contrition before God, He is claimed as the exclusive ally of our contingent self.[42]

---

41. Augustine, *Sermons on New Testament Lessons* 41.5 (*NPNF*, 1st ser., 6:399).
42. Reinhold Niebuhr, *The Nature and Destiny of Man* (2 vols.; New York: Charles Scribner's Sons, 1941), 1:200–201.

# 12:41–44

## *The Widow's Contribution*

Everyone used to know what this story means, but some contemporary scholars have challenged that interpretation. Jesus and his disciples are sitting in the temple, watching people drop their contributions into "the treasury." Many rich people make large gifts, and then a poor widow puts in two copper coins, worth only a penny; but, since they were all she had, Jesus says that she has given more than all the rest. We do not know how public the giving was, if Jesus could see how many coins she put in, and, for that matter, how Jesus knows that this is all the money she has.

The standard interpretation is that, as Eugene Boring puts it, Jesus is holding the woman up as an example.[43] She gives all that she has, just as Jesus is about to give all that he has, his very life—and this is a model for Christians. Calvin writes that the passage teaches the poor that their gifts are valuable even if small, and the rich that they should not be proud just because their gifts are large.[44] This is a good lesson for debates in local churches today about who gave the most to the annual pledge drive.

In a 1982 article, however, Addison Wright argued that Jesus lamented the widow's contribution. Jesus has just made the point, Wright noted, that the temple system is full of corruption—the widow's gift will likely be used for purposes far less worthy than feeding herself. Moreover, in the very next passage, Jesus declares that the temple is about to be destroyed. "Her contribution was totally misguided, thanks to the encouragement of official religion, but the final irony of it all was that it was also a waste."[45] Anything contributed to temple upkeep will soon have its fruits demolished by Roman soldiers. In sum, then, Wright concludes, while Jesus pities the widow rather than condemning her, he "condemns the value system that motivates her action, and he condemns the people who conditioned her to do it."[46]

43. Boring, *Mark*, 352.
44. Calvin, *Harmony of the Evangelists*, 3:114.
45. Addison G. Wright, "The Widow's Mite—Praise or Lament?" *CBQ* 44 (1982): 263.
46. Ibid., 262.

Wright's account (followed by Ched Myers and others) seems to rest on too pragmatic a basis. Do we really want to "lament" every good deed that does not result in a useful payoff? Early martyrs died for their faith rather than putting a pinch of incense on the altar of the emperor. Some inspired others to become Christians, but some died with their heroism unknown or soon forgotten. Some Christians today put long efforts into trying to turn around the life of a child who has been subject to years of abuse and neglect—and largely fail. Can we not say, as Jesus will soon say of the woman who anoints his head at the house of Simon the leper, "she has done what she could," and celebrate what she has done?

Nevertheless, this alternate interpretation carries with it a good warning. Giving to the church is not always the right thing to do with one's money. We have other responsibilities too. Churches should therefore not always urge without qualification that people give sacrificially before thinking about how much the church needs the money and what other needs it might serve. Further, those who spend money given to the church should always remember that it comes, always figuratively and sometimes literally, from "coins people put in the collection plate," and exercise prudent stewardship.

## 13:1–8
### *Foretellings (1): The Destruction of the Temple*

In chapter 13 Jesus' teaching moves from public controversies to private lessons for his disciples. Chapter 13 speaks in the language of apocalyptic, with predictions and warnings about the future, especially about future catastrophes. It was a language familiar to Jesus' audience and to Mark's, a style of thinking that had given up on practical reforms to look forward to transformation by divine intervention. In difficult times, with prophecy seemingly at an end and no more kings of Israel, Jews turned increasingly to apocalyptic texts, often cast as secret texts revealed long ago to famous figures in Israel's history and predicting a series of catastrophes that would culminate in the end of the present age and the beginning of God's reign.

Yet there are ways in which Mark 13 is not an apocalyptic text. Jesus, as usual, speaks on his own authority, without appeal to the secret messages of some ancient sage. He cites no visions. Careful reading of the text makes clear just how few specific predictions it makes; indeed, its conclusion is that even Jesus does not know the exact shape of the future. The point is to be ready whenever it comes.

Jesus begins with a specific prediction: the temple and surrounding buildings will be destroyed; "not one stone will be left here upon another." Indeed, this is roughly what happened in 70, though Josephus reports that some towers and a portion of the city wall remained standing.[47] Indeed, the western wall of the temple, the so-called Wailing Wall, remains standing today. Historians trying to figure out whether Mark was written before or after 70 cite evidence on both sides: he must have written after 70, since he has Jesus predict the destruction of the temple; no, he must have written before 70, since he does not offer many details and gets some of what happened wrong.

Neither sort of argument seems entirely persuasive. The emperor Caligula planned to erect a statue of himself in the temple around 40, and this would have produced a violent response. With wars and threats of war constantly in the air, even if one doubts that Jesus had some special ability to see into the future, it would have been a good guess that Roman armies would soon be fighting in Jerusalem, and that their victory would lead to the destruction of the temple. On the other hand, if the temple had been destroyed by the time Mark was writing, it is contrary to his style here to fill in a list of accurate details. Indeed, the basic theme of Jesus' "predictions" is, "Do not think you have figured out the details; do not assume that the first disaster is a sign of the imminent end. All sorts of things are going to happen first." In that sense, it is almost anti-apocalyptic.

It is understandable that Jesus' disciples, mostly from the countryside, would have been impressed by the temple Herod had built. It occupied a platform of over 900 by 1,500 feet, and the front of the temple building itself stood 150 feet tall and 150 feet wide, made of white stone, much of it covered with silver and gold, by far the most

---

47. Josephus, *Jewish War* 7.1–4.

impressive building any of them had seen, glowing in the sunlight. Little wonder that they were amazed by it all—and then little wonder at Jesus' frustration that they had not yet understood his teaching that God was now present in him and not in the temple. "Look, Teacher," they say at the magnificence of the temple, much as Peter said, "Rabbi, look! The fig tree that you cursed has withered." They do not understand that the temple will be destroyed just as the fig tree was. Peter, James, John, and Andrew draw Jesus aside for a question. Andrew had dropped from the inner circle, but now, near the end of Jesus' ministry, he reappears in the place he occupied at that ministry's very beginning.

They want to know what is going to happen, and Jesus says that many terrible things will happen (a safe bet in first-century Palestine), but that they should not jump to the conclusion that bad times announce the immediate end of the present age. Preachers throughout Christian history have been eager to identify some particular event as the precursor of the end, but Jesus warns specifically against this. Many will come saying, "I am he"—again the "I am" that echoes God's self-revelation in Exodus 3:14. About the time Mark was written, indeed, leaders of the Jewish rebellion like Menahem and Simon bar Giora were claiming to be, or being identified by their followers as, the Messiah. Mark is not imagining a purely theoretical possibility. Christians in any period who see the end at hand need to remember that such predictions came within a generation of Jesus' death and have been coming, on and off, ever since.

# 13:9–13

## *Foretellings (2): Persecution*

Jesus next predicts that those who follow him will be persecuted. The book of Acts records nearly all the events he describes as having happened in the early church before Mark was written—beatings, standing before governors, divisions within families, becoming the objects of hatred. Here too, though, if following Jesus meant claiming that the Messiah had come in a totally unexpected form and challenging both religious and political authority, it surely did not take much insight to expect persecution. And "following Jesus" is what he expects those he is addressing to do, for they will be "handed over," the verb used repeatedly for what is about to happen to Jesus.

Jesus' account of the horrors to come reaches a climax with reference to betrayals within families: "brother will betray brother to death, and a father his child, and children will rise against parents and have them put to death." It is worth remembering how often conversion to Christianity divided families. A Christian in the family was like a critic of the government in the family under Stalin or Hitler; everyone else's career and respectable social position might be damaged. Sacrifices to various gods were an ordinary part of political and social life. Suddenly, one member of the family could not take part, and this in a society where obedience within the family was generally taken for granted. Worst of all would be if the new Christian was a woman, who would have been thought to have almost no independent rights. Perpetua, martyred in North Africa in 203, tells how her father begged her to abandon Christianity, and, when she refused, "was so angered by the word 'Christian' that he moved towards me as though he would pluck my eyes out." Later he begs her, "Do not abandon me to be the reproach of men. Think of your brothers, think of your mother and your aunt, think of your child, who will not be able to live once you are gone. Give up your pride! You will destroy all of us!"[48] But she would not bend.

## FURTHER REFLECTIONS
### *The Holy Spirit*

The Holy Spirit here makes one of only a few appearances in Mark. After the Spirit's presence at Jesus' baptism (and John's declaration that Jesus will baptize with the Holy Spirit, Mark 1:8), the Spirit drives Jesus into the wilderness (1:12), and there is the cryptic warning against the unforgivable sin against the Holy Spirit (3:29). At 12:36 Jesus describes David as inspired "by the Holy Spirit" in writing

---

48. *The Martyrdom of Perpetua*, in *The Acts of the Christian Martyrs*, trans. Herbert Musurillo (Oxford: Oxford University Press, 1972), 109, 113.

the Psalms, and here he reassures his disciples that, when they are brought to trial and "handed over," they will know what to say, "for it is not you who speak, but the Holy Spirit." The Spirit functions, then, (1) in baptism, (2) in inspiring the authors of Scripture, and (3) in inspiring Christian witness in times of trial.

Certainly Mark does not assert that the Holy Spirit is God, let alone that the Spirit is one of three persons in the divine substance. He does write out of an experience of the Spirit, and, as Eduard Schweitzer wrote, "Long before the Spirit was a theme of doctrine, He was a fact in the experience of the community."[49] Indeed, as the contemporary Orthodox theologian Pavel Florensky puts it, "It is quite evident that the holy fathers know something from their own experience; but what is even clearer is that this knowledge is so deeply hidden away, so 'unaccountable,' so unspeakable, that they lack the power to clothe it in precise language."[50]

Mark would have experienced the power of the Holy Spirit. Living in a community at least under threat of persecution, he knew that Christians had unexpected courage and articulateness when they faced such threats. He saw the strange power of baptism to shape Christians' lives. All the allusions he makes to the Hebrew Scriptures make clear that he found them speaking God's word. In his narrative he tells how the Spirit is inspiring and guiding Christ, so that the logic would be that one cannot say less of the Spirit than one says of Christ. Thus as Basil asked centuries later, "When we speak of the dispensations made for man by our great God and Saviour Jesus Christ, who will gainsay their having been accomplished through the grace of the Spirit? ... In the first place He was made an unction ... After this every operation was wrought with the co-operation of the Spirit."[51] Thus in the fourth century Gregory Nazianzus finally took the step of declaring the Spirit to be God:

49. Eduard Schweitzer, "*pneuma*," *Theological Dictionary of the New Testament*, ed. Gerhard Kittel and Gerhard Friedrich, trans. G. W. Bromiley (Grand Rapids: Eerdmans, 1968), 6:396. Since I wrote this book as Kilian McDonnell Writer in Residence at the Collegeville Institute, it is a particular pleasure to give credit for much of what follows to Kilian McDonnell, *The Other Hand of God* (Collegeville, MN: Liturgical Press, 2003).
50. Pavel Florensky, "On the Holy Spirit," in *Ultimate Questions: An Anthology of Modern Russian Religious Thought*, ed. Alexander Schmemann (New York: Holt, Rinehart, and Winston, 1965), 141.
51. Basil, *On the Holy Spirit* 16.39 (*NPNF*, 2nd ser., 8:25).

> For if He is not to be worshipped, how can He deify me by
> Baptism? But if He is to be worshipped, surely He is an Object
> of adoration, and if an Object of adoration he must be
> God.... Look at these facts: Christ is born; the Spirit is His fore-
> runner. He is baptized; the Spirit bears witness; He is tempted;
> the Spirit leads Him up. He works miracles; the Spirit accom-
> panies them.... What great things are there in the idea of God
> which are not in His power?[52]

The Spirit is the divine person who most directly encounters
people. Christian experience begins with the Holy Spirit, who leads
us to the Word, who leads us in turn to the Father. Christ is God's
self-revelation, but it is only through the Spirit that we can understand who Christ is. As Irenaeus says, "Without the Spirit it is not possible to see the Word of God, and without the Son one is not able
to approach the Father, for the knowledge of the Father is the Son,
and the knowledge of the Son of God is through the Holy Spirit."[53]
In the times of trial that Jesus is promising lie ahead, times of trial
Mark may have known firsthand, it was that knowledge that would
sustain Christians.

# 13:14–23
### *Foretellings (3): The Desolating Sacrilege*

Mark's account of the horrors to come now apparently moves from
the general to the specific—there will be "the desolating sacrilege set
up where it ought not to be." For the only time in the Gospel Mark
addresses his readers directly; he steps outside the framework of the
story to insert an authorial parenthesis: "(let the reader understand)."
Mark's original audience must have been able to catch a quite specific
reference. Modern readers, unfortunately, cannot. The "desolating
sacrilege" comes from Daniel 12:11, where it presumably refers to an
altar to Zeus set up in the Jerusalem temple by the Hellenistic king

---

52. Gregory of Nazianzus, Oration 31.28–29 (*NPNF*, 2nd ser., 7:327).
53. Irenaeus, *On the Apostolic Preaching*, trans. John Behr (Crestwood, NY: St. Vladimir's
    Seminary Press, 1997), 44.

Antiochus Epiphanes in 168 BCE as part of his effort to hellenize the Jewish people, an effort that led to the Maccabean rebellion (see 1 Macc. 1:54–59). So Mark is referring to another event like that one, an event his first readers will recognize. "Sacrilege" is a neuter noun, but "set up" is a masculine perfect participle; this inconsistency *might* imply a statue—a thing that could be treated as a person. A number of candidates can be considered possibilities. The emperor Caligula threatened to erect a statue of himself in the temple in 40; the plan came to nothing only because of his death. When the Zealots took over the temple in 67 or 68, they used it as a military headquarters, allowing the animals they were using for food to graze all around. Critical as they were of the established temple authorities, who had cooperated with the Romans, they invested a man named Phanni as high priest in a satiric ritual. In 70, when Titus's Roman soldiers took the temple, they set up the standards of their legion and made sacrifices to them. Mark, and any pious Jew, would have found any of these events a "desolating sacrilege."

Whatever the sacrilege may have been, Mark's advice to his readers is that, when it has been set up, they ought to flee, and as quickly as possible. Most modern scholars have rejected the historicity of a tradition that Christians fled from Jerusalem to Pella early in the Jewish War in response to an oracle, but a few recent writers have made a case for its truth.[54] Still, it is hard to think that Mark is referring to a historical event here. It makes little sense to urge people to "flee to the hills" (my trans.) from Jerusalem, which is already as high up as the surrounding territory, and in the crucial stages of the war Jerusalem was under siege and one could not have fled. In general the situation Mark describes does not fit the details of what happened during the Jewish War. Moreover, once again Jesus here, having issued warnings about the future, in turn warns against jumping to conclusions. People will say, "Look! Here is the Messiah!" or "Look! There he is!" but Mark, paraphrasing a similar passage in Deuteronomy 13:1–5, urges his readers not to believe them. The ability to produce signs and omens proves nothing. What matters is to be alert.

54. See Vicky Balabanski, *Eschatology in the Making* (Cambridge: Cambridge University Press, 1997).

## 13:24–27
### Foretellings (4): The Coming of the Son of Man

Mark's story is not just one of judgment and tribulation, nor is it confined to the environs of Jerusalem. He is telling us the story of the presence in this world of God, the Creator of all things. The story thus culminates with the darkening of the sun and moon and the falling of stars from heaven. Will this plunge the world into darkness? No, Barth says, quoting Isaiah:

> The sun shall no longer be your light by day,
>     nor for brightness shall the moon give light to you by night;
> but the LORD will be your everlasting light.
>
> (Isa. 60:19)

Or, in the words of Revelation 22:5, "the city has no need of sun or moon to shine on it, for the glory of God is its light, and its lamp is the Lamb."[55] This is obviously symbolic language. At minimum it means that, no matter what catastrophes may come, God's protection will remain. God's power reaches beyond the power of Roman armies to the whole universe.

The Son of Man promised in Daniel 7:13 will in the end come, and Mark's readers will now have inferred that Jesus is that Son of Man. His coming is not about judgment but about rescue. Notice that in Mark 13:20 no one would be saved if the Lord did not cut short the days of suffering and bring the Son of Man, as it were, ahead of schedule. Both verses 20 and 27 refer to a gathering of "the elect," but Mark does not here specify who they are, and he makes no mention of a corresponding class of nonelect. What is clear is that they will come "from the ends of the earth to the ends of heaven." As Howard Kee has written, "there are not social or ethnic prerequisites for admission to the covenant community."[56] Jesus is drawing on the universalistic theme in Judaism, represented by Isaiah's promise:

---

55. Barth, CD III/1:121.
56. Howard Clark Kee, *Community of the New Age: Studies in Mark's Gospel* (Philadelphia: Westminster, 1977), 115.

Do not let the foreigner joined to the LORD say,
　"The LORD will surely separate me from his people. . . ."
And the foreigners who join themselves to the LORD,
　to minister to him, to love the name of the LORD, and to be
　　his servants,
all who keep the sabbath, and do not profane it,
　and hold fast my covenant—
these I will bring to my holy mountain,
　and make them joyful in my house of prayer. . . .
Thus says the Lord GOD,
　who gathers the outcasts of Israel,
　I will gather others to them
　besides those already gathered.

　　　　　　　　　　　　　　　　(Isa. 56:3a, 6–7a, 8)

The "four winds" represent all the nations of the world. In one of his more imaginative bits of exegesis, Augustine notes that the Greek names for the four winds begin with A, D, A, and M, thus spelling out the name of the first human. Adam, humanity, has been scattered over the whole earth like leaves blown in the wind.[57] But at the coming of the Son of Man, they will be regathered, beginning with the outcasts of Israel.

## 13:28–37
### *Foretellings (5): Summary*

In Israel the budding of the fig trees is the first sign that summer is coming. People watch for the soft buds on the bare branches with eager anticipation. It might seem an odd analogy for the list of disasters Mark has been describing, but he emphasizes, as always, that his message is gospel, good news. His focus is not on the tough times but on the divine blessings that lie beyond them. It will all happen soon: "This generation will not pass away until all these things have taken place."

---

57. Augustine, *Expositions on the Psalms* 96.15 (*NPNF*, 1st ser., 8:474).

The contemporary German theologian Wolfhart Pannenberg addresses the matter bluntly: "There is no doubt that Jesus erred when he announced that God's Lordship would begin in his own generation. . . . It was fulfilled by himself, insofar as the eschatological reality of the resurrection of the dead appeared in Jesus himself. It is not yet universally fulfilled in the way in which Jesus and his contemporaries had expected."[58] Calvin, on the other hand, pointed out that within fifty years of Jesus' death Jerusalem was destroyed, the temple was razed, and the church was suffering persecution. "What Christ said was true, that, before the close of a single generation, believers would feel in reality and by undoubted experience, the truth of his prediction."[59] Whether we judge Jesus wrong in his prediction depends on what we think he predicted. Certainly Jerusalem was destroyed, the temple was razed, and the church suffered persecution. Jesus returned from the dead. But his return was not part of a visible cosmic transformation. The key to any final judgment seems to involve putting verse 30 together with verse 32. Having made a temporal prediction, Jesus says he does not know the time. Subsequently, his final conclusion seems to be that, not knowing, we should be prepared as if the last events were about to occur.

Verse 32, however, raises some of the hardest theological puzzles in this whole chapter. "About that day or hour no one knows, neither the angels in heaven, nor the Son, but only the Father." In the second century Irenaeus granted that the text means what it says. In critique of his gnostic opponents, who claimed to know everything, he pointed out that "even the Lord, the very Son of God," admits not knowing the time of the day of judgment.[60] As the doctrine of the Trinity developed more fully, however, it grew harder to allow that the Father could know things hidden from the Son. Athanasius points out that Jesus clearly does know the time, since he has just described what will happen beforehand, and, if I know where the house just before your house is, then I know where your house is as well. The Son is the framer of the whole universe, he continued; how

58. Wolfhart Pannenberg, *Jesus—God and Man*, trans. Lewis L. Wilkins and Duane A. Priebe (Philadelphia: Westminster, 1968), 226.
59. Calvin, *Harmony of the Evangelists*, 3:151.
60. Irenaeus, *Against Heresies* 2.28.6 (*ANF* 1:401).

could he not know its boundaries, temporal as well as spatial?[61] So how to interpret the passage at hand? Augustine said that it means not that the Son himself does not know, but that he is using a "kind of figurative language"[62] to say that he is not enabling us to know. "For he is ignorant of this, as making others ignorant."[63] Aquinas followed suit.[64] But this seems an inadequate solution. "I don't know" seems a dishonest way of saying, "I'm not going to tell you."

Gregory Nazianzus, on the other hand, said that the remark applied only to the Son's human nature.[65] In a technical sense, this looks like a mistake. "Knowing" is the sort of thing that, to use technical terminology, applies to the whole person, not to one or the other of the two natures. But it does open the question of whether there are different ways in which the same person can know or not know. Karl Rahner discusses the point. Knowing, he points out, is not a univocal concept. "A man can have several different types of knowledge which cannot be translated from one to another. Why not admit that one can really know something in a certain way, while the very same thing, even as it is in itself, may remain unknown in another way?" As one with God, Christ presumably knows everything, but maybe this is not the case "in that dimension of the human spirit in which one is conscious of articulate, express, individual items of knowledge."[66] I can know that a company is doing well without being able to cite last quarter's earnings, or know that Switzerland is a democracy without remembering when they had their last election. So, presumably, Jesus could know that God will intervene at the appropriate time to end the sufferings of the present age without knowing when that time will be.

More recent theology has also explored the possibility that the Son really did not know. Rahner proposed, "In certain circumstances, a certain kind of ignorance could . . . be a more perfect thing, in contrast to knowledge."[67] If we start with the assumption that God

61. Athanasius, *Discourses against the Arians* 3.28.42–45 (*NPNF*, 2nd ser., 4:416–18).
62. Augustine, Letter 180 (*NPNF*, 1st ser., 1:547–48).
63. Augustine, *On the Trinity* 1.12.23 (*NPNF*, 1st ser., 3:30).
64. Aquinas, *Summa theologica* 3a.10.2 ad 1, 2081.
65. Gregory of Nazianzus, *Oration* 30.15 (*NPNF*, 2nd ser., 7:315).
66. Karl Rahner, "Exegesis and Dogmatic Theology," in *Dogmatic vs. Biblical Theology*, ed. Herbert Vorgrimler (Baltimore: Helicon, 1964), 49–50.
67. Ibid., 49.

is first of all love, and that in that love the Son comes to be servant to all, then he might manifest that love by accepting limitations. After all, he accepts the physical limitations of a human body; might he accept the limitations of a human mind as well, and in so doing be more complete in his loving, and thereby more perfect? As Barth says, "We must not measure Him by a preconception of what is divine. . . . This is how it is when the Son of the Father becomes a guest in the world."[68] It is hard to think, for instance, that he knew Chinese or quantum physics while still affirming his full humanity. Why assume that he knew the end time? What would it mean to be perfectly human? Balthasar argues that it would mean two things simultaneously: "he looks ahead to the reality that will come without fail, and he possesses the place of the man who unhurriedly performs his tasks each day that is granted him."[69] To abandon his ultimate trust in God would be wrong, but to live with such a detailed foreknowledge that he had no need of trust would also be wrong.

> If the Word became flesh, if God became man, He necessarily existed as a man in a human history, and trod a human way, and on this way had human wants, was subject to human temptations and influences, shared only a relative knowledge and capacity, and learned and suffered and died as a man. . . . Here, in the flesh, there dwells the eternal Word, and His glory is seen—in the exaltation of human essence.
> —Karl Barth
>
> CD IV/2:95, 96.

He was "the Brother of all men who as such, even in the weakness of His human essence, was the Son of God."[70]

These two themes can fit together. The Son manifests the perfection of his love by choosing to become a fully human servant who does *not* know all things. He can know enough about the general shape of things to trust fully in God without knowing details. The conclusion of this passage emphasizes, indeed, that one need not know details. We are to keep alert, live as if the end were close at hand, precisely because we do not know when it will come.

68. Barth, *CD* IV/2:95–96.
69. Hans Urs von Balthasar, *Theo-drama*, vol. 3, *Dramatis Personae: Persons in Christ*, trans. Graham Harrison (San Francisco: Ignatius Press, 1992), 92.
70. Barth, *CD* IV/2:95.

# 14:1–15:47

# Arrest, Torture, Death

## 14:1–2
### The Plot Begins

"The chief priests and the scribes" have appeared before, but they become more prominent as Jesus' opponents in the next two chapters. Intellectuals and religious leaders who reflect on this story do well to remember that the leaders of the plot against Jesus were not politicians or military leaders or businesspeople but intellectuals and religious leaders, victims of what Reinhold Niebuhr called intellectual and spiritual pride.[1] They wanted Jesus' arrest to happen sometime other than the Passover festival, when crowds filled Jerusalem and the chance of a popular rebellion grew accordingly. But, Calvin writes, God wanted Jesus to die at Passover for the symbolic meaning, and "Christ was not unexpectedly dragged to death by the violence of his enemies, but was led to it by the providence of God."[2] Nevertheless, Calvin notes that this does not absolve them because: "[It is] not that Judas's act of betraying ought strictly to be called the work of God; . . . [rather] God turned the treachery of Judas so as to accomplish His own purpose." The strange story of Jesus' death is an account of how evil human plotting fulfills God's plan. Judas "and all wicked men" are forced to obey divine providence; "men can do nothing but what God has appointed."[3]

---

1. Reinhold Niebuhr, *The Nature and Destiny of Man* (2 vols.; New York: Charles Scribner's Sons, 1941), 1:194–203.
2. Calvin, *Harmony of the Evangelists*, 3:186.
3. Ibid., 200.

# 14:3–9

### *A Woman Anoints Jesus*

Mark presents one more intercalation or sandwich, switching from the plot against Jesus to the woman who anoints him and then back again to the plot, pressing us to think about these two stories in relation to each other. Jesus and his disciples have gone from the city to the Mount of Olives (13:3) and now to the nearby town of Bethany, where they are having supper at the house of Simon the Leper. "Leprosy" can refer in the Gospels to a number of skin diseases, some of them curable, so Simon may have retained his name from a disease of which he is now cured; we do not know. What we do know is that Jesus, now apparently rather famous, recently honored in a triumphant if odd entry into Jerusalem, is eating at the home of a man identified with a disgusting disease that rendered its victims ritually unclean. Jesus, friend of outcasts and critic of ritual purity laws, will eat with a leper.[4]

A woman comes with a jar of costly ointment, breaks it open, and anoints Jesus' head. Like many of the most admirable disciples in Mark, she remains anonymous. After all, the way to become a true follower of Jesus involves losing oneself (8:35). Peter recognized Jesus as the Christ, the anointed one. She does not speak, but she enacts his anointing. Anointing is the ritual ceremony for kings, priests, and prophets, but it is also what one did for a dead body, so she is symbolically both honoring him and preparing him for death. Indeed, he is a king whose royal function is to die, a priest who is also the sacrifice, a prophet who has predicted his own death. Mark brackets his account of Jesus' passion with two stories about women and anointing—this woman at Bethany, and the women who come to Jesus' tomb to anoint his body. Both stories mention Jesus' absence: "You will not always have me" (14:7). "He is not here" (16:6).

Elisabeth Schüssler Fiorenza entitled her classic book *In Memory of Her* from this story, and she is worth quoting at length here:

---

4. John Chrysostom, *Homilies on Matthew* 80.1 (*NPNF*, 1st ser, 10:480).

Despite their differences, all four Gospels reflect the same
basic story: a woman anoints Jesus. This incident causes objec-
tions which Jesus rejects by approving of the woman's action.
If the original story had been just a story about the anointing
of a guest's feet, it is unlikely that such a commonplace gesture
would have been remembered and retold as the proclamation
of the gospel. Therefore, it is much more likely that in the original story the woman anointed Jesus' head. Since the prophet
in the Old Testament anointed the head of the Jewish king, the
anointing of Jesus' head must have been understood immediately as the prophetic recognition of Jesus, the Anointed, the
Messiah, the Christ. According to the tradition it was a woman
who named Jesus by and through her prophetic sign-action. It
was a politically dangerous story. . . .

Whereas according to Mark the leading male disciples do
not understand this suffering messiahship of Jesus, reject it,
and finally abandon him, the women disciples who have followed Jesus from Galilee to Jerusalem suddenly emerge as
the true disciples (*akolouthein*) who have understood that his
ministry was not rule and kingly glory but *diakonia*, "service"
(Mark 15:41). Thus the women emerge as the true Christian
ministers and witnesses. The unnamed woman who names
Jesus with a prophetic sign-action in Mark's Gospel is the paradigm of the true disciple. While Peter had confessed, without
truly understanding it, "you are the anointed one," the woman
anointing Jesus recognizes clearly that Jesus' messiahship
means suffering and death.[5]

Given later legends and the temptation to draw from other Gospels, it is worth emphasizing that Mark tells us nothing about this
woman. John tells a similar story about Mary, the sister of Lazarus.
Luke, not Mark, says she is a sinner (7:37), but the New Testament
never refers to her as a prostitute. No one seems to have identified
her with Mary Magdalene until the fourth century.[6] She has spent
a lot of money—three hundred denarii would have been nearly a

5. Elisabeth Schüssler Fiorenza, *In Memory of Her: A Feminist Theological Reconstruction of Christian Origins* (New York: Crossroad, 1984), xiii–xiv.
6. Boring, *Mark*, 381.

year's wages for an ordinary laborer. Eugene Boring calculates that it could have bought meals for 7,500 people.[7] It is understandable that "some who were there" (the disciples? but why not say so?) complain about the waste. They "scold" her, with a verb related to the snorting of horses. We assume that the "some who were there" were men—at a public dinner served at Simon's house—and, as nearly always in Mark, when men and women confront each other, the woman is in the right (even if the man is Jesus!). The NRSV weakens Jesus' response a bit by saying, "She has performed a good service for me," for *kalos* is not just a generic good but something *beautiful*.

You will always be able to help the poor, Jesus says, "but you will not always have me." So Calvin, in a characteristically Puritan mood, acknowledges that the woman acted appropriately when Jesus was alive but insists that, now that Jesus is no longer bodily with us, God "desires us to bestow on *the poor* what superstition foolishly expends on the worship of God."[8] He raises a hard question. (John's Gospel stacks the deck by having Judas scold the woman for her waste of money, but in Mark the objection comes simply from "some who were there.") Some who visit Assisi see the vast Basilica of St. Francis, with its marvelous Giotto frescoes, and are filled with admiration and awe. Others think of Francis and his commitment to poverty and simplicity and are appalled by the ostentation. Neither reaction seems entirely wrong. As Jesus says, we do have the poor with us, and they need our help. But is there not also a place for doing beautiful things for God, even if some of them get rather expensive? Every church building campaign raises such questions, and perhaps the most important thing is that we should realize that there are no easy answers. For this anonymous woman, however, there was no ambiguity. Jesus was there, she did something beautiful for him, and Jesus' prediction is true: wherever the gospel is proclaimed, what she did is told.

7. Ibid., 382.
8. Calvin, *Harmony of the Evangelists*, 3:190.

# 14:10–11
## *Judas's Betrayal*

The chief priests and scribes have been looking for a way to arrest Jesus in secret, and now we are back to that story—Judas offers them their opportunity. When we first met Judas, in the list of the Twelve, Mark identified him as "Judas Iscariot, who betrayed him" (3:19). Now at the moment of betrayal, he is "Judas Iscariot, who was one of the twelve." He has never been mentioned in the interim. Judas's function in the story is to be one of the Twelve and to betray Jesus. He is nowhere singled out as the reprehensible or weak disciple; he is simply "one of the twelve." The first real action in Jesus' betrayal, then, comes, not from the Romans or the Jewish leaders, but from one of Jesus' own followers, and thus as Karl Barth says, from "the Church": "And at this first and decisive place that the Church stands and acts in identity with the Israel which rejected its Messiah, together with the heathen world which allied itself with this Israel, and made itself a partner in its guilt."[9] Particularly in the face of the horrible history of Christian anti-Semitism, but also in the face of the general Christian instinct toward self-satisfaction, Christians need to remember that the ball that rolled down the hill toward Jesus' crucifixion got its initial push from one of Jesus' own followers, one of "us."

Mark tells us nothing about Judas's motive. The chief priests promise to give him money, but he does not ask for it. Modern retellings of the story imagine him as an idealist or political revolutionary somehow disappointed at the path Jesus is taking. Theodore Jennings suggests that Mark resists providing Judas with a motive because that would allow us to classify him as one particular type of villain, and he would thereby lose his generic role as simply the betrayer.[10] Indeed, the word the NRSV translates "betrayed" could equally be rendered by the more neutral "handed over." Mark brings no emotion to what he says about Judas—it is all just statement of fact.

9. Barth, *CD* II/2:460. Barth's whole forty-page section on Judas here is a model of theological commentary.
10. Theodore W. Jennings Jr., *The Insurrection of the Crucified* (Chicago: Exploration Press, 2003), 244.

The woman at Bethany gave Jesus the ointment—nothing expected in return. The high priests offer Judas money, but they expect something in return, and indeed they are not prepared to pay until he has completed his task. Contemporary philosophers have debated the possibility of a truly authentic gift—is it in the nature of human relations that we always want *something* in return, if only gratitude or recognition?[11] But this woman's action comes as close to pure gift as one can imagine. Mark's intercalation of her story and Judas's certainly invites us to think about the contrast between these two exchanges. Historians debate just what Judas was offering the high priests. After all, Jesus was easy enough to find, teaching in the temple. Presumably they feared the popular reaction to any attempt to arrest him in public and needed help in locating him at a private moment.

## 14:12-25

### Passover Meal with the Disciples

Jews came to Jerusalem for Passover, like New Yorkers flooding Times Square on New Year's Eve, so it was customary for Jerusalemites to rent out rooms to visitors for the Passover meal. Again, however, as when Jesus sent the disciples to get a young donkey for his ride into Jerusalem, we encounter mystery. Who will be their host? How does Jesus know to send them off to follow a man carrying a jar of water? We do not know. In the traditional sense of the word, Jesus works no miracles in Jerusalem, but he certainly manifests remarkable powers. Carrying water was usually a woman's task, and men, if they carried it at all, would have used a bottle rather than a jar, so a man carrying a jar of water would be a sufficiently distinctive sight to serve as a sign, and a sign that took the form of a reversal of traditional gender roles. When Samuel anointed Saul as Israel's first king, he gave him two signs of the authenticity of his call: he would find the asses for which he had been searching, and he would get

---

11. Marcel Mauss, *The Gift*, trans. Ian Cunnison (New York: Norton, 1967); Jacques Derrida, *The Gift of Death*, trans. David Wills (Chicago: University of Chicago Press, 1995).

two loaves of bread from three men, one of them carrying a jug of wine (1 Sam. 10). Here Jesus, the anointed one, sends his disciples after a donkey and a man carrying a jar who will lead them to a meal culminating in bread and wine.

A Passover meal involved detailed tradition, and the main course was always lamb, in memory of the lambs killed in Egypt to mark Hebrew houses with blood over the front door so that the angel of death would pass them over as he killed the firstborn of the Egyptians. But Mark does not mention any lamb. Does he just skip over most of the meal? Or is the lamb to be sacrificed on this occasion God's firstborn, Jesus? Jesus tells his disciples that one of them will betray him, "one of the twelve," "one who is dipping bread into the bowl with me." Matthew (26:25) identifies this reference as pointing to Judas, who was then presumably sitting next to Jesus, and Mark may mean the same thing, but he may just refer to someone from the whole group that is eating with Jesus. Somewhere in the background may be a memory of Psalm 41:9, "Even my bosom friend in whom I trusted, who ate of my bread, has lifted the heel against me." The others, at any rate, do not spot a reference to Judas, and all say, "Surely, not I?" The Greek particle at the beginning of the sentence indicates that the questioner expects a negative answer. More colloquially, "It isn't me, is it?" Yet the asking of the question implies at least a shadow of doubt. As Origen sees it, "It may happen, in the struggle against principalities and powers and rulers of this world of darkness, that one may fall quite unexpectedly into evil. . . . Thus, each disciple feared lest it might be he who was foreknown as betrayer."[12] This is part of the memory we preserve when we repeat Jesus' actions in the Eucharist; as Vernon Robbins puts it, "After Mark, no Christian can eat the holy meal without asking himself, 'Am I myself a betrayer of Jesus?'"[13] None of us can be sure of our innocence, though we can know our guilt. In Bach's *St. Matthew Passion* the question "Is it I?" is repeated eleven times. Judas does not need to ask.

12. Origen, *Commentary on Matthew* 50, in *Ante-Nicene Exegesis of the Gospels*, ed. H. D. Smith (London: S.P.C.K., 1925), 5:236.

13. Vernon K. Robbins, "Last Meal," in *The Passion in Mark: Studies on Mark 14–16*, ed. Werner Kelber (Philadelphia: Fortress, 1976), 40.

In 1 Corinthians 11, writing perhaps fifteen years before Mark wrote his Gospel and twenty to twenty-five years after Jesus' death, Paul describes what the Lord Jesus did "on the night when he was betrayed" in ways very similar to Mark's account of the bread and wine. Paul claims to report an earlier tradition of which he is just the messenger, something "I received from the Lord" that "I also handed on to you." Unlike Paul, Mark reports no instructions about repeating the ritual, but it must have been already an important ritual in the church.

Jesus blesses the bread and gives thanks for the cup. In Luke he gives thanks for the bread as well. Figuring out this variation, Luther says, "I leave to those who find pleasure in troubling themselves over such problems."[14] Christian churches have differed about exactly what happened and happens in this ritual, from those who understand Jesus' words metaphorically to those, like Luther, who "believe and teach that in the Supper we eat and take to ourselves Christ's body truly and physically" but go on to say, "How this takes place or how he is in the bread we do not know and are not meant to know,"[15] to those who think the theory of transubstantiation offers some measure of understanding as to how the transformation takes place. Tempting as it is for a theologian to explore these distinctions, the truth is that Mark had simply not thought about such distinctions, so that on such matters an honest theological commentary on Mark can only cite the narrative and leave open questions of its interpretation.

Reading the story in Mark's own context, however, does provide some insights. A Passover meal followed a quite specified ritual, and Jesus here did something new, not only contrary to the Passover tradition but, so far as we know, something he had never done before. He wanted to capture his disciples' attention, to indicate that what followed was important.[16] This is not the first bread Jesus has shared. In the feedings of five thousand and four thousand he fed both Jews

14. Martin Luther, "Confession Concerning Christ's Supper," trans. Robert H. Fischer, *Word and Sacrament III*, LW 37 (Philadelphia: Muhlenberg, 1961), 313.
15. Martin Luther, "That These Words of Christ, 'This Is My Body,' etc., Still Stand Against the Fanatics," trans. Robert H. Fischer, ibid., 29.
16. Luther, "Confession Concerning Christ's Supper," 311–12.

and Gentiles, multitudes, everyone who came. When Jesus welcomes you to the table, Wolfhart Pannenberg notes, everything that separated you from God is removed.[17] Indeed, even his betrayer is at the table for this meal. As the final "feeding story" in Mark, this narrative focuses us on Jesus' suffering and death, not his miraculous powers, as the key to understanding all these stories.[18] The word he uses for "cup" (*potērion*), on the other hand, often refers to pain and suffering. Earlier in the Gospel, when James and John requested places of honor, he asked if they were able "to drink the cup that I drink" (10:38). Psalm 75:8 warns,

> in the hand of the LORD there is a cup
> with foaming wine, well mixed;
> he will pour a draught from it,
> and all the wicked of the earth
> shall drain it down to the dregs.

A number of prophets pick up this theme of a cup of punishment (see, for instance, Isa. 51:17; Lam. 4:21; Ezek. 23:31–35). The cup is filled with wine, of which Frederick Buechner says, "Wine is booze, which means it is dangerous and drunk-making. It makes the timid brave and the reserved amorous. It loosens the tongue and breaks the ice.... It kills germs. As symbols go, it is a rather splendid one."[19] In sum: what happens at this meal is important; all are welcome, yet taking part is possibly dangerous and certainly exciting.

In *Jesus Christ Superstar*, Jesus sings, "For all you care, this could be my body.... For all you care, this could be my blood." As an interpretation of Mark (or any other Gospel), that bitterness is just wrong, but it does capture something of the darkness of the moment. The place of the Eucharist in Christian tradition leaves us oblivious to the horror of the literal image. One of the worst things their Roman enemies could say about the early Christians was that they were cannibals who ate human bodies and drank human blood. For Jews,

---

17. Pannenberg, *Systematic Theology*, 3:285.
18. Robbins, "Last Meal," 21.
19. Frederick Buechner, *Wishful Thinking* (New York: Harper & Row, 1973), 96.

whose rules of kosher center around draining blood from the dead animal, the idea of drinking *any* blood would be particularly abhorrent. This Passover meal is the beginning of something, and the narrative that follows will have terrible things to tell.

Jesus says, "This is my blood of the covenant, which is poured out for many." The English word "many," incidentally, more or less implies "but not all." If I tell my students that many passed the exam, I am implying that some failed. The Greek word *pollōn* is more open-ended; it means, "more than a few; maybe not all, but maybe even all." The pouring out of blood evokes some sort of sacrificial ritual; but a covenant sacrifice, Pannenberg argues, is not the same thing as an expiation. In Genesis, when Jacob and Laban agree to go their separate ways in peace, they erect a pile of stones, "and Jacob offered a sacrifice on the height" (Gen. 31:54). The sacrifice invokes God to serve as a sort of United Nations force to police the agreement; it is not about any repentance for sin.[20] But between whom is the covenant here? If it is between God and humankind, then it can hardly be a matter of specifying appropriate boundaries, and indeed part of it must concern human sin. Pannenberg therefore seems to put too much emphasis on the word "covenant."

Mark tells the story of how Jesus went to his death. He assumes that Jesus' way is part of God's plan, so Jesus' suffering and death must accomplish something God wants to accomplish. But Mark is very thin on the what, much less the how, of that accomplishment. At 10:45 Jesus says the Son of Man came "to give his life a ransom for many," and here at 14:24 he says, "This is my blood of the covenant, which is poured out for many." Somehow (implied in the idea of ransom) Jesus' death will free some or all of humankind. Somehow it will function like the blood poured out at a sacrifice. If we are honest, that is just about all Mark has to tell us on this topic.

20. Pannenberg, *Systematic Theology*, 2:417.

# 14:26–31
## *Desertion and Denial*

We are again reminded that this is not a story of Jesus and his follow-ers against his opponents. The Twelve will all desert him too. The Twelve are men; we will see that women disciples are more faithful, but even they run away in the end. These prophecies of denial on the Mount of Olives evoke the episode in 2 Samuel 15, where David's trusted advisor Ahithophel has deserted him to join the rebellion of David's son Absalom. "But David went up the ascent of the Mount of Olives, weeping as he went, with his head covered and walking barefoot; and all the people who were with him covered their heads and went up, weeping as they went" (2 Sam. 15:30). Jesus has been ambivalent about the title, "son of David," wanting to make clear that he does not come as a political-military leader. Yet how strange it is that Israel's greatest king, in the midst of his reign, should have been portrayed centuries before as a man of sorrows, abandoned and rejected, climbing the Mount of Olives barefoot, as if he were anticipating the very different kind of anointed one Jesus will be.

Jesus also cites Zechariah once more, paraphrasing (rather than quoting) the prophecy that the sheep will all be scattered when the shepherd has been struck (Zech. 13:7). Almost casually, he slips in the promise that he will go before the disciples to Galilee after he has been raised up. No one seems (I am talking about Mark's nar-rative, not about any history behind it) even to notice the remark, so focused are they on denying Jesus' prophecies of desertion and betrayal. As usual, Peter is the impetuous spokesman for the Twelve, assuring Jesus of his faithfulness even after Jesus has promised that Peter will deny him three times.

# 14:32–42
## *Grieving in Gethsemane*

Nowhere else in Mark do we more directly confront Jesus' human-ity. He and the now eleven (Judas will soon return, so he must some-time have slipped away, though Mark makes no mention of it) go to "a place called Gethsemane" on the Mount of Olives. Only John's Gospel (18:1) calls it a "garden"; a "place" could refer to any unoccupied field or space. The name "Gethsemane" might refer to an olive press. Mark, often vague about locations earlier in the Gospel, now begins to get quite specific. His first readers could have gone to Gethsemane, the courtyard of the governor's palace, and Golgotha. This is their world; this is real.

As often in Mark, the English translation if anything understates the force of the Greek. Jesus shudders in distress, in anguish, in horror. The NRSV captures the energy by saying, "he threw himself on the ground." It is the picture of a man right on the edge of complete emotional collapse—as Eugene Boring says, "barely in control, on the verge of panic."[21] This was not the ancient ideal of how a hero should face his death. A calm Socrates drank the poison and continued to chat with his friends. The Maccabean martyrs provided "a noble example of how to die a good death willingly and nobly" (2 Macc. 6:28), going to their deaths "as all ought to go who have the courage" (2 Macc. 6:20). Celsus, the great second-century critic of Christianity, asked how Christians could view as divine this Jesus, who mourned and lamented and prayed to escape the fear of death.[22]

Calvin rejects that ideal for human nature. Even among Christians, he admits, "there are also new Stoics, who count it depraved not only to groan and weep but also to be sad and care-ridden. . . . Yet we have nothing to do with this iron philosophy which our Lord and Master has condemned not only by his word, but also by his example. For he groaned and wept."[23] Christians should not be ashamed of emotion. Nor should we treat the case of Jesus as an exception to the rule, for his full humanity is part of the story of our salvation. Calvin admits, "As it appears to be inconsistent with the divine glory of Christ, that he was seized with trembling and sadness, many commentators have labored with toil and anxiety to find some way of evading the difficulty. But their labor has been ill-judged and of no use; for if we are ashamed that Christ should experience fear and

---

21. Boring, *Mark*, 397.
22. Origen, *Contra Celsum* 2.24, trans. Henry Chadwick (Cambridge: Cambridge University Press, 1953), 88.
23. Calvin, *Institutes* 3.8.9.

sorrow, our redemption will perish and be lost."[24] Just as the physical agony on the cross was real and no fake, so with this emotional agony.

Jesus prays, "*Abba, Patēr*"—Mark has him say "Father" in both Aramaic and Greek. *Abba* appears three times in the New Testament— here, Galatians 4:6, and Romans 8:15. In both Pauline passages, it occurs in the context of passionate Christian prayer. A generation of scholars made much of these passages, arguing (1) that they pointed to a word used by the historical Jesus, (2) that *abba* was a term of unusual informality and intimacy, meaning something like "Daddy," and (3) that only Jesus used this term of God. Thus *abba* captures Jesus' uniquely intimate relation with the one he called his Father. Edward Schillebeeckx, for instance, centered his whole Christology around the idea of "Jesus' *abba* experience."[25]

All three of the premises of this argument have come under criticism. (1) While it is true that the use of a Hebrew or Aramaic word suggests the possibility of direct quotation from Jesus, the Pauline passages do not claim to be quotations from Jesus, and one passage from Mark seems a weak foundation on which to base an argument about the practice of the historical Jesus. (2) Other uses show that, while *abba* is a shortened form, it is not necessarily a sign of great informality or intimacy; "Daddy" is not the right translation. (3) Passages calling God *abba* have been found in other Jewish texts.[26] Jesus here is indeed praying passionately to one to whom he feels close— no need to try to draw further conclusions from the word *abba*.

For many contemporary Christians, it is in this story that Jesus feels most real, most like us. As Raymond Brown writes, "This combination of human suffering, divine strengthening, and solitary self-giving has done much to make Jesus loved by those who believe in him."[27] It is therefore worth remembering how problematic this

---

24. Calvin, *Harmony of the Evangelists*, 3:226.
25. Edward Schillebeeckx, *Jesus*, trans. Hubert Hoskins (New York: Crossroad, 1981), 256–68; see also Joachim Jeremias, *The Central Message of the New Testament* (London: SCM, 1965), 9–30.
26. See James Barr, "'*Abbā* Isn't 'Daddy,'" *Journal of Theological Studies* 39 (1988): 28–47; Mary Rose D'Angelo, "*Abba* and 'Father': Imperial Theology and the Jesus Traditions," *JBL* 111 (1992): 611–30.
27. Brown, *Death of the Messiah*, 1:216.

passage was for theologians throughout much of Christian history.[28] Such distress seemed inconsistent with their ideal image of a strong human being or divine figure. Part of the answer emerged in the debate between monothelitism and dithelitism in the seventh century. The monothelites held that Christ has only one will. He is one person in two natures, and a will, they said, is a thing that belongs to a person. This was a politically advantageous position to take at the time, because it seemed a possible compromise with the monophysite Christians living in Egypt and nearby territories, who believed that Christ had only one nature. They were under threat from the rising power of Islam, and such a compromise would make a united Christian opposition to the Muslims much easier. The pope at the time, Honorius I, even seems to have supported the one-will position.

Mark 14 and its parallels in other Gospels provided the dithelites, who eventually carried the day, their clearest biblical support. When Jesus prays, "not what I want, but what you want," he is clearly distinguishing two different wills who want different things. One might suppose he is distinguishing between the will of the Father and the will of the Son (indeed, to be honest, that seems the most natural reading of the text), but a majority of theologians argued that for the Father and Son to have different wills would violate the unity of the Trinity. If there are two wills but only one divine will, then there must be two wills in the divine-human person of Christ, one corresponding to each nature, and this was finally affirmed by the Sixth Council of Constantinople in 680. Centuries later, Aquinas laid out the classic argument: "For it is manifest that the Son of God assumed a perfect human nature. . . . Now the will pertains to the perfection of human nature, being one of its natural powers. . . . Hence we must say that the Son of God assumed a human will, together with human nature. Now by the assumption of human nature the Son of God suffered no diminution of what pertains to His Divine Nature, to which it belongs to have a will. . . . Hence it must be said that here are two

28. Kevin J. Madigan, *The Passions of Christ in High Medieval Thought* (New York: Oxford University Press, 2007), 65.

wills in Christ, i.e. one human, the other Divine."[29] Christ would not be fully human without a human will or fully divine without a divine will; hence the one person has two wills, and one can struggle with the other in Gethsemane.

Jesus really prays that the "cup" be removed from him, but then accepts the divine will: "not what I want, but what you want." Raymond Brown cites a number of recent theologians who have tried to "interpret the passage so that Jesus is not trying to avoid crucifixion and death." Jesus was worried that he would die before he reached the cross, and such an anticlimax was the fate he was praying to avoid. Or, he was not praying that he would not die on a cross, but that the agony on the cross would not last too long.[30] Brown rightly concludes that such interpretations are rather desperately trying to avoid the natural meaning of the text.

Some medieval theologians addressed the problem by making some fine distinctions. In *On the Four Wills of Christ*, Hugh of St. Victor claims that not only did Christ have a divine will and a human will, but his human will was divided into a will of reason, a will of piety, and a will of the flesh or sensitive will. Thus, in a case like this, he would understand (will of reason) that, yes, he must die on the cross, and accept (will of piety) conformity to God's wishes, while still, at an emotional or bodily level (sensitive will) not wanting to die.[31] Such a multiplication of wills may just complicate the issue (and introducing several human wills risks blurring the clear distinction between the human and divine wills), but in its cumbersome way it captures something true about Jesus' situation. He knows and accepts that he needs to die as part of God's plan, but he is scared. To ask, "Is there some way this could not happen?" is to articulate that fear, without which he would not be fully human, even though he willingly accepts his fate. Barth puts it well:

> He only prays. He does not demand. He does not advance any claims. . . . He prays only as a child to the Father, knowing that He can and should pray, that His need is known to the

---

29. Aquinas, *Summa theologica* 3a.18.1.
30. Brown, *Death of the Messiah*, 1:166.
31. Madigan, *Passions of Christ*, 78–79.

> Father, is on the heart of the Father, but knowing also that the
> Father disposes what is possible and will therefore be, and that
> what He allows to be will be the only thing that is possible and
> right.[32]

At the beginning of his ministry, after all, Jesus was tempted. To be
tempted is not to sin; it is to see the wrong path and recognize its real
attractions before rejecting it. That is what happens in Gethsemane.
Catherine of Siena once cried out, "Where were you, my God and
Lord, when my heart was full of darkness and filth?" Then she heard
God's reply, "My daughter, did you not feel it? I was in your heart."[33]
That in us which is tempted also lies in God's presence.

Indeed, to return to Barth, Jesus' fear "is not to be understood
as an inclination to disobedience but as an element in the obedience of Jesus. He did not throw away His life as if it were worthless.
He sacrificed it as something precious from which it was not easy
for Him to part."[34] A Jesus who did not fear death would not have
been following God's plan. What was it he was afraid of? Most often
human flesh instinctively shrinks back from death. One might also
think that it was not death itself but the painful process leading to it
that he feared. Both Luther and Calvin, in contrast, held that Jesus,
bearing all of humankind's sins, feared the judgment that awaited
him. Here is Calvin: "He had no horror at death, before, simply as
a passage out of this world, but because he had before his eyes the
dreadful tribunal of God, and the Judge himself aroused with incon-
ceivable vengeance; and because our sins, the load of which was laid
upon him, pressed him down with their enormous weight."[35] In a
systematic theology one would have to take this idea seriously. Paul
declares that God made Christ "to be sin who knew no sin, so that in
him we might become the righteousness of God" (2 Cor. 5:21). Not
that Christ pretends to take on our sins, or accepts the punishment
for them, but that he really becomes the worst of all sinners. But

32. Barth, *CD* IV/1:270.
33. Quoted in Jürgen Moltmann, *The Way of Jesus Christ: Christology in Messianic Dimensions*,
    trans. Margaret Kohl (San Francisco: HarperSanFrancisco, 1990), 180.
34. Barth, *CD* III/4:401.
35. Calvin, *Harmony of the Evangelists*, 3:228.

such ideas go further than a theological commentary on Mark can justify. Eugene Boring puts it this way: "Mark reports the ultimate mystery of God's saving act in the weakness and death of the truly human Jesus of Nazareth, and acknowledges the mystery of God's acting through the sinful acts of those who betray, condemn, and execute him. Mark affirms and narrates this mystery, but does not elaborate or explain it, does not incorporate it within some larger theological system."[36] This is inevitably frustrating to the theological commentator.

Jesus comes back from his prayerful struggles and finds his disciples asleep. As Robert Fowler points out, "The disciples have failed Jesus, but they have also failed us. No one in the story stayed awake and heard the prayer. Only the reader of the storyteller's discourse has fulfilled the role of the faithful follower. The master storyteller knits us into the fabric of his narrative at the same time that he unravels the disciples' role inside the story."[37] One could argue that Mark is sloppy and has forgotten that there is no witness to record what he is describing. Fowler offers a more sophisticated analysis. The narrative thrusts us as readers into the story, if we are willing to accept the role, as the only faithful witnesses (just as only the audience can save Tinkerbell by applauding at the right moment in *Peter Pan*, or only the boy reading the book can save the enchanted land in *The Neverending Story*). And Mark makes that point while at the same time showing the disciples failing Jesus once more.

Jesus asks *Peter*, "*Simon*, are you asleep?" The juxtaposition of the names (they are right next to each other in the Greek too) calls our attention to the fact that Jesus does not use the name he has given this disciple, "Peter." On one interpretation, this is because "Peter" is his name-as-disciple, and as one who has fallen asleep and is soon to deny Jesus, he no longer deserves that name. I am less persuaded of this analysis because I follow the minority view that in Mark "Peter" originally evoked the rocky ground on which seeds grow but briefly rather than the church's solid foundation. It is not a high

36. Boring, *Mark*, 398.
37. Robert M. Fowler, "Reader-Response Criticism: Figuring Mark's Reader," in *Mark and Method: New Approaches in Biblical Studies*, ed. Janice Capel Anderson and Stephen D. Moore (Minneapolis: Fortress, 1992), 71.

compliment one could cease to deserve. Moreover, this is the only time in Mark Jesus directly addresses *anyone* by name. I thus read it as a desperately human gesture. No more nicknames or titles. The night is dark, and Jesus is facing death. He reaches out to a friend, calling him by name.

Three times, in classic folktale style (there are also Jesus' three predictions of his passion and Peter's three denials), Jesus comes back to the disciples, and three times he finds them asleep. As Barth says, "In other words, the apostolate, the community, Christendom, the Church . . . sleeps. . . . Jesus makes it alone. There is no one to bear the burden with Him. There is none to help."[38] "Are you still sleeping and taking your rest? Enough!" Jesus says. "The hour has come; the Son of Man is betrayed into the hands of sinners. Get up, let us be going." One imagines a painting by Caravaggio—everything dark but suddenly a bright light as Judas and the soldiers arrive.

The passage raises a number of issues in translation. Jesus' reference to the disciples' still sleeping can be taken as an indicative ("You are still sleeping!"), an ironic interrogative ("Are you still sleeping?"), or an imperative, delivered even with a touch of compassion ("Rest while you can"). The last of these, which will probably strike most readers today as the least likely, is the interpretation offered by Chrysostom and Augustine, perhaps concerned for the disciples' partial rehabilitation, though both Raymond Brown and the NRSV favor the interrogative interpretation.[39] "Enough" (*apechei*) raises further problems. Its ordinary usage was to conclude a business transaction, where it could mean something like, "The account is settled." As such, it could refer to Judas, who is about to complete his side of his deal with the high priests and is owed his money. In a looser sense, it could just mean, "It's done." Whatever chance Jesus might have had to escape into the countryside is gone now, and he will have no further opportunities to turn away from his destiny.

"The hour has come" carries a great deal of eschatological freight. Mark here uses the same verb (*ēngiken*) he used at 1:15, "The reign

38. Barth, *CD* IV/1:267.
39. Brown, *Death of the Messiah*, 1:207–8.

of God is at hand" (my trans.). He is about to start doing what he has most come to do, and it is this that makes his life the beginning of the new age. If that verb harks back to the cosmic meaning of these events, the next is a very human reference. At Mark 1:38 Jesus first called Simon, "Let us go." Now he uses the same words to call his disciples as he meets his betrayer.

Mark is telling a very human story about a man and his unreliable friends, and a story about the transformation of the world by God. Even in his apparently casual choice of words, he keeps both stories before us.

> The time is fulfilled, and the kingdom of God has come near; repent, and believe in the good news.
>
> —Mark 1:15

## 14:43–52

### *Betrayal, Arrest, and a Naked Young Man*

One more scene begins with Mark's favorite word, "Immediately." Judas is again identified as "one of the twelve" (had we forgotten?). The authorities arrive with "a crowd with swords and clubs"—how often officials descend on protesters with far more troops and weaponry than the situation requires. Jesus asks if they think he is a bandit (*lēstēs*), a word that could refer either to ordinary robbers or to Robin Hood–like figures stirring up trouble in hopes of a coming revolution. Judas betrays Jesus with a kiss. Jesus has, as he says, been in the temple every day, but perhaps there are local bullies here sent to round him up who do not spend their time in the temple and would not recognize him. They need an identifying sign from Judas. Dionysius of Alexandria, writing in the third century, imagines the gentleness of Jesus' response: "The Lord . . . even kissed his own traitor, and spoke words even softer than a kiss! For he did not say, 'O you abominable one, utterly abominable traitor, is this the return you make to us for such great kindnesses?' But, somehow, He simply says, 'Judas,' using his first name, which was the address that would be used by one who commiserated with a person, or who wished to call him back, rather than of one in anger."[40] (Luke has Jesus call Judas by name; in Matthew he calls him "Friend.") Jesus accepts his destiny—"let the scriptures be fulfilled"—in words that indicate the clearest "reason" Mark offers for why Jesus has to die—to fulfill the prophecies of Scripture, a reason that begs the question of why this pattern of things was set out in Scripture in the first place.

In the midst of the confusion, someone draws a sword and cuts off the ear of one of the high priest's servants. Lack of an ear would have been a disqualification for the priesthood, but it is unclear whether this servant (the word could also mean, as the NRSV renders it, "slave") would be or would hope to be a priest. Some have suggested that Mark is vague about details here since the ear cutter was still alive, and Mark wants to protect him from arrest.[41] This is one of those odd details Mark gives us that adds to the verisimilitude of the story, since it is hard to think of a reason for saying it other than that it actually happened; and the same is true of the young man following Jesus, "wearing nothing but a linen cloth." The guards grab his wrapping, and he breaks loose and flees, naked, into the night. These two verses have, to put it mildly, occasioned many different interpretations.

1. The version I learned in Sunday school is that the young man was Mark himself, here appearing anonymously, as the portly figure of Alfred Hitchcock always turns up somewhere in his films. Nothing in the text supports (or, to be fair, counts against) this interpretation.

2. In the early 1970s the distinguished Columbia University scholar Morton Smith reported the discovery of a previously unknown letter by Clement of Alexandria, in which Clement describes a longer, "more spiritual" version Mark wrote of his Gospel after he had completed the standard version we have. The letter then quotes a passage from this "secret Gospel" that follows what we know as Mark 10:34. In this passage Jesus, visiting Bethany, raises a rich young man from the dead. The young man loves Jesus and begs to follow him, and

40. Dionysius of Alexandria, "An Interpretation of the Gospel according to Luke" (fragment), *The Works of Gregory Thaumaturgus, Dionysius of Alexander, and Archelaus*, trans. S. D. F. Salmond (Edinburgh: T. & T. Clark, 1871), 256, translation revised.
41. Taylor, *Mark*, 560.

after six days goes to Jesus at night, wearing a linen garment over his naked body. During the night, Jesus instructs him in "the mystery of the kingdom of God."[42] Presumably the young man in Mark 14:51– 52 represents a parallel case. Smith hypothesizes a secret baptismal initiation characteristic of early Christianity and invites his readers to wonder about the possibility of homosexual activity amid this nighttime nakedness. Though Smith's account received wide accep- tance, there is also a strong argument that he, annoyed with his fel- low scholars on many grounds, forged the manuscript of the letter from Clement as a kind of joke.[43]

4. At the end of Mark, when the women come to the tomb, they encounter a young man wearing a white garment who tells them that Jesus has been raised. The word for "young man" (*neaniskon*) is the same as in 14:51. Is this mysterious observer who flees from Gethse- mane (a young man? an angel?) the same as the one who meets the women at the tomb? The evidence is, to say the least, limited.

4. The literary critic Frank Kermode relates Mark's young man to the figure of "the man in the Macintosh" (a sort of raincoat) who appears at several points in James Joyce's *Ulysses*. Joyce used to annoy scholars who studied his works by asking them what they made of this figure, and Kermode infers that Joyce simply inserted him in the story, which is otherwise full of symbolic connections, with no par- ticular meaning at all. Such an authorly joke seems uncharacteristic of Mark, but Kermode's deeper point is that, as readers, we are driven to try to make sense of the elements of a text. Maybe a young man did run away naked that night, and so Mark reports it. Maybe Mark is making his narrative seem more "real" by adding irrelevant details. We should be suspicious, Kermode says, of our readerly instinct to "make sense" of every element in a story.[44]

Confused? None of these interpretations seems demonstrably wrong (except for Smith's if it indeed rests on a forgery) or right.

42. Morton Smith, *Clement of Alexandria and a Secret Gospel of Mark* (Cambridge: Harvard University Press, 1973); idem, *The Secret Gospel* (New York: Harper & Row, 1973); and Kermode, *Genesis of Secrecy*, 57–58.
43. See Stephen C. Carlson, *The Gospel Hoax: Morton Smith's Invention of Secret Mark* (Waco, TX: Baylor University Press, 2006).
44. Kermode, *Genesis of Secrecy*, 49–59.

Even the text itself has its mysteries. In 14:50 Mark declares that everyone has fled. But in the next two verses the young man is initially still there, and flees only after his garment has been grabbed. Nakedness is a matter of shame, particularly among ancient Jews (an idea that has survived in the Middle East and used against Iraqi prisoners), and several scholars interpret the young man's running away naked as the ultimate shame, in which he "chooses shame over fidelity to Jesus."[45] Yet the young man remained when everyone else fled, and giving up everything to follow is, elsewhere in Mark, a sign of the faithful follower. In the texts from the Hebrew Scriptures sometimes cited as parallels, such as Joseph fleeing naked when Potiphar's wife attempts to seduce him (Gen. 39:12), or Amos warning that "those who are stout of heart among the mighty shall flee away naked in that day" (Amos 2:16), nakedness is the attribute of the morally pure and the "stout of heart." If nothing else, the story drives home the point that *everyone* has at this point abandoned Jesus.

> No man but Jesus has ever known the true breadth and depth, the true essence and darkness, of human misery.
> —Karl Barth
> CD IV/2:487.

## 14:53–65

### Jesus at the Council

Mark offers us one more textual sandwich, shifting back and forth between Jesus and Peter. The crowd takes Jesus to the high priest, and Peter "followed him at a distance" (note the pain implied in the tension between "followed" and "at a distance"!).

The task of a theological commentary is generally to interpret the text rather than to probe behind it to discover some "real history." This is one of the cases where that rule needs at least to be bent. Jesus was crucified—a Roman penalty (Jewish law prescribed stoning for those sentenced to death). Yet Christians have a long, horrible his-

---

45. John R. Donahue and Daniel J. Harrington, *The Gospel of Mark*, SP (Collegeville, MN: Liturgical Press, 2002), 417; for the same point, Boring, *Mark*, 403.

tory of accusing "the Jews" of killing Jesus. Paul's First Letter to the Thessalonians, which may be the earliest Christian writing we have, already writes of "the Jews, who killed both the Lord Jesus and the prophets" (1 Thess. 2:14–15). As an early Christian writing in times of actual or threatened persecution, Mark would have had good reason to minimize the Roman role in Jesus' death. If he was killed by order of the Roman governor, Romans would have suspected that he was some sort of political troublemaker, and wondered if his followers also represented a threat to the political order and ought at least to be investigated. On the other hand, if the real impetus for killing Jesus came from Jewish leaders, and the local Roman officials merely acquiesced and carried out the sentence, then Romans might be more open to listening to Jesus' story.

Thus there is reason for some initial skepticism when Mark describes how Jesus was tried by the Jewish council before being taken to Pilate. Some argue that Mark's account of the trial before the Sanhedrin raises additional grounds for suspicion. First, if the Jewish council found him guilty, why did they not sentence and execute him themselves? Philo indicates that Jews could carry out death sentences for cases, for instance, that involved violation of the temple.[46] In contrast, an anecdote told by Josephus seems to imply that (at least in 62) a man who violently misbehaved in the temple was taken to the Roman authorities because Jewish officials could not impose a death sentence.[47] Scholars continue to debate the matter.

What seems less debatable is that the trial as described by Mark violates all the rules of Jewish procedure. Capital trials were to take place only in the daytime, but this one is at night. No legal procedures were to take place on a Sabbath or feast day, but this one does. A death sentence could not be pronounced on the same day as the trial, as this one is. A charge of blasphemy could be brought only if someone were accused of speaking the sacred divine name, which Jesus is not. Trials were to be held in the official council chamber, while this one meets in the high priest's house. Prior examination of witnesses was required, but it does not take place in Mark's

---

46. Philo, *On the Embassy to Gaius* 39.
47. Josephus, *Jewish War* 6.300–309.

account.[48] Mark, therefore, some would argue, cannot be describing an actual event.

To this point several responses can be made. First, the legal procedures cited come from the Mishnah, brought together several centuries later, and may not represent the reality of Jesus' own time. Second, trials of threatening troublemakers in all centuries frequently break the rules of legal procedure to get the desired results; we have no reason to assume the first century was different in this respect. Third, Mark describes "the chief priests and the whole council" as present but never identifies what transpires as an official trial or meeting of the council. He may have been indifferent to or unaware of such distinctions. But he may also be describing a preliminary hearing or informal inquiry rather than an actual trial, and in that case it is not surprising that trial rules were not followed. Indeed, if the Jewish authorities could not execute people but had to send them on to the Romans, then an inquiry as to whether they should do so in this case would be quite appropriate.[49]

Historical conclusions? We cannot be sure that such a trial or hearing took place. I have not even considered the question of how Mark would have found out about it. The arguments that Mark's account is *impossible* do not hold up, but here as elsewhere we should focus on what Mark wants to show us about Jesus through telling us this story rather than the story's accuracy. It is particularly important to detach the question of the historicity of this story from issues about "blaming the Jews." As Vatican II declared, "What happened in His passion cannot be blamed upon all the Jews then living, without distinction, nor upon the Jews of today."[50] Indeed, it may be dangerous to get too caught up in debating whether there actually was a Jewish trial, as though if some Jewish leaders two thousand years ago condemned Jesus, that would have any implications at all for how we ought to treat our Jewish neighbors—or how appalled we should be at the history of Christian anti-Semitism.

48. John R. Donahue, "Temple, Trial, and Royal Christology," in *Passion in Mark*, ed. Kelber, 61.
49. For an interesting attempt at a historical reconstruction, see Pannenberg, *Systematic Theology*, 2:340.
50. *Declaration on the Relationship of the Church to Non-Christian Religions (Nostra aetate)* 4, *The Documents of Vatican II*, ed. Walter M. Abbott (Piscataway, NJ: New Century Publishers, 1966), 666.

Mark's first point here is that Jesus faced a kangaroo court. As the psalmist had written,

> wicked and deceitful mouths are opened against me,
>> speaking against me with lying tongues.
> They beset me with words of hate,
>> and attack me without cause.
>
> (Ps. 109:2–3; see also Ps. 35)

His judges "were looking for testimony against Jesus to put him to death, but they found none." Nevertheless the proceedings continued.

Some witnesses give false testimony, but what they say is inconsistent. Given that plotting against Jesus began in chapter 3, the case against him seems remarkably ill-prepared. The witnesses do focus on Jesus' critique of the temple. Indeed, he had prophesied its destruction, though Mark has recounted nothing that sounded like, "and in three days I will build another, not made with hands." But Jesus did present himself as the successor to the temple as the site of God's presence, and did promise that he would be raised from the dead after three days, so the testimony could be confused reports of remarks not understood rather than sheer invention. Raymond Brown suspects that the witnesses and judges were motivated by "an admixture of insincerity, self-protective cunning, honest religious devotion, conscientious soul-searching and fanaticism."[51] In other words, they acted as many religious leaders, and other sorts of leaders, do, bending the truth a bit because they know their cause is good (they really do believe that); and, besides, they will be in real trouble if they lose the argument.

But the witnesses are quite inconsistent. The prosecution has no case. At least that is the situation until Jesus speaks, and gives his accusers what they want. In a few words, he confesses himself to be the Messiah, the Son of the Blessed One, the one who can say, "I am," and the Son of Man who sits on God's right hand and will come in judgment. It is the climax of this Gospel. All the good reasons

---

51. Brown, *Death of the Messiah*, 1:434.

for concealing his identity have come to an end. There is no danger he will be mistaken for a great political-military leader, successful by the world's standards, when he is a prisoner being prepared for execution. He can speak the truth. That he does so makes clear that he is still oddly in charge. Whatever Judas or the council or Pilate do, the moment when Jesus is first condemned flows out of Jesus' own choice.

"Son of the Blessed One" appears nowhere else in the New Testament, and indeed nowhere else in Jewish literature of the time, though its meaning is clear.[52] "Bless the Lord" and "Blessed be the Lord" are common phrases in the Psalms and elsewhere. In these few words, then, Jesus identifies himself as (1) the Son of God, God's chosen representative with a special relationship to God; (2) the Messiah, the one Israel has awaited, who will bring an end to oppression and injustice; (3) the Son of Man, the figure who will come from God to end the present age; and (4) one who can say "I am," the words God uses to identify himself. Mark's goal is to show us who Jesus is, and, to the extent that titles can do the job, he here achieves that goal. What remains is to narrate what it all means in practice.

As already indicated, it is unclear if what Jesus said met the technical standards of the time for a charge of blasphemy. Mark seems to assume that it did. Through his ministry, Jesus had claimed the power to forgive sins, criticized the law, said that people would be judged in God's coming reign at least in part in terms of their relation to him, and criticized the temple and presented himself as its replacement as the site of God's presence. If one kind of blasphemy involves claiming to be God, this all adds up to something pretty close. The high priest, at any rate, thinks he has won his case. Ordinarily several witnesses would be required to convict, but, since they have heard the blasphemy themselves, the judges can also serve as witnesses. The high priest tears his clothes. This gesture was originally a sign of passionate grief (Gen. 37:34; 2 Sam. 1:11–12); but on the claim, actual or theoretical, that hearing something offensive to

---

52. Norman Perrin, "The High Priest's Question and Jesus' Answer," in *Passion in Mark*, ed. Kelber, 87.

God would generate emotion as great as that caused by passionate grief, it had also become an act appropriate on hearing blasphemy (2 Kgs. 18:37; 19:1). Indeed, the Mishnah would later specify as the required end of a trial for blasphemy that the chief witness state the exact blasphemous words the accused had used and the judges then stand up and tear their garments.[53] Who can ever discern how much real emotion lies behind such ritual actions?

## 14:66–72
### *Peter by the Courtyard Fire*

While Jesus has been facing inquisition, Peter has been down in the courtyard of the high priest, "sitting with the guards, warming himself at the fire." Mark presents the two stories—Jesus' and Peter's—as happening simultaneously, shifting back and forth between them. No doubt the night was chilly—the guards had started a fire—but Peter must also have been seeking the warmth that helps overcome fear, and the comfort of human companionship. Few human gestures are as universal as that of gathering around a fire in the dark of night. Peter must be torn between wanting to stay near this man who has so inspired and puzzled him, so often left him feeling both love and awe, and the simple fear of a stranger in a city with a funny provincial accent, a follower of a man under arrest, a human being worried he too might end up dead. The other disciples simply fled. Peter follows at a distance, and falls farther than any.

Three times a servant girl of the high priest identifies him as a follower of Jesus. "The man from Nazareth," she says the first time—probably a dismissive reaction from a Jerusalemite about a hick town in a notoriously lawless part of the country. ("That guy from Big Foot, Texas," we might say.) Three times, with growing force, Peter denies it. First, he says he does not understand her. Second, he specifically denies what she says. Third, he denies any relation with Jesus by a curse. Then he hears a cock crow a second time and

53. *Sanhedrin* 7:5; *The Mishnah*, trans. Jacob Neusner (New Haven: Yale University Press, 1988), 597–98.

remembers that Jesus had prophesied Peter would deny him three times before the cock crowed twice. The guards have been beating Jesus, spitting on him, and calling on him to prophesy, and right there in the courtyard one of his prophecies has come true. Those who admire empirical research will be glad to know that scholars have in fact stayed awake through the night in Jerusalem to find out when the cocks crow. Times run from as early as 2 till as late as 5:15[54]—the time of the night, at any rate, when spirits run lowest. It does not take much, Calvin remarks on this passage, to overcome a human being's virtue, "for any man, who is not supported by the hand of God, will instantly fall by a slight gale [or breeze] or the rustling of a falling leaf."[55] So for Peter, on a cold night, it takes only the accusations of a serving maid to lead him to deny Jesus with a curse.

Writers in the early church made two points in particular about this passage. First, they noted the testimony to the disciples' (in this case Peter's) honesty in passing down stories that no one would have known apart from their reports. As Eusebius writes, "Surely, then, men who . . . handed down in writing slanders against themselves to unforgetting ages, and accusations of sins, which no one in after years would ever have known of unless he had heard it from their own voice, by thus placarding [or exposing] themselves, may justly be considered to have been void of all egoism and false speaking."[56] Even some modern scholars appeal to this text as evidence of Peter as a particular source for Mark's Gospel, on the grounds that no one in the early church but Peter himself would have dared spread such an embarrassing story about this great church leader.[57]

Second, early Christians saw the story as a warning against pride and evidence of the possibility of forgiveness. Listen to Gregory the Great:

> Why did almighty God permit the one he had placed over the whole church to be frightened by the voice of a maidservant, and even to deny Christ himself? This we know was a great

54. Brown, *Death of the Messiah*, 1:606–7.
55. Calvin, *Harmony of the Evangelists*, 3:261.
56. Eusebius, *The Proof of the Gospel* 3.5, trans. and ed. W. J. Ferrar (repr. Grand Rapids: Baker, 1981), 1:140.
57. Taylor, *Mark*, 551.

> dispensation of the divine mercy, so that he who was to be
> the shepherd of the church might learn through his own fall
> to have compassion on others. God therefore first shows him
> to himself, and then places him over others: to learn through
> his own weakness how to bear mercifully with the weakness
> of others.[58]

It is still good advice, surely, to choose leaders who are conscious of their own faults and therefore likely to be more forgiving of the faults of others. Moreover, particularly if Mark was written in Rome, he wrote in the aftermath of a persecution in which many Christians denied their faith in order to avoid torture and death. To them Peter's story offers hope: someone else who denied Christ ended up the greatest leader of the early church.

The twentieth-century literary critic Erich Auerbach used this story as one of his examples of the particular literary character of the Bible. It fits none of the genres of classical literature. In Greek and Roman literature, serious stories had to do with kings and queens and warriors. Lower-class folks, if they appeared at all, were the stuff of comedy. Yet here is Peter, "a fisherman from Galilee, of humblest background and humblest education. The other participants in the night scene in the court of the High Priest's palace are servant girls and soldiers. From the humdrum existence of his daily life, Peter is called to the most tremendous role. Here, like everything else to do with Jesus' arrest, his appearance on the stage—viewed in the world-historical continuity of the Roman Empire—is nothing but a provincial incident, an insignificant local occurrence, noted by none but those directly involved." Yet Mark's claim is that the fate of humankind is here being played out.[59] Mark invents a new literary genre, according to Auerbach, not for some literary purpose. Rather, his style "was rooted from the beginning in the character of Jewish-Christian literature; it was graphically and harshly dramatized through God's incarnation in a human being of the humblest social station, through his existence on earth amid humble

---

58. Gregory the Great, *Homilies on the Gospels* 21, cited in Oden and Hall, *Mark*, 222.
59. Erich Auerbach, *Mimesis*, trans. Willard R. Trask (Princeton: Princeton University Press, 1953), 41–42.

everyday people and conditions, and through his Passion which, judged by earthly standards, was ignominious."[60] The character of Mark's story, and nowhere more than here, mirrors Mark's Christology, what Mark has to tell us about who Jesus is. If God is enfleshed in a particular wandering Jewish rabbi, then a story of ordinary folks struggling in the lower parts of society is the only way to show God's self-revelation. A Gospel has to be more like a short story by Flannery O'Connor or Richard Price than like a television show about the secrets of the celebrities or a news broadcast about the presidential election.

## 15:1–15

### Before Pilate

We simply do not know the legal or personal relations between Jewish high priest and Roman prefect in Palestine in the early 30s. Joseph Caiaphas was high priest from 18 to 36 and Pontius Pilate was prefect from 26 to 36, both of them in offices that usually turned over every couple of years. (An inscription found in 1961, incidentally, provides archaeological evidence that Pilate was prefect.) They must have been successful, and the fact that Caiaphas lost his job shortly after Pilate lost his suggests they may have found an effective way of working together. There had been a rebellion in 6, and there would be political trouble in 37, but the early 30s when Jesus was killed represent the end of a long period of stability in this most fractious of Roman provinces. Pilate was in charge of keeping order, Caiaphas presumably found it to his advantage to help, and they were apparently good at their jobs. Mark's narrative certainly imagines religious and political authorities at some level cooperating in the case of Jesus.

Pilate had bad press among his contemporaries. Philo described him as "naturally inflexible, a blend of self-will and relentlessness," and said his tenure was characterized by "briberies, insults, robberies, outrages, and wanton injuries, executions without trial con-

60. Ibid., 41.

stantly related, and ceaseless and supremely grievous cruelty."[61]
Josephus likewise pictures him as stubborn and cruel.[62] Raymond
Brown thinks they may have been unfair. He considers the recorded
controversies. In 26, new to the job, Pilate sent troops into Jerusalem with busts of Caesar on their standards. Jews were offended, and
he had the busts removed. Between 29 and 31, troops' use of pagan
symbols in a number of contexts produced protests but no riots.
About this time, he used some money from the temple treasury to
start building an aqueduct, and this seizure of temple money led to
riots. But the aqueduct was needed and the treasury funds were in
part intended for the construction of public works. A few years later
he dedicated some golden shields to Caligula, but carefully did not
put the imperial image on them.[63] All in all, he was an imperial official in a tough job, sometimes insensitive to local customs but willing to compromise. He lasted a long time. Brown's summary: "Jesus
had not met either the best or the worst of Roman judges."[64] Jesus
did not face an individual monster, but a career politician doing
what imperial powers think they need to do to keep order, then and
now. Pilate's "greatest anxiety was to preserve the kingdom in a state
of quietness," Calvin wrote. "Would to God that the world were not
now filled with many Pilates."[65]

It might seem implausible that the prisoner and his guards would
turn up to see Pilate just as dawn was breaking, but we have independent evidence that Roman trials did regularly begin at daybreak.[66]
Mark does not tell us what the guards said about the charges against
Jesus. Presumably blasphemy would be of little interest to a Roman
prefect. Pilate asks, "Are you the king of the Jews?" and Jesus replies,
"You say so." It is one of the rare places where all four Gospels report
an exchange in exactly the same words. A Roman prefect *would* have
been interested in someone claiming to be "king of the Jews." Imperial officials were in general nervous about claimant kings; in Judea

61. Philo, *On the Embassy to Gaius* 38, *Philo* 10, trans. F. H. Colson, LCL (Cambridge: Harvard
   University Press, 1962),151.
62. Josephus, *Jewish War* 2.169–77. *Jewish Antiquities* 18.55–62.
63. Brown, *Death of the Messiah*, 1:698–703.
64. Ibid., 722.
65. Calvin, *Harmony of the Evangelists*, 3:276, 285.
66. See Seneca, *On Anger* 2.7.3.

the Maccabeans had claimed the title, and Herod Antipas lost his job and went into exile because he was pressing for it. "King" was a sensitive word, and, if Jesus claimed to be Messiah, was that not close enough to claiming to be king?

In Mark's narrative Pilate's question signals a major shift. A few verses earlier, before the high priest and the council, Jesus acknowledges the titles that had been attributed to him earlier in the Gospel—Messiah, Son of God, "I am," Son of Man. In chapter 15 "king" becomes the central term—see 15:2, 9, 12, 18, 26, and 32. As Norman Perrin once wrote, "If there is a single place in Mark 15 where the Evangelist could have used 'King' in reference to Jesus and failed to do so, then I cannot imagine where it might be."[67] In Galilee and, until this point, in Jerusalem, Jesus has been debating, with religious terms defining the debate. Now he confronts political forces, and the terms have to change.

What comes next is a very odd story. It seems unlikely that a Roman prefect in a territory always on the edge of rebellion would have let the crowd pick a prisoner to be released once a year during the tensest time, when the city was packed with visitors at the Passover feast, much less that he would encourage them to release someone who "was in prison with the rebels who had committed murder during the insurrection." "Abba" was a personal name, so "Bar-abbas" could mean "son of a man named Abba," but it could also mean "son of the father," a slightly unnerving name for an alternative victim offered instead of Jesus, the Son of the Father. It adds to the strangeness that some early manuscripts of Matthew give his name as "Jesus Barabbas." Are both Mark and Matthew playing a deep game of symbolic meanings?

If so, no one has ever penetrated their meaning. Right on its surface, Mark's narrative tells us something about Pilate and the crowd. Pilate clearly does not want to send Jesus off to his death. He is willing to risk the release of a known terrorist instead. Perhaps Mark is trying to keep Christians in his own time out of trouble by showing that the representative of the Roman government really did not want to kill Jesus, whatever death by crucifixion might seem to

67. Perrin, "High Priest's Question and Jesus' Answer," 94.

imply, so Christianity's founder was not some sort of traitor. But Mark's account does not let Pilate off the hook. The high priest and the council, however mixed their motives, did believe among other things that Jesus was guilty of horrible blasphemy. Pilate thinks he is innocent, but he is willing to send him off to an excruciating death anyway, for no better reason than that the crowd is restless, and killing this man will quiet things down, at least for a while.

As for the crowd—crowds are fickle. The crowd *shouts*, "Crucify him!" The last time Mark used that word "shout" (*krazein*) was at 11:9, where a crowd, only a few days earlier, was shouting "Hosanna" and laying down branches as Jesus entered Jerusalem. Whatever Mark is teaching us, it is not that, in the face of the corruption of officials, one should trust in the faithfulness and good judgment of the masses of ordinary folks.

# 15:16–21

## *Mockery*

After Jesus' hearing before the high priest and council, his guards blindfolded him and called on him to prophesy. Now, after Pilate has sent him off to be crucified, the soldiers put a purple cloak (purple was the royal color) and a crown made out of twisted thorn branches on him, and salute him, "Hail, King of the Jews." Perhaps they are in part getting rid of frustrations about the Jewish "locals," who cause the legion so much trouble. But the central point is ridicule—ridicule of religious claims in the first instance and of political ones in the second. In both cases Mark's narrative reverses the irony. Just as Jesus is being sarcastically called on to prophesy, his prophecy that Peter would deny him three times before the cock crowed twice is being fulfilled. So now, as the soldiers ridicule Jesus as a king, Mark's readers recognize that he is acting out his royal calling. Cyril of Jerusalem put it this way:

> When they "clothed him in purple," it was in mockery, yet ironically it was a fulfillment of prophecy, for he indeed was a king, so even their parody indirectly served divine revelation.

Even though they did it in a spirit of derision, still they did it, and his regal dignity was by that symbolically heralded. So, likewise, though it was with thorns they crowned him, it was still a crown.[68]

Yet the humiliation is real humiliation. As Barth says, "The Almighty exists and acts and speaks here in the form of One who is weak and impotent, the Eternal as One who is temporal and perishing. . . . The Holy One stands in the place and under the accusation of a sinner with other sinners. The glorious One is covered with shame."[69]

The mockery in the courtyard complete, the soldiers begin to lead Jesus to the place of crucifixion. Traditionally, the victim carried his own cross. More precisely, an upright was probably in place at the site of execution, and the one to be crucified carried the crossbeam. Mark offers no explanation of why Jesus was spared this part of the ritual. He died a good bit more quickly than most victims of crucifixion, suggesting that he was fairly near to collapse even before he was nailed to the cross, and perhaps they feared that this exhausted man might die on them before they even crucified him, thus embarrassing the troops and preventing the sentence from being properly performed. At any rate, they dragoon a passerby to carry the cross. Innocence provides no way out when imperial troops decide they want your help. Mark identifies this man as "Simon of Cyrene, the father of Alexander and Rufus." Since Alexander and Rufus appear nowhere else in the Gospel, and are mentioned here only as the children of a very minor character, Mark's mention of them suggests they were otherwise known to his original audience. At this most dramatic moment in his narrative, he says to his audience, "And that man's sons were Alex and Red, those guys you know." This story is real, and it happened among people like you.

68. Cyril of Jerusalem, "Sermon on the Paralytic" 12, *The Works of Saint Cyril of Jerusalem*, trans. Leo P. McCauley and Anthony A. Stephenson, 2 vols., FC 61, 64 (Washington, DC: Catholic University of America Press, 1970), 2:217.
69. Barth, CD IV/1:176.

# 15:22–32

## Crucifixion

Death by crucifixion, Josephus writes, is "the most pitiable of deaths."[70] Given that thousands were killed on crosses, we have surprisingly few details about the process. Intellectuals, the sort of people who write books, probably did not want to know just how crucifixion worked, just as Americans today would rather not know the details of waterboarding and other forms of torture our forces use. As Cicero said, "The very word 'cross' should be far removed not only from the person of a Roman citizen but from his thoughts, his eyes, and his ears."[71]

As a method of execution, crucifixion was both painful and shameful. The penalty was reserved for lower-class criminals and dangerous rebels. Nails were driven through the wrists and ankles to hold the body in place. Though these matters are debated, the best guess is that one could stay alive by holding one's torso up until complete exhaustion set in, the body drooped, and the flow of fluids to the lungs led to asphyxiation, though there is also an argument for death by shock through dehydration and loss of blood.[72] Sometimes the end did not come for several days. In contrast to many artistic representations of the crucified one as high in the air, the feet might only be a foot or so off the ground, and half-wild dogs and other animals could chew on the feet. Insects would be attracted to a sweaty body already bloodied by beatings. Sensitivity to the Jewish horror of nakedness probably led to some cloth around the waist in this province, but the body's natural processes would, over the hours, run their course.

All that said, it is worth noting how little emphasis Mark puts on Jesus' physical suffering. As Barth notes, other human beings have "suffered more grievously and longer and more bitterly" than Jesus,[73] and Mark's first audience was likely less sheltered from such

70. Josephus, *Jewish War* 7.203, *Josephus* 3, trans. H. St. J. Thackeray, LCL (New York: G. P. Putnam's Sons, 1928), 563.
71. Cicero, "In Defense of Rabirius," *The Speeches: Pro Lese Manilia et al.*, trans. H. Grose Hodge, LCL (New York: G. P. Putnam's Sons, 1927), 467.
72. F. T. Zugibe, "Two Questions about Crucifixion," *Bible Review* 5 (1989): 34–43.
73. Barth, *CD* IV/1:245.

stories than most of us are. Jesus refuses to drink a mixture of wine and myrrh that might have decreased his pain. He had promised (14:25) not to drink wine again until he drank it in God's reign, and he presumably did not want to avoid full exposure to the pain that awaited him. He is stripped of his clothes, and the soldiers cast lots to see who gets what, one of many references Mark makes to the Psalms:

> A company of evildoers encircles me.
> My hands and feet have shriveled;
> I can count all my bones.
> They stare and gloat over me;
> they divide my clothes among themselves,
> and for my clothing they cast lots.
> (Ps. 22:16–18)

This from a psalm Jesus himself will soon quote.

The theme of Jesus as king, characteristic of these last chapters, continues, with the inscription on the cross to identify his crime reading, "The King of the Jews." One can imagine Pilate writing it in cynicism about this troublemaker's pretensions and perhaps also in frustration at the people of this backwater province far from Rome where his career had led him. Perhaps surprisingly, some historians made a good case for the authenticity of the inscription. Jesus is crucified between two "bandits"—*lēstai* (bandits or outlaws), rather than *kleptai* (common thieves, who would not have been punished by crucifixion). Such bandits not only broke the law; they controlled some wilderness areas and threatened public order. "Terrorists" might be an appropriate contemporary translation. James and John sought the places at Jesus' right and left hand—now we see what that might mean in human terms before one could contemplate its meaning "in glory."

The high priests and scribes, as well as passersby, ridicule Jesus by calling on him to save himself by coming down from the cross. After all, he claimed he could destroy the temple in three days. As Calvin says, they call on him to prove his divinity by coming down from the cross, but he shows it precisely by continuing to suffer.[74] In suffering, he shows his obedience and his love. His human journey was meant to end with this ignominious death. In dying like this, he accomplishes the salvation of humankind. But why and how? To repeat the point, Mark offers by way of answer only a narrative, not a theory explaining that narrative. Barth's theology most carefully sticks to commentary on the narrative without developing a theory.

> Jesus did not come to reveal God's power, God's might, God's victory. Rather, Jesus came . . . into the pain, the passion, and the wonder of creation itself. Jesus accepted the vocation of being truly human in the image of an enigmatic God.
>
> —Carter Heyward
>
> *Our Passion for Justice: Images of Power, Sexuality, and Liberation* (Cleveland: Pilgrim Press, 1984), 28.

## FURTHER REFLECTIONS
### *Why Did Jesus Die?*

Barth presents God as "the one who loves in freedom." Thus his "glory obviously consists in the fact that because He is free in His love He can be and actually is lowly as well as exalted." False gods are "lords who cannot and will not be servants."[75] But "God shows Himself to be the great and true God in the fact that He can and will let His grace bear this cost, that He is capable and willing and ready for this condescension, this act of extravagance, this far journey. . . . God is not proud. In His high majesty He is humble."[76] As we read Mark's narrative, a Jesus who did come down from the cross or who demolished soldiers and priests and passersby alike in an explosion of fireworks as he rose to heaven would be less loving, less committed to the full extravagance of his journey into human lands than the humble Jesus who suffers and dies on the cross. Thus, if we understand God as the one who loves in freedom, then "in Jesus

---

74. Calvin, *Harmony of the Evangelists*, 3:305.
75. Barth, *CD* IV/1:130.
76. Ibid., 159.

Christ God—we do not say casts off his Godhead, but (as the One who loves in sovereign freedom) activates and proves it by the fact that He gives Himself to the limitations and suffering of the human creature."[77] However improbably, this poor Jew on a cross is what it looks like to be God.

But to what purpose? First, there is solidarity. No human being now, in the midst of suffering pain, loneliness, abandonment, can say that God does not understand. No one need feel, when everyone else has turned away, that God has turned away too. God has become "the brother of man, threatened with man, harassed and assaulted with him, with him in the stream which hurries downwards to the abyss, hastening with him to death."[78]

Second, Barth argues, Jesus takes on our sins so that we are freed from them. Does this go beyond Mark's narrative? Mark has Jesus say that he came as a ransom. At the Last Supper, he says that the wine is "my blood of the covenant, which is poured out for many." Then he goes on to die the death of a condemned criminal. "Jesus Christ has taken his [humankind's] place as a malefactor. . . . The sentence on him as a sinner has been carried out. It cannot be reversed. It does not need to be repeated. It has fallen instead on Jesus Christ."[79] The fate that ought to have fallen on us, sinners that we are, has fallen on him, and therefore we need not bear it. Calvin made the same point:

> "He was reckoned among the transgressors." . . . yet from his shining innocence it will at the same time be obvious that he was burdened with another's sin rather than his own. He therefore suffered under Pontius Pilate, and by the governor's official sentence was reckoned among criminals. Yet not so—for he was declared righteous by his judge at the same time. . . . This is our acquittal: the guilt that held us liable for punishment has been transferred to the head of the Son of God.[80]

It is what Paul calls a blessed exchange.

77. Ibid., 134.
78. Ibid., 215.
79. Ibid., 93.
80. Calvin, *Institutes* 2.16.5.

The Gospel narrative is thus one in which Jesus takes on our sins. We are characters in this story, and Jesus is. Neither the Father nor the devil is. Thus the two classic theories of the atonement both go beyond what Mark offers us. In contrast to Anselm, Mark does not present a "Father" who accepts the death of his Son as recompense for human sin. If anything, Mark's story would imply, as Barth says, "primarily it is God the Father who suffers in the offering and sending of His Son, in His abasement."[81] At the same time, there is no devil in this story by whom we are entrapped and who has any legitimate rights over us.

# 15:33–41
## *The Death of God's Son*

With Jesus slowly dying on a cross, darkness comes over the whole *gē*—a word that could refer either to the land of Israel or the whole world—for three hours. Raymond Brown plausibly maintains that Mark probably believed that this darkness actually occurred but that his primary interest in it is symbolic and theological.[82] It is fair to note that contemporaries to this event like Seneca and Pliny, who regularly report remarkable natural phenomena, never mention this one.[83] Symbolically, as Barth says, "The cosmos had to register the strangeness of this event."[84] The three hours of darkness recall the three days of darkness in the plague of Exodus 10:21–23, and darkness often appears in the prophets as a threatened punishment.[85] But it does not take specific texts to sense that darkness is a bad thing—cutting off the life-giving sun, making it hard to see, turning the world colder.

What was Jesus thinking as the sky turned dark and exhaustion set in? Rudolf Bultmann bluntly declares, "How things looked in the

81. Barth, CD IV/2:357.
82. Brown, *Death of the Messiah*, 2:1034.
83. Ibid., 1040.
84. Barth, CD IV/1:239.
85. Jer. 15:9; Zeph. 1:15; Joel 2:2; 3:15; Amos 8:9–10.

heart of Jesus I do not know and do not wish to know."[86] From a more conservative point of view, E. L. Mascall agreed, "It is both ridiculous and irreverent to ask what it must have been like to be God incarnate."[87] Mark offers no comments. He does tell us what Jesus *says*: "My God, my God, why have you forsaken me?" reported both in Greek and in Aramaic. It is a remark full of complex tensions. He feels forsaken, abandoned by God, but he still cries out to God. It is the first time in the Gospel that he does not call God "Father," but he does address "*my* God." He is quoting the beginning of Psalm 22, and scholars have pointed out the more positive note on which that psalm ends and argued that, in quoting the opening, Jesus implies the whole. Morna Hooker, though, rightly notes that such interpreters "fail to grasp the significance of Mark's picture of Jesus as utterly desolate. Jesus now experiences the most bitter blow which can befall the religious man: the sense of being abandoned by God."[88] A Jesus who knew all the while that God was with him, that he would shortly be in paradise, would not have suffered anything like the worst that humans endure. But this Jesus suffers all the fears and doubts that death brings to many of us as well as the physical pain. "Death must show what it can do on Him supremely, as in a masterpiece. No place must be left for foolish dreams, as though everything were bound to come right in the end."[89]

Some of the greatest of Christian mystics, from John of the Cross to Mother Teresa, report experiences of God's silence, the eclipse of God, the dark night of the soul. Such experiences are not, they insist, signs that they have lost their way or turned aside from God but part of the path that will lead them to God, a somehow necessary stage in coming to know the fullness of God's love.[90] How much more this must have been true of Jesus on the cross.

---

86. Rudolf Bultmann, *Faith and Understanding*, trans. Louise Pettibone Smith (New York: Harper & Row, 1969), 132.
87. Quoted in Hans Urs von Balthasar, *Theo-drama: Theological Dramatic Theory*, vol. 3, *The Dramatis Personae: The Person in Christ*, trans. Graham Harrison (San Francisco: Ignatius Press, 1992), 165.
88. Hooker, *Mark*, 375.
89. Barth, *CD* III/2:602.
90. See Moltmann, *Way of Jesus Christ*, 167; Balthasar, *Theo-drama*, 3:197.

As Jesus dies, with a loud cry, the curtain in the temple is torn in two, from top to bottom. Joseph Fitzmyer counts thirteen curtains or veils in the temple,[91] one dividing the Holy of Holies from the Holy Place within the temple, and one dividing the whole temple from the courtyard outside. The first of these was the most sacred one, but the second was far larger—about ninety feet high, woven in four colors to represent the four elements that make up the whole cosmos. Scholars have made cases for either of them as the one to which Mark refers; it is even possible that his ambiguity is intentional. The important element in this story is the "tearing" or "ripping" of the curtain, a verb Mark has not used since 1:10, where the heavens were torn apart and the Spirit descended on Jesus at his baptism. For ancient Judaism, if one can specify any location for God, that location would be either the heavens above or the Holy of Holies within the temple. At the beginning and end of Jesus' story, the barrier between the place of God's presence and the rest of the cosmos is ripped apart. Further, Jesus has claimed that he, rather than the temple, is now the place of God's presence in the world, and it would refute that claim if he were to die while the temple stood unharmed. In the episode at the beginning of Jesus' ministry, there was a voice from heaven, and the Spirit gently descended like a dove. Now the sky is dark and there is only silence. The ripping open that seemed at the beginning a sign of hope now seems to signal judgment.

> Christ is the new holy place where God's presence is manifest—now not just to Israel but to the world.
> —William C. Placher
>
> *Jesus the Savior* (Louisville, KY: Westminster John Knox Press, 2001), 137.

Watching Jesus' death from nearby, a centurion, an officer of high enough rank that he would likely be the commander of the troops present, declares, "Truly this man was God's Son." The Greek of this apparently simple assertion has occasioned much debate. Literally it is, "This man is son of God," without either "a" or "the" before "son." For a Greek-speaking Roman soldier, "a son of God" could mean just

---

91. Joseph A. Fitzmyer, *The Gospel According to Luke*, 2 vols., AB (Garden City, NY: Doubleday, 1981–1985), 2:1518.

a pious, worthy person, while "the Son of God" affirms all of Mark's claims about Jesus. Several generations ago, E. C. Colwell asserted "Colwell's rule": "definite predicate nouns which precede the verb usually lack the article," and this has become a standard principle for scholars of NT Greek.[92] In other words, if the text does not have a "the" in this context, we can assume one. The context in Mark seems to me to offer an even stronger argument. The Gospel begins with Jesus declared *the* Son of God—it would be a very odd anticlimax to end with him recognized as *a* Son of God. Given Mark's subtlety, however, one might read here a deliberate ambiguity. Just as, earlier, the soldiers mocked Jesus as prophet and king while he really was prophet and king, so here perhaps the centurion means to say only that Jesus was a righteous man, while he inadvertently acknowledges far more.[93]

The centurion, at any rate, is the person with real power, the emperor's chief representative on the scene. He sees a man die a horrible and shameful death and declares, "Truly, *this man* was God's Son." Not the emperor, not the Jewish high priest, not the priest of Jupiter Capitolinus back in Rome, but *this man*. All assumptions about human power and divine character are thereby transformed. The last time Mark used the word translated "truly" (*alēthōs*) was back in 14:70–71, where Peter was accused of "certainly" being one of Jesus' followers, to which Peter asserted, "I do not know *this man*." Mark thus ties together Peter's denial and the centurion's confession. The leader of Jesus' disciples denies him, and the least likely person on the scene recognizes who he is; and the reference to Peter reminds us that by now all the male disciples have fled.

But some women remain, looking on from a distance. Mark identifies them by name—Mary Magdalene, Mary the mother of James the younger and Joses, and Salome. They are the first women followers of Jesus whose names we have learned, and, while they have not appeared in the story before, they become prominent here at

92. E. C. Colwell, "A Definite Rule for the Use of the Article in the Greek New Testament," *JBL* 52 (1933): 20–21; qualified a bit in P. B. Harner, "Qualitative Anarthous Predicate Nouns," *JBL* 92 (1973): 75–87.
93. See Harner, "Qualitative Anarthous Predicate Nouns," 81.

the end. Yet Mark tells us they are not newcomers: "These used to follow him and provided for him when he was in Galilee, and there were many other women who had come up with him to Jerusalem." The male disciples have misunderstood Jesus consistently and abandoned him at the end. Now we learn that all along there were women followers too, and they are still present.

One of them raises particularly interesting questions. Mark has already mentioned a Mary who was the mother of sons named James and Joses—those are the names of the brothers of Jesus cited at 6:3. Within the names Mark has given us, then, this woman would be Mary the mother of Jesus. Most scholars reject this idea; why would Mark not specify that she is Jesus' mother? This must be some other woman named Mary. But, as Eugene Boring says, reaching this conclusion too hastily "may do less than justice to Mark's evocative subtlety."[94] Back in 3:31–35 Jesus declared that those who followed him and did the will of God were his true mother and brothers and sisters, and he rejected Mary and the brothers and sisters waiting for him outside. If we take that exclusion seriously, then his mother Mary was the mother of James and Joses but still absent from the family of Jesus' followers.

What is more important than that puzzle is the sudden importance of these women in the story. They have been there all along, "providing for" (or "serving") Jesus, but the followers we heard about were the clumsy male disciples, with all their misunderstandings. Only after the male disciples fled do we hear about these women, who have "served" Jesus—the very term he used to James and John in 10:43, when he told them, "whoever wishes to become great among you must be your servant." For that matter, it is the word used of the first woman we met in the whole Gospel, Simon Peter's mother-in-law, who began to "serve" them as soon as Jesus had cured her. Women in Mark get it; they understand that greatness in following Jesus means serving.

---

94. Boring, *Mark*, 438.

## 15:42–47
### Burial

In the evening after Jesus died, Joseph of Arimathea, "a respected member of the council," goes to Pilate and asks for the body of Jesus so he could bury it. Mark describes the action as "bold," and the verb for "asked" carries connotations of begging a favor. After all, Jesus had just been killed as a dangerous troublemaker; asking for his body for burial took courage. Romans usually left the bodies of the crucified to rot on their crosses or tossed them somewhere where dogs and carrion birds could devour them. But Jews were horrified by such practices. The Law (Deut. 21:22–23) specified that bodies should be buried on the day of death. Sometimes, at least, exceptions were made and the burial of crucified criminals was permitted.[95]

Mark tells us nothing about Joseph of Arimathea apart from this one episode. He describes him as "one waiting expectantly for the reign of God" (my trans.), a phrase reminiscent of the praise offered the "good scribe" in 12:34. On the other hand, Mark emphasizes that the actions of the council were unanimous—all sought testimony against Jesus, all condemned him, the whole council delivered him to Pilate, and Joseph was a member of the council. He could be acting out of a measure of sympathy for Jesus (simple human sympathy? sympathy for his cause?), but he could also simply be attempting to follow Jewish law concerning prompt burial. Characteristically, Mark says nothing about motives.

Symbolically Joseph plays a number of roles in the story. There is a kind of parallel as the centurion, representative of Rome's power, proclaims Jesus God's Son, and then a member of the Jewish high council intervenes to give him burial. Like the scribe whom Jesus praised, Joseph reminds Mark's readers that not all the leaders of the Jews in Jerusalem were bad people. He also reminds us of Jesus' total abandonment. John the Baptizer was buried by his own disciples. Jesus was abandoned by his disciples and had to be buried by one of those who had voted to condemn him.

95. Josephus, *Jewish War* 4.317.

# 16:1–8

# *Afterword*

Is this the promis'd end?
—Shakespeare, *King Lear* 5.3

Most scholars now agree that the original text of Mark ends at 16:8. Verses 9–20, considered part of the Gospel for most of Christian history, do not appear in the earliest surviving manuscripts. Early theologians like Origen, Tertullian, and Cyprian make no reference to these last verses. That might just be an accident; more significantly Eusebius (probably relying on Origen) and Jerome both say that all the manuscripts known to them end at 16:8. Though these judgments are inevitably more subjective, particularly when considering such a short text, studies of the vocabulary and style of 16:9–20 suggest that it was not written by the same author as the rest of the Gospel. (Dropping these verses loses the only biblical reference to snake handling, but that is a price most scholars seem willing to pay!)

This conclusion, however, leaves us with an ending odd in both content and grammar. Three women find Jesus' tomb empty and get a message from a young man there, but Mark provides no account of anyone seeing the resurrected Jesus, which one might have expected to be the climax of the story. Moreover, at the very end the women run away and (to translate the negatives literally) say "nothing to no one." Thus, as Robert Fowler indicates, "The story *in* the Gospel seems to preclude the telling *of* the Gospel."[1] The only witnesses are silent. As to grammar, the last sentence ends with the preposition *gar* ("for"). "They were afraid was why" is perhaps the closest one can get to the original in English. In a highly inflected language like

---

1. Robert M. Fowler, *Let the Reader Understand: Reader-Response Chriticism and the Gospel of Mark* (Minneapolis: Fortress, 1991), 250.

Greek, sentence order is more flexible, and there are examples of texts or sections of texts ending with a *gar*.[2] But this is indisputably an odd way to end a whole book.

At this point consensus comes to an end. Given the oddities just noted, many scholars propose that there must have been a longer original ending, now lost. Very early in the process of transmission, maybe when there was just one copy of the Gospel, the last page somehow fell off or was destroyed.[3] The melodramatically inclined have even proposed Mark dropping dead just as he was about to finish his book.[4] On the other hand, Adela Yarbro Collins, in her massive commentary on Mark, probably reflects the views of the current scholarly majority when she concludes, "In light of the evidence it seems best to regard v. 8 as the original ending of Mark.... The alternative is to argue that (1) the author was prevented from completing his Gospel, or (2) that he did continue after 16:8, but that the continuation was lost or detached at an early date. These hypotheses have already been refuted decisively."[5] As an amateur in these matters, I am in agreement though less certain than she of this conclusion. How can one refute *decisively* the possibility of a lost last page? Still, there is no way to interpret a text we do not have, and, given strong arguments that the text we have is the original ending, what can we make of it? At this point, things get interesting.

Reading Mark as a literary critic, Frank Kermode concludes, "The conclusion is either intolerably clumsy; or it is incredibly subtle."[6] Eager to refute the claim that 16:8 is the real ending, W. L. Knox argues that that would imply "that by pure accident" Mark "happened to hit on a conclusion which suits the technique of a highly sophisticated type of modern literature."[7] Indeed, a number of the masterworks of the twentieth century—Kafka's *Trial* and *Castle*,

---

2. For instance, Plotinus, *Ennead* 5.5; Plato, *Protagoras* 328a; Musonius Rufus, *Twelfth Tractate*.

3. Bruce M. Metzger, *A Textual Commentary on the Greek New Testament*, 2nd ed. (New York: United Bible Societies, 1998), 105; see also N. Clayton Croy, *The Mutilation of Mark's Gospel* (Nashville: Abingdon, 2003).

4. See this, just as one hypothesis, in Reginald H. Fuller, *The Formation of the Resurrection Narratives* (New York: Macmillan, 1971), 64.

5. Collins, *Mark*, 799.

6. Kermode, *Genesis of Secrecy*, 68.

7. W. L. Knox, "The Ending of St. Mark's Gospel," *Harvard Theological Review* 35 (1942): 22–23.

Pound's *Cantos*, and others—are unfinished in ways that seem not accidents but somehow appropriate to their greatness and their fit to a century unsuited to closures and completions. But it is more than that.

One perhaps "subtle," even "sophisticated," approach uses the tools of reader response criticism.[8] What is it like to read this text? What is the reader experiencing? What happens to that experience at the end? Robert Tannehill proposes, "The Gospel is open ended, for the outcome of the story depends on decisions which the church, including the reader, must still make."[9] Mark does not end leaving its readers, whether in the first century or the twenty-first, feeling that the story is wrapped up with nothing left to do but rejoice in its outcome. Rather, to quote Robert Fowler again, the reader can respond to the story "in a multitude of ways, among them the option of telling the story that was never told. The burden of response-ability lies wholly on those of us standing outside the story."[10] In accord with the principles of reader response criticism, "The key to understanding the ending of Mark is not to understand the women and men in the story but to understand what is happening in the women or men reading the story."[11] It is as if the Gospel were saying, with the mystic poet Angelus Silesius:

> Friend, let this be enough; if you wish to read beyond,
> Go and become yourself the writ and yourself the essence.[12]

If the story is to continue, its continuation lies in part in the hands of its readers.

Another contemporary way of reading Mark's ending centers around various "postmodern" discussions of absence and presence,

---

8. For an anthology of key texts, see Jane P. Tompkins, ed., *Reader-Response Criticism: From Formalism to Post-Structuralism* (Baltimore: Johns Hopkins University Press, 1980).

9. Robert Tannehill, "The Disciples in Mark," *Journal of Religion* 57 (1977): 404.

10. Fowler, *Let the Reader Understand*, 250.

11. Robert M. Fowler, "Reader-Response Criticism," in *Mark and Method: New Approaches in Biblical Studies*, ed. Janice Capel Anderson and Stephen D. Moore (Minneapolis: Fortress, 1992), 80.

12. Angelus Silesius, *The Cherubinic Wanderer* 6:263, quoted in Jacques Derrida, *On the Name*, trans. Thomas Dutoit et al. (Stanford: Stanford University Press, 1995), 41.

most interestingly developed in the complex works of Jacques Derrida. To oversimplify radically, Derrida accuses virtually the whole history of Western philosophy of having fallen victim to a "metaphysics of presence." Starting with Plato, philosophers have distinguished appearance from reality and sought to penetrate behind the merely apparent to the truly real (in Plato's case, behind particular objects to the Forms), to get what is present before us. Similarly, modern philosophy from Descartes to Husserl has assumed that we can become fully present to ourselves. Clear away all the false beliefs, bracket all the problematic assumptions, and how could I not know who I myself am?

Derrida, however, thinks both these quests are doomed. Everything we experience is always interpreted, all the way down. I experience the apple sitting on my desk in ways shaped not only by the light in the room and the perceptual apparatus of my eye (the image on my retina, for example, is upside down compared with what I "experience") but also by my love of apples' taste, my traumatic experience of once in childhood seeing a worm in an apple I was about to eat, and my admiration for Cézanne's still lifes and the way they capture apples with paint. Similarly, at least since Freud we have learned the conditionedness and limitations of our understandings of ourselves.

Derrida particularly focuses on what he considers a kind of prejudice against written texts. The argument has been that we write because both the subject about which we are writing and the person to whom we are writing are not present. If both the apple and you were here, I could show you the apple, and that would be so much better than writing to you about it. Not so, Derrida insists. Even if we were all present, an interpreted I would be presenting an interpreted apple to an interpreted you. Writing can do that too. Writing is of course different in various ways from showing an object, but not because one is representation and the other is real—one takes place in absence and the other in presence.[13]

So Mark writes a Gospel, and we read it. "If only I could have been there. . . ." Well, yes and no. I would have known what the servant girl was wearing when Peter encountered her in the courtyard, but I would not have had Mark's juxtaposition of the fulfillment of

13. Jacques Derrida, *Writing and Difference* (Chicago: University of Chicago Press, 1978) and *Grammatology* (Baltimore: Johns Hopkins University Press, 1974).

Jesus' prophecy about Peter's denial with the soldiers' demand that Jesus prophesy, or Gregory the Great's reflection on how Peter's struggles with his own cowardice must have helped him become a better leader of the church. Conversely, Mark ends his story without an account of the presence of the resurrected Jesus. But Mark's first audience and Christians today have ways of encountering Jesus in the sacraments, in prayer, and in the sufferings of the poor. Such modes of presence are ambiguous, but a text by an anonymous author describing events of two thousand years ago—events that seem inevitably to defy description—would not be without ambiguity either. A more confident story with better "closure" would comport less well with faith that in its nature lacks confidence and closure, or it would not be faith.

> The experience of the resurrected one is shrouded in mystery, but the message is clear: Go. Tell. Be witnesses. Proclaim. Feed my sheep.
>
> —William C. Placher
>
> *Jesus the Savior* (Louisville, KY: Westminster John Knox Press, 2001), 181.

## 16:1–8

### *The Empty Tomb*

On the Sunday morning after Jesus' death, the three women who were looking on from a distance as he died go to his tomb to anoint him with spices. Two of them were just mentioned as having seen where Joseph of Arimathea laid the body. *Women*—one last time, Mark privileges women as the more faithful followers and reverses the standard social hierarchies of his culture. In Jewish law, women's testimony was not accepted in court "because of the levity and temerity of their sex,"[14] but in Mark they are the only witnesses to the evidence of Jesus' resurrection.

In the only Christian texts we know were written before Mark, Paul's Letters, we hear about appearances of the resurrected Jesus

---

14. Josephus, *Jewish Antiquities* 4.219, *Josephus* 4, trans. Louis H. Feldman, LCL (New York: G. P. Putnam's Sons, 1930), 581.

but not about an empty tomb. In Mark there are promises from Jesus (14:28) and now from a mysterious young man (16:7) that Jesus will go before his followers to Galilee, but there is no account of an appearance. Instead, Mark tells this story of an empty tomb. Jesus was in the tomb, and he will be in Galilee, but just now, as the Gospel ends, he is absent.

No NT text purports to narrate the resurrection itself. In the later Gospels, people see the resurrected Jesus, but they still do not see Jesus being resurrected. Paul lists those to whom Jesus appeared, but he does not describe what it was like to see the risen Jesus. We remember Luke's later account of Paul's experience on the road to Damascus, but Paul himself says only—cryptically, and in a subordinate clause—"when God . . . was pleased to reveal his Son to me" (Gal. 1:15–16). No description, no narrative. "How could it be otherwise?" Barth asks. "Recollection of the pure presence of God, recollection of a time which cannot be past and has no future before it, recollection of eternal time, as this recollection obviously purports to be—what sort of recollection is this?"[15] How does one describe the indescribable? T. S. Eliot proposes that the answer can only lie in a life lived:

> to apprehend
> The point of intersection of the timeless
> With time, is an occupation for the saint—
> No occupation either, but something given
> And taken, in a lifetime's death in love,
> Ardour and selflessness and self-surrender.[16]

What is remarkable, one could argue, is not that Paul and Mark resist the effort to narrate encounters with the resurrected Jesus, but that later Gospels attempt it.

Those attempts are full of inconsistencies—about chronology, geography, and the experience itself. The shift between the relative

---

15. Barth, *CD* I/2:115.
16. T. S. Eliot, "Four Quartets: The Dry Salvages," *The Complete Poems and Plays* (New York: Harcourt, Brace, 1952), 136.

clarity of the narratives of Jesus' last days and hours and the shifting, puzzling character of the "resurrection narratives" is dramatic, as if "the stories themselves are about difficulty, unexpected outcomes, silences, errors, about what is not readily accessible or readily understood."[17] One could argue that these strange narratives point in the same mysterious direction as Mark's silence.

As noted, Paul does not mention the empty tomb. Is it a way of talking about what happened after Jesus died that arose later, perhaps with Mark himself? Or did Paul simply take it for granted—if someone is resurrected, his tomb is of course empty. The absence of the body could have been due to a plot or a mistake; Paul may not have thought it provided the important evidence that Jesus had been raised, and therefore he turned straight to the appearances. With Barth, I believe, "The content of the Easter witness, the Easter event, was not that the disciples found the tomb empty . . . but that when they had lost Him through death they were sought and found by Him as the resurrected. . . . Christians do not believe in the empty tomb but in the living Christ."[18] For what it is worth, at one point in my life I had persuaded myself that the empty tomb story was a legend that developed after Paul, and that conviction did not seem to make much difference to the rest of my Christian faith.

I have, however, come to think otherwise. Given that age's suspicion of the testimony of women, the most plausible explanation for why Mark has women discover the empty tomb is that it happened that way. No one would have invented the story in this form. Moreover, from as early as we know, Christians gathered for worship on the first day of the week, not the Jewish Sabbath. Given the centrality of the Sabbath in Jewish life

> The resurrection is in part about the sheer toughness and persistence of God's love. . . . The resurrection displays God's triumphant love as still and for ever having the shape of Jesus.
>
> —Rowan Williams
>
> *Tokens of Trust* (Louisville, KY: Westminster John Knox Press, 2007), 91.

---

17. Rowan Williams, "Between the Cherubim: The Empty Tomb and the Empty Throne," in *Resurrection Reconsidered*, ed. Gavin D'Costa (Oxford: Oneworld, 1996), 91.
18. Barth, *CD* III/2:453.

and teaching, this seems a more remarkable fact than is generally acknowledged. Something important would have to trigger such a change, and the explanation early Christians constantly offer is that they were honoring the day of Jesus' resurrection, which at least suggests a discovery of the empty tomb early Sunday morning as Mark describes.

Theologically, the empty tomb secures the reality of the resurrection of Jesus' *body*. Writing about the time of Jesus, the Roman philosopher and statesman Seneca expressed his hope of being freed from "this clogging burden of a body, to which nature has fettered me."[19] Plato and many another Greek and Roman would have said the same—the body was a prison from which to escape. In contrast, as Jews began to hope for life after death, their hope was that dead bodies would be resurrected. Ezekiel's valley of dry bones comes back to life (Ezek. 37:1–14). An anonymous prophecy in Isaiah declares:

> Your dead shall live, their corpses shall rise.
> O dwellers in the dust, awake and sing for joy.
> (Isa. 26:19)

Like Paul, Jewish texts from around Jesus' time refer to a "spiritual body" very different from our physical bodies, but they nevertheless assume that our bodies are transformed and not discarded. God made our bodies too, Tertullian insisted in the third century, and God would not simply "abandon to everlasting destruction" something he had made and pronounced good.[20] His contemporary Athenagoras agreed: "If no resurrection were to take place, the nature of human beings as human beings would not continue."[21] A great deal of suffering and misguided advice down the centuries might have been avoided if Christians had remembered that the human body is

---

19. Seneca, *Ad Lucilium Epistulae Morales* 24.18, trans. Richard M. Gunmere, LCL (New York: G. P. Putnam's Sons, 1917), 177.
20. Tertullian, *On the Resurrection of the Flesh* 9 (ANF 3:551–52).
21. Athenagoras, *The Resurrection of the Dead* 15 (ANF 2:157, translation revised).

a good thing. The empty tomb provides an important way of affirming that bodies are not something we should hope to cast aside.[22]

In contrast to the allusions to Hebrew Scriptures that fill his passion narrative, Mark's last verses are spare and straightforward. The three women coming to the tomb to anoint Jesus with the spices appropriate to a dead body realize on the way that they may have trouble moving the large stone that covers the tomb's entrance, but they find it has been rolled away. A young man in the tomb greets them. Eugene Boring says confidently, "The figure is clearly an angel."[23] Like angels as described in Jewish texts of the time, he is wearing white and sitting on the right side, has supernatural knowledge, gives authoritative commands, and assures those who see him that they should not be afraid. He tells them that Jesus has been raised, and that they should tell "his disciples and Peter" (is there just a hint here that Peter, who had denied being a disciple, does not at the moment quite count as one of the disciples?) to go to Galilee where they will see Jesus, "just as he told you."

Terror and amazement, however, seize the women, "and they said nothing to no one; they were afraid was why" (my trans.). All through Mark, women have been faithful when men failed to be, and these women have come to the tomb to minister to Jesus' body when the male disciples are long gone, but in the end no human beings are completely faithful. Fear captures us all. So when Joseph could be silent no longer and revealed himself to the brothers who had sold him into slavery, the brothers he had saved from famine, his brothers were reduced by amazement to silence—in the Septuagint, that sentence too ends with *gar* (Gen. 45:3). So at the transfiguration, amazement reduces Peter, James, and John to silence (Mark 9:6). Mark ends faithful to his own cryptic, dark theology, in a way none of the other Gospels will be able to tolerate. As Werner Kelber has written, "A Christology which peaks in the lowness of the cross, subordinates resurrection to crucifixion, and refrains from

---

22. Pannenberg, *Systematic Theology*, 2:359; Jürgen Moltmann, *The Way of Jesus Christ*, trans. Margaret Kohl (San Francisco: HarperSanFrancisco, 1990), 256; Barth, *CD* IV/1:341.
23. Boring, *Mark*, 445. Similarly, Calvin, *Harmony of the Evangelists*, 3:343; Brown, *Death of the Messiah*, 1:300.

displaying the Resurrected One (while stressing his absence) is too harshly focused on the paradox of negation to be of enduring attraction."[24] Yet perhaps it is just these features of Mark that make a particular appeal in our own age of uncertainty, when a Gospel that ends with Christ triumphantly present is harder to reconcile with the horrors of the world around us and the doubts within us. Mark throws the ball to us, as he did to his first readers. The three women run away silent, but we have heard the story; it is up to us, in our lives and our testimony, to tell it and keep it alive.

---

24. Werner H. Kelber, "Conclusion: From Passion Narrative to Gospel," in *The Passion in Mark*, ed. Werner H. Kelber (Philadelphia: Fortress, 1976), 164.

# Selected Bibliography

Aquinas, Thomas. *Summa theologica*. Translated by Fathers of the English Dominican Province. 5 vols. Repr. Westminster, MD: Christian Classics, 1981.

Barth, Karl. *Church Dogmatics*. Edited by G. W. Bromiley and T. F. Torrance. 4 vols. in 13. Edinburgh: T. & T. Clark, 1936–1977.

Boring, M. Eugene. *Mark*. NTL. Louisville: Westminster John Knox, 2006.

Brown, Raymond E. *The Death of the Messiah*. 2 vols. New York: Doubleday, 1994.

Calvin, John. *Commentary on a Harmony of the Evangelists, Matthew, Mark, and Luke*. Translated by William Pringle. Calvin's Commentaries 16–17. Repr. 3 vols. in 2. Grand Rapids: Baker, 1989.

———. *Institutes of the Christian Religion*. Edited by John T. McNeill. Translated by Ford Lewis Battles. LCC 20–21. Philadelphia: Westminster, 1960.

Collins, Adela Yarbro. *Mark*. Hermeneia. Minneapolis: Fortress, 2007.

Hooker, Morna D. *The Gospel of Mark*. BNTC. London: A. & C. Black, 1991.

Juel, Donald H. *The Gospel of Mark*. IBT. Nashville: Abingdon, 1999.

Kermode, Frank. *The Genesis of Secrecy: On the Interpretation of Narrative*. Cambridge: Harvard University Press, 1979.

Luther, Martin. *Luther's Works*. Edited by Jaroslav Pelikan. American edition. 55 vols. St. Louis: Concordia; Philadelphia: Muhlenberg/Fortress, 1958–1986.

Marcus, Joel. *Mark*. 2 vols. AB. New York: Doubleday, 2000–2009.

Meier, John P. *A Marginal Jew: Rethinking the Historical Jesus*. 4 vols. New York: Doubleday, 1991–2009.

Oden, Thomas C., and Christopher A. Hall, eds. *Mark*. Ancient Christian Commentary on Scripture: New Testament 2. Downers Grove, IL: InterVarsity Press, 1998.

Pannenberg, Wolfhart. *Systematic Theology*. Translated by Geoffrey W. Bromiley. 3 vols. Grand Rapids: Eerdmans, 1991–1998.

Perkins, Pheme. "Mark." In *New Interpreter's Bible*, edited by Leander E. Keck, 8:507–733. Nashville: Abingdon, 1995.

Taylor, Vincent. *The Gospel according to Mark*. 2nd ed. New York: St. Martin's Press, 1966.

Tolbert, Mary Ann. *Sowing the Gospel: Mark's World in Literary-Historical Perspective*. Minneapolis: Fortress, 1989.

# Index of Ancient Sources

# Index of Subjects